Intelligent Buildings

Intelligent Buildings

Applications of IT and Building Automation to High Technology Construction Projects

UNICOM

APPLIED INFORMATION TECHNOLOGY REPORTS

Editor **Brian Atkin**

KOGAN
PAGE

First published in Great Britain in 1988 by
Kogan Page Limited, 120 Pentonville Road, London N1 9JN
in association with Unicom Seminars Limited

British Library Cataloguing in Publication Data
Intelligent buildings.
1. Building industries. Application of computer systems
I. Atkin, Brian   II. Series
670′.028′5
ISBN 1-85091-683-7

Printed and bound in Great Britain by
Billings & Sons, Worcester

CONTENTS

PREFACE

With the passage of time, buildings are becoming more complex living environments that need to respond to changing circumstances. New demands on office buildings have become apparent through the increasing use of information technology. These demands are, in their turn, creating problems for building owners and users that were not envisaged a few years ago. As a result, owners and users are beginning to take a physiological account of their buildings, rather than a purely anatomical view. Each new building design has to accommodate higher levels of servicing than before to support communication, energy management, fire and security protection systems. 'Intelligent buildings' is the term that has been coined for these 'high technology' building environments. But they are intended to be more than high technology spaces for accommodating commerce, containing, as they do, their own sophisticated technology to monitor and control the internal environment.

This book brings together many experts from across the world, offering a broad spectrum of experience in the design, construction, planning and management of these potentially sophisticated living environments. It contains twenty-four chapters covering key issues in the areas of building technology, information technology, building automation, systems and facilities management.

Whilst the future always presents us with uncertainty, there can be no doubt that the poorly equipped buildings of yesteryear will never return to the designer's drawing board. New skills, covering a wide range of disciplines, are needed to solve the real problems associated with intelligent buildings. It is highly likely that the future will be dominated by those individuals and organisations who are able to identify and exploit the opportunities that the intelligent buildings' concept offers. It is hoped that this book will make a modest contribution to our understanding of the problems facing those who would wish to promote intelligent buildings.

Brian Atkin
Summer, 1988
Reading, England

Chapter 1
Progress towards intelligent buildings

B. L. ATKIN

1.1 INTRODUCTION

1.1.1 Why intelligent buildings?

Today, almost every new building has to accommodate higher levels of servicing than ever before. Although some buildings completed recently have been labelled intelligent, there is still a fair way to go before integrated 'smart' devices are likely to be capable of maintaining optimal internal environments. However, this issue is just one of many that must be considered when attempting to characterise intelligent buildings.

Several different types of technology need to be present before any building could be termed intelligent. They exist in many buildings already, although have often been introduced as after-thoughts, instead of resulting from the identified needs of owners and occupants. What is usually missing is the ability to bring technology together - integration is the missing link. However, many of the problems are not related to the technology - this provides the solutions - rather they are related to the needs of owners and occupants.

1.1.2 What are intelligent buildings?

A recent report on the Japanese construction industry (Bennett *et al.*, 1987) identified three attributes that an intelligent building should possess.

1. Buildings should 'know' what is happening inside and immediately outside.
2. Buildings should 'decide' the most efficient way of providing a convenient, comfortable and productive environment for the occupants.
3. Buildings should 'respond' quickly to occupants' requests.

These attributes may be translated into a need for various technology and management systems. The successful integration of these systems will produce the intelligent building, containing:

1. *Building automation systems:* to enable the building to respond to external factors and conditions (not just climatic, but also fire and security protection); simultaneous sensing, control and monitoring of the internal environment; and the storage of the data generated, as knowledge of the building's performance, in a central computer system.

2. *Office automation systems and local area networks (LANs):* to provide management information and as decision support aids, with links to the central computer system.

3. *Advanced telecommunications:* to enable rapid communication with the outside world, via the central computer system, using optical fibre installations, microwave and conventional satellite links.

A consequence of this integration is that intelligent buildings will have more in common with engineering projects than those of traditional construction. They require many different skills and an understanding of technology in a broader context than has hitherto been the need within the construction industry.

1.1.3 Demand for intelligent buildings

The notion of the intelligent building is linked increasingly with big business, where being a part of a world market demands considerable inter-organisation communications and a building that can deliver them. A culture of high salaries and ultra-dependence upon extensive, expensive information technology has become common after the 'Big Bang' in the UK.

The potential obsolescence inherent in anything containing a computer means that operating costs for these buildings can be many times greater than those of just a few years ago. Internal environments have to be controlled more precisely; the penalty for any failure in communications, for instance, can be catastrophic. Furthermore, the capital cost of some of these buildings could conceivably be less than one day's trading on the international market. This is the real backdrop for many potential intelligent building projects. They are demand led by clients who can probably afford better buildings than the industry is currently able to offer.

1.2 SOME EXAMPLE PROJECTS

1.2.1 Japanese progress

Toshiba's headquarters, constructed by Shimizu in Tokyo, is a showcase of modern electronic systems, which is hardly surprising given the range of products manufactured by them. The major facilities within this building are essentially information technology based, although high levels of servicing are also present:

1. Local area network linking individual workstations and based on optical fibre installations running vertically through the building, with coaxial cables running horizontally on each floor. An electronic mail system and electronic telephone directory are incorporated.

2. *Toshiba Total On-Line System* linking 120 external locations through 4,000 terminals to accumulate all domestic plant operation data, plus branch sales and general business data.

3. Telephone network.

4. FAX network linking 100 locations throughout Japan and 70 across the world.

5. Decision rooms with advanced audio-visual and computer-based equipment.

6. *Business Information Center* document filing system using optical laser discs.

7. ID card system for time recording and cash transactions.

The implications for designers and constructors of these facilities is that cabling requirements must be co-ordinated fully with the building's design. This means bringing the constructor's expertise in planning and co-ordination into the design phase of the project. Potential problems must be headed off early, through a managed design phase, rather than leaving them to the constructor to solve during the construction phase.

Apart from Toshiba, other Japanese corporations (for example, Hitachi, NTT, Fujitsu and NEC) have very diverse interests and are making significant inroads into integrating their products within single, large scale projects. The result will be that a single Japanese corporation can not only design and construct a complex building, but can also supply virtually all of its components. This is in stark contrast to the UK where the industry is highly fragmented, with relatively large numbers of suppliers and contractors coming together on an *ad hoc* basis for each new building project.

Other corporations involved with developments into intelligent buildings include Ohbayashi, who have developed the 'Super Energy Conservation Building', and Shimizu who have completed a prototype office building that eliminates the wiring problems of ordinary computer networks. Both organisations are part of the so called Big Six of Japan's contractors, emphasising the involvement of the construction industry in research and development projects on a large scale.

In another example, a mock-up hotel bedroom has been developed. Here, the guest could lie in bed and 'tell' the room to perform all kinds of chores. For instance, the room can be 'told' to run a bath of water of a stated temperature and depth, to make a cup of tea, switch on the television to a stated channel, record and type simple spoken messages, draw the curtains and raise or lower the lights. A further example is based on an apartment, where the telephone, television, video camera, voice control, burglar alarms, fire and gas detectors, lighting, air conditioning, the front door, curtains, cooker, dishwasher, bath, voice synthesiser, computer and control panels are interconnected. It provides the equivalent of a very competent and compliant servant 24 hours a day.

1.2.2 Other progress

It would be wrong to give the impression that all progress was confined to Japan. But the truth is that few notable projects are to be found outside Japan. Exceptions include the Epcot Center in Florida (Walt Disney Enterprises) and the Lloyd's of London building in the City of London, the Royal Bank of Scotland building in Islington and several buildings on the Milton Keynes Energy Park. Doubtless, there are other projects, although none would seem to approach the size of Japan's plans for the 25,000 acre Tokyo Bay development, costed at $387 billion.

1.3 SYSTEMS IN ACTION

1.3.1 High technology designs

A further trend evident from a study of the Japanese industry is the extent of prefabrication and industrialised buildings; an approach that evokes many unhappy memories in the UK. Bad experiences of industrialised building systems still linger and are not helped by periodic reminders occasioned by the demolition of yet another local authority tower block.

But industrialised systems are different today. One important distinction is that yesterday's industrialised buildings were concerned mainly with the prefabrication of entire building superstructures, incorporating relatively primitive services installations. Nowadays, prefabrication is likely to mean the provision of complete, highly serviced areas within the building and systems for retaining flexibility in the layout of internal spaces.

A trend towards a component-based approach to design is also evident, encouraged to an increasing extent by computer aided design (CAD) techniques. By using CAD systems, it is possible to compose designs from standard components held in an on-line library. As a result, drafting time and cost can be reduced significantly on some projects. High technology, component-based designs using large proportions of dry, mostly rigid materials may also mean that the traditional wet trades may be eliminated from these building projects.

A further distinction today is that superstructures can be constructed rapidly using means other than the prefabrication of major components. The use of innovative procurement methods and designs that deliberately take account of the construction process are just two examples, and are often used in combination.

The cost of services within many buildings has swung from well below half of the capital cost to significantly above it. The role of the general contractor as prime contractor is being rightly challenged by those with the responsibility for the largest, single element of the contract: the environmental services. Furthermore, the proportion of time attributable to the superstructure is now often outweighed by the construction time for the services installations.

1.3.2 Building automation

HVAC, lighting, power, lifts, security and protection systems are present in many buildings today. However, these systems have not necessarily been integrated for the benefit of the occupant. Partially integrated installations have sometimes been badly disrupted by interference from occupants themselves, concerned (usually justifiably) with local comfort conditions. The addition of sensors, and the means for responses to be effected via controllers, on a zone by zone basis, has begun to create environments that can accommodate constantly varying demands. When coupled with an ability to monitor against the external environment, through a central computer, the resultant knowledge-base becomes a valuable commodity for the manager of the facilities and the planner or designer examining new uses and/or functions for the building.

The detailed monitoring of the environment, and an ability to sense and effect responses on a relatively small zone basis, is likely to lead to lower energy consumption and wastage. The interaction of sensing, control and monitoring systems, complemented by energy management programs, can be regarded, therefore, as a form of intelligence. The Royal Bank of Scotland building in Islington, London provides an interesting and relevant case study of energy management in a modern office building, and is discussed elsewhere in this volume.

A consequence for the client, designer and constructor of these additional systems is that capital costs are significantly higher than for most recent building designs. Cost/price databases will need to be expanded beyond merely recording the details of yesterday's designs, which may provide no really useful benchmark for predicting tomorrow's construction costs/prices. As the technology advances, the design life of many components and systems will become shorter (for example, built in obsolescence). Historical cost/price data will no longer be as valuable a commodity as it is today. Databases will need to be dynamic, current and comprehensive. Links to external sources of data will be essential.

1.3.3 Office automation and telecommunications

Other demands on buildings have become apparent through the dependence upon information technology. These demands are creating problems for building occupants that were not envisaged a few years ago. For instance, the Lloyd's of London building has, in terms of its design and construction life, spanned the entire microcomputer era.

From a position where computing facilities in many buildings were provided for a few occupants, and met largely from centralised processing, the demands from occupants today have reached the point of one terminal per desk. Distributed processing, file servers and printer spooling have rapidly become the norm, with local area networks (LANs) connecting relatively large numbers of workstations. Effective cable management has proved to be a headache for some occupants located in buildings without the advance provision of trunking or raised floors. The latter need is an interesting one, since, not so very long ago, raised flooring systems were almost entirely associated with mainframe computer installations. The advent of the desk top computer was seen by some as signalling the end of the need for such a requirement. This has proved to be far from the situation. Furthermore, the aim today is to deliver a number of quite different services directly to the workstation. In particular, the increase in the use of electronics equipment has created serious problems of heat dissipation that designers must resolve, if comfort and safety are to be assured.

1.4 CONCLUSIONS

Buildings in the foreseeable future will be very different to those of just a few years ago. The design of many types of building today are the result of evolution, with some features having changed very little over decades. However, technology will help to revolutionise the ways in which the interiors of buildings are used and the extent to which buildings as complete systems can respond and adapt to man and the external environment. The design and construction team must be able to apply themselves to this rapidly advancing field by anticipating owners' and occupiers' changing demands.

True intelligent buildings may not be here yet, but they are inevitable. Designers and constructors should recognise that these buildings are moving construction closer to engineering. The construction industry needs to adopt a serious approach to the long term implications of these highly serviced environments. Intelligent buildings are not a fad, but simply progress.

1.5 REFERENCE

Bennett, J., Flanagan, R. and Norman, G. (1987), *Capital and Counties Report: Japanese Construction Industry*, Centre for Strategic Studies in Construction, University of Reading, Reading.

Chapter 2

The need: intelligent building for building intelligence

P.A.D. MILL, F.S. DUBIN, V. HARTKOPF and V. LOFTNESS

2.1 BUILDING PERFORMANCE REQUIREMENTS

2.1.1 Productivity and interior environments

Productivity in the workplace is dependent upon a series of factors including: management; job satisfaction; income; status; context (state of the economy); time spent in buildings; as well as interior environmental conditions. Over the past few years, several research efforts have begun to establish the strength of the relationship between the last factor, interior environmental conditions, and productivity. Steelcase and Louis Harris completed a study in 1980 on comfort and productivity in the office of the 1980s (Harris, 1980).

(Number of respondents	Total (1,004)	Industry							Job Type			
		Manufacturing (190)	Government (147)	Health And Education (74)	Communications And Public Services (94)	Business And Profesional Services (82)	Insurance And Real Estate (108)	Banking And Investments (80)	Executive, Manager, Supervisor (23)	Professional (162)	Secretarial (89)	Clerical (384)
	%	%	%	%	%	%	%	%	%	%	%	%
Good lighting	88	89	90	92	90	86	89	88	91	85	94	89
A comfortable chair	73	75	76	81	71	66	67	75	78	71	88	76
Good circulation of air	70	64	72	74	77	66	70	71	65	64	75	69
Right temperature	69	66	71	66	66	56	79	79	48	59	83	72
Machines and reference materials within reach	69	72	69	68	69	60	70	70	57	64	79	70
Opportunity to stretch and move around	67	61	77	65	73	62	71	66	61	64	62	70
A place to work to concentrate	63	58	63	69	63	71	60	66	74	65	62	56

Table 2.1: Steelcase and Harris Polls ranking of comfort factors

This study outlines the comfort factors most important to office workers: good lighting; a comfortable chair; good circulation of air, at the right temperature; machines and reference materials in reach (see Table 2.1). Osborne and Gruneberg (1983) were able to correlate operator's abilities with environmental demands (such as visibility, noise/distraction) (see Figure 2.1).

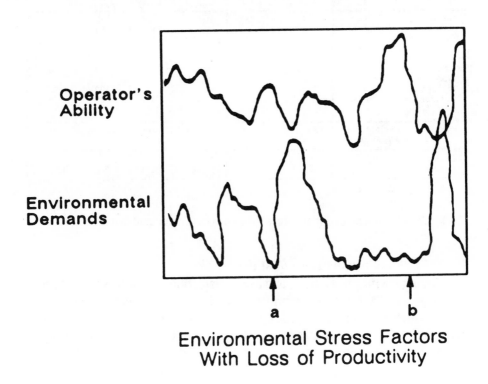

Operator's Ability

Environmental Demands

a   b

Environmental Stress Factors With Loss of Productivity

Figure 2.1: Correlation of operator's abilities with environmental demands

Most recently, Brill *et al* (1984), in a joint industry study, were able to assign productivity value in dollars to various environmental factors in the workplace (see Table 2.2).

All of this is explored with the full knowledge that although suitable environmental conditions are necessary for increased productivity in industrialised countries today, they are not sufficient. However, the recent and increasingly widespread introduction of automated information processing technology, into both existing and new workplaces, has highlighted the importance of the quality and control of environmental conditions on user satisfaction and productivity (Kaplan, 1985).

FACETS	JOB TYPES					
	Managers (Avg. Salary $41,500)		Professional/ Technical (Avg. Salary $31,600)		Clerical (Avg. Salary $17,400)	
Facets that Relate to Job Satisfaction	Annual Value	NPV 5 Yrs	Annual Value	NPV 5 Yrs	Annual Value	NPV 5 Yrs
Noise	472	1,789	282	1,068	148	560
Temperature Fluctuation	270	1,023	162	613	85	322
Glare	275	1,023	165	625	87	329
Comfort	–	–	234	886	–	–
Floor Area	–	–	–	–	–	–
Relocation Frequency	450	1,705	271	1,026	142	538
Work Surface Width	–	–	–	–	–	–
Storage (Personal)	–	–	–	–	630	2,387
Ease of Communication	75	284	45	170	23	87
Participation	–	–	–	–	–	–
Facets that Relate to Job Performance	Annual Value	NPV 5 Yrs	Annual Value	NPV 5 Yrs	Annual Value	NPV 5 Yrs
Enclosure	3,423	12,971	2,606	9,873	1,438	5,447
Layout	2,491	9,438	1,646	6,236	1,046	3,964

Table 2.2: Assignment of dollar values to various environmental factors

2.1.2   Critical performance qualities

In improving productivity and user satisfaction, it is necessary to define a manageable list of critical performance qualities for office environments, for their evaluation, programming, design, construction, maintenance and use. In many instances, building diagnostics (for determining our collective professional competence inherent in our existing building practices) is our first priority before we effectively predict requirements for future building intelligence performance. A minimum of six performance criteria might capture the performance qualities we want to find in the workplace today: spatial (or functional) quality, thermal quality, air quality, aural quality, visual quality, as well as building integrity against degradation (Hartkopf *et al.* 1983) (see Table 2.3).

First, there has been a fundamental mandate over the centuries for building integrity - protection of the buildings appearance and critical properties from degradation through moisture, temperature shifts, air movement, radiation, chemical and biological attack, human attack, and natural disasters (fire, flood and earthquake). Established by concerns for health, safety, welfare, resource management (energy, materials, manpower and money) and image, the requirements of building integrity are bound by limits of 'acceptable' degradation - ranging from slight decay (of the buildings visual, mechanical and physical properties), to debilitation in the ability to provide weathertightness or environmental conditioning for the function, to total devastation.

Secondly, there are a series of mandates relating to interior occupancy requirements (human, animal, plant, artifact and machine) and their elemental needs for health, safety, and welfare (comfort and protection for the five senses), that is, the thermal quality, air quality, aural quality, visual quality and spatial quality.

I.   FUNCTIONAL/SPATIAL QUALITY = SATISFACTORY:
based on knowledge of the building occupancies, occupancy functions, and organizational structures

    A. Individual Space Layout Quality
      useable space, furnishings, layout efficiency, access, anthropometrics, ergonomics, image, flexibility/growth, occupancy controls
    B. Aggregated Space Layout Quality
      proximities, access, compartmentalization, useable space, layout efficiency, image, amenities, flexibility/growth
    C. Building Siting Layout Quality
      access, public interface/image, indoor–outdoor relationships, outdoor space layout, flexibility/growth
    D. Quality of Convenience and Services
      sanitary, firesafety, security, transportation, electrical, telephone, informational technology, flexibility/growth

II.   THERMAL QUALITY = SATISFACTORY:

    A. Air Temperature
    B. Mean Radiant Temperature
    C. Humidity
    D. Air Speed
    E. Occupancy Factors and Controls

III.   AIR QUALITY = SATISFACTORY:

    A. Fresh Air
    B. Fresh Air Distribution
    C. Restriction of Mass Pollution   % – gases, vapours, micro–organisms, fumes, smokes, dusts
    D. Restriction of Energy Pollution – ionizing radiation, microwaves, radio waves, light waves, infrared
    E. Occupancy Factors and Controls

IV.   AURAL QUALITY = SATISFACTORY:

    A. Sound Source – Sound Pressure Levels and Frequency
    B. Sound Source – Background Noise
    C. Sound Path – Noise Isolation (air and structureborne)
    D. Sound Path – Sound Distribution; absorption, reflection, uniformity, reverberation
    E. Occupancy Factors and Controls

V.   VISUAL QUALITY = SATISFACTORY:

    A. Ambient Light Levels – artificial and daylight
    B. Task Light Levels – artificial and daylight
    C. Contrast and Brightness Ratios
    D. Colour Rendition
    E. View, visual information
    F. Occupancy Factors and Controls

VI.   BUILDING INTEGRITY = SATISFACTORY:
based on knowledge of loads, moisture conditions, temperature shifts, air movement, radiation conditions, biological attack, manmade and natural disasters

    A. Quality of Mechanical/Structural Properties
      compression, tension, shear, abuse
    B. Quality of Physical/Chemical Properties
      watertightness, airtightness, transmission, reflection, absorption of heat, light and sound energy, firesafety
    C. Visible Properties
      colour, texture, finish, form, durability, maintainability

---

Table 2.3: Expanded outline of critical performance qualities

For the office environment, 'total building performance' is the simultaneous provision of these five qualities, and the provision of building integrity for the integrated system, over time. The programming, design, construction and operation of buildings for total building performance is intended to ensure: the immediate suitability of the integrated setting for the building occupancies and functions (all performance qualities); the long term reliability of the integrated setting to perform as intended through the life of the facility (given appropriate maintenance and use); and flexibility to accommodate changing functions and occupancies, maintaining suitability throughout the building's life cycle.

2.1.3 Acceptable limits for environmental quality

Codes and standards are the traditional guarantee for environmental quality in the workplace, embracing certain aspects of spatial, thermal, air, visual and aural quality, as well as building integrity. However, there are some severe shortcomings with these limits of acceptability:

1. They focus primarily on physiological (health and safety) limits of acceptability (Woods, 1982).
2. The standards are set, measured and assessed for one performance quality at a time, whereas the occupant is a complex sensor of all the environmental qualities simultaneously.
3. They do not quickly reflect state-of-the-art understandings of conditions below which spatial quality, thermal quality, visual quality, aural quality and building integrity are known to be unacceptable.

Today, limits of acceptability for environmental quality can be discussed in terms of physiological, psychological, sociological, and economic (resource) needs of the occupants and surrounding community (Blanchere, 1972). With respect to human occupancy, physiological requirements aim to ensure the physical health and safety of the building occupants, sheltering basic bodily functions - sight, hearing, breathing, feeling and movement - from wear or destruction over time (against such conditions as fire, building collapse, poisonous fumes, high and low temperatures, and poor light). Psychological requirements aim to support individual mental health through appropriate provisions for privacy, interaction, clarity, status, change etc.. Sociological requirements (also referred to as socio-cultural requirements) aim to support the well-being of the community with which the individuals act, relating the needs of the individuals to those of the collective. Finally, economic requirements aim to allocate resources in the most efficient manner in the overall goal to serve user needs within the wider social context (see Table 2.4).

	PHYSIOLOGICAL NEEDS	PSYCHOLOGICAL NEEDS	SOCIOLOGICAL NEEDS	ECONOMIC NEEDS
Performance Criteria Specific to Certain Human Senses, in the Integrated System				
1 FUNCTIONAL/ SPATIAL QUALITY	Ergonomic Comfort Handicap Access Functional Servicing	Habitability Beauty. Calm. Excitement, View	Wayfinding, Functional Adjacencies	Space Conservation
2 THERMAL QUALITY	No Numbness. Frost- bite. No Drowsiness, Heat Stroke	Healthy Plants, Sense of Warmth, Individual Control	Flexibility to Dress w/the Custom...	Energy Conservation
3 AIR QUALITY	Air Purity. No Lung Problems, No Rashes, Cancers	Health Plants, Not Closed in. Stuffy No Synthetics	No Irritation From Neighbours Smoke, Smells	Energy Conservation
4 AURAL QUALITY	No Hearing Damage. Music Enjoyment Speech Clarity	Quiet, Soothing, Activity, Excitement "Alive"	Privacy, Communication	Conservation of Productive Environments
5 VISUAL QUALITY.	No Glare, Good Task Illumination, Way- finding. No Fatigue	Orientation, Cheer- fulness, Calm, Initi- mate, Spacious, Alive	Status of Window, Daylit Office "Sense of Territory"	Energy Conservation
6 BUILDING INTEGRITY	Fire Safety; Struct. Strength + Stability; Weathertightness, No Outgassing	Durability, Sense of Stability Image	Status/Appearance Quality of Const. "Craftsmanship"	Material/Labour Conservation
Performance Criterial General to All Human Senses, in the Integrated System				
	Physical Comfort Health Safety Functional Appropriateness	Psych. Comfort Mental Health Psych. Safety Esthetics Delight	Privacy Security Community Image/Status	Space Conservation Material Conservation Time Conservation Energy Conservation Money/Investment Conservation

Table 2.4: Performance criteria for evaluating the integration of systems

2.2 TECHNOLOGICAL DEVELOPMENTS AND THE WORKPLACE

Present day discussions of artificial intelligence for 'smart' buildings centre on the advancement of the infrastructure, or central servicing system and their controls, without assuming any major technological advancement in the design of architectural enclosure or interior systems. Moreover, the question of whether certain levels of control must be given to the buildings' occupancy, in order to ensure total building performance in the face of changing spaces and functions, is left unspoken. Evidence now indicates that technologically advanced buildings must begin to incorporate today's advancements in com- puter technology, communication technology, and control technology at each environmental scale in the building, from the macro scale of the whole building to the micro scale of the individual's environment.

Studying the advancements in office design over the past five years, one might conclude that there are three basic approaches to designing the 'intelli- gent office':

1. Using the technology as controller.
2. Using the environment as controller.
3. Enabling the individual user to be controller of interior office environments.

With state-of-the-art technology as controller (now called the intelligent or smart building), voice, data and environmental information travel through one integrated path to a consolidated management system for security, fire, telephone, data processing, energy management, environmental control (HVAC and lighting) and so on (see Figure 2.2) (Honeywell, 1985).

Figure 2.2: Honeywell's vision of the integrated building

With the environment as controller (potentially labelled decentralised building intelligence), repetitive local environmental sensors, controls and even systems are able to manage security, fire, data processing and environmental needs. These environmental controllers can also provide energy management (thermostats to control unitary heat pumps, solar/temp cells to control local sunshades and daylight sensors to control perimeter lighting).

With the individual user as controller (potentially labelled the 'user-intelligent' building), local environmental sensors, often tied to central information processors, inform occupants to locally manage/control security, fire, data and environmental conditions (heating, cooling, air movement, lighting) for energy efficiency and/or comfort.

2.3   PROBLEMS IN TECHNICALLY CONTROLLING BUILDING INTELLIGENCE

The present intelligent building approach basically represents a technologically-centred idea, not a human-centred one, extending the notion that building occupants detrimentally affect environmental performance. However, current central management and control systems (ECMS) already fail to perform as envisaged, without the added complexity of data and telecommunication management. In numerous large scale building performance evaluations in Public Works Canada (PWC), the following problems have been found repeatedly in occupied buildings:

1. Sensors not calibrated.
2. Line connections between sensors and central management not functioning.
3. Central computer systems not installed or not operated as intended (lack of training).
4. Local controls (for example, VAV dampers) not adjusted for the occupancy.
5. Local sensors not corresponding with local controls due to frequent spatial/layout changes.

Moreover, current centrally managed environmental control systems have not demonstrated capability in coping with major changes in building functions, rapid changes in activities, or rapid changes in exterior environmental conditions (for instance, when the sun comes out). Instead they demonstrate unacceptable sluggishness in the face of dynamic environments.

The goals of a building are to protect occupants from weather, noise, excess heat and vibration. In order to attain effective building performance for building intelligence, it is necessary to know more about the effects from all of these interacting factors, in particular, illumination and indoor air pollution. PWC's extensive field studies have shown that problems in the long term integrity of buildings arise from moisture migration into the structure, excessive energy consumption, poor visual environment, poor air quality and inadequate maintenance procedures and practices (Public Works Canada, 1981). Therefore, one should acknowledge that:

1. Buildings are not designed to adapt to human needs.
2. People are not adequately protected from visual discomfort, noise or from interior air pollution and electro-magnetic radiation.
3. Human needs for privacy, variety, interaction and identity are not met.
4. Buildings do not always contribute appropriately to the fabric of the surrounding community.

Consequently new knowledge about building assemblies and the performance limits for our contemporary social and technical thresholds, inherent in any building utilising artificial intelligence, requires a new and emerging transdisciplinary responsibility known as building diagnostics. The authors believe this is a critical forum for professional activity during the late 1980s.

2.3.1 Building diagnostics: a tool for intelligent building

Building diagnostics observes deficiencies in a building so that corrections can be made, and determines the cause of the deficiencies in order to publicise the results as new design guidelines or performance standards that will reduce the likelihood of their repetition. Aspects of a building that are examined include:

1. System design and performance: temperature and humidity, illumination, air quality, distribution and circulation and acoustics.
2. Enclosure design and performance: connection between components, the durability and serviceability of materials.
3. Functional performance (mini-environmental requirements): electronic systems and organisational effectiveness, environmental systems, ergonomics and individual health and well-being.

Designing for building intelligence must begin with the very first conceptual ideas, assuring responsive and dynamic siting, configuration, spatial layout, enclosure and fenestration design, as well as the overall systems integration traditionally associated with building intelligence (Hartkopf *et al,*

1985). It should come as no surprise that unintelligently designed buildings (conceived as a static entity) can never be made to work by mechanical or electronic wizardry, which already fails to perform its much more limited task. Contemporary procedures for investigation and intervention therefore need transdisciplinary studies of existing buildings with a view to improving building performance that accommodates artificial intelligence in the areas of:

1. Serviceability.
2. Durability.
3. Energy efficiency.
4. Economical operation.
5. Cost effectiveness.
6. User satisfaction and productivity.

The overall goal and main objective is to improve building quality in order to accommodate building intelligence requirements. However, several levels of diagnostic objectives exist that permit a variety of intelligent building approaches. The first requires studies of how effectively we build today, which will have a bearing on how one intervenes and standardises the variety of choices and building approaches before appropriate total building performance for artificial intelligence in buildings is achieved. A menu of these building diagnostic objectives is listed below.

1. Plan/Archive Analysis		
2. Expert Walkthrough		
3. Occupancy and Use Analysis		
4. Simple Instrumentation	what looked at:	
5. Complex Instrumentation	1. Documentation	
	2. Component-Component Interfaces	
	3. Occupant-Component Interfaces	records kept:
	4. Occupant-Occupant Interfaces	1. Checklists
		2. Counts
		3. Annotated Plans
		4. Photos/videos
		5. Plots (curves, charts)
		6. Tables

Table 2.5: Levels of measurement

(a) Investigation (see Table 2.5)

1. To find out about the work environment; to understand how health and well-being are affected by air, noise and light systems, by space planning, and by the social organisation of the work environment.

2. To find out systematically everything that does and does not work in a building, in terms of its operating efficiency, the effect of one system on others, and the overall effect of one or a combination of components on the net quality of the environment.

1. Expert/Informed Judgement
2. Pattern Recognition
3. Simple Algorithms (scalar, curve fit)
4. Statistical Assessment
5. Complex Algorithms (multiple indices)
6. Expert Systems
7. Mock-up Sensory Assessment

thresholds compared to:
1. Codes/Standards
2. Guidelines
3. Project Brief
4. Accepted Practice
5. Research Results

recommentation types:
1. Specific Retrofit
2. Organize/Use Change
3. M + O Change
4. Generic Retrofit
5. PDS Change
6. Codes and Stds. Change
7. Data Base Development
8. Further Testing

Table 2.6: Levels of assessment and intervention

(b) Intervention (see Table 2.6)

1. To devise ways of redesigning or re-structuring elements of existing buildings to optimise the quality of the environment in terms of improved user well-being; improved efficiency of systems operation; and improved building maintenance.
2. To devise recommendations for the design and construction of new buildings to optimise the quality of future work environments.

(c) Standardisation

1. To synthesise performance standards from a systematic approach of Total Building Performance Analysis that can be disseminated and applied to a variety of building intelligence programmes and as an approach to building quality control.
2. To standardise this practical approach with a theory of transdisciplinary communication related to Total Building Performance Analysis.

The approach and consequences of these previous three steps can be illustrated in the following example, when insulation is used in most buildings to control heat flow, by showing that it does matter where in the wall the insulation is located. Building investigations further show that although it does not matter where a membrane barrier is placed when it is used to control only air flow without temperature changes, it does matter if that air is moving to colder temperatures and is at a high temperature with a high humidity.

The placement of the insulation and/or the air barrier to each other's positioning will have considerable effect on each other's function and the ability to control such factors as water vapour accumulations and resulting water flow, which greatly affects the durability of some other elements of the wall. Thermographic building investigations since 1977 have given profile to this problem which has reduced condensation problems in current Canadian building insulation programmes.

Other responses to this problem awareness have also shown that the designer may often ease the requirements of future designs for the various materials and elements of the building assembly before making judicious selections and new design arrangements (Public Works Canada, 1981). This has enabled diagnostics to become a springboard for future building innovations.

The enclosure of a building is traditionally limited in its design to resist flows of energy instead of responding to these energy flows. Generally, the enclosure consists of a rigid and fixed structural skeleton, and a fixed exterior skin or shell of exterior walls and roof. It is an assembly of thousands of small pieces. Problems of enclosure failure arise, from the dimensional, physical and chemical tolerance limits when these pieces fit together, that is, from lack of understanding of the long range performance of materials. Building enclosure defects can be both visible and invisible. They are approached as follows:

1. Presence is determined through measurement.
2. Cause is determined through analysis of design documents.
3. Design of corrective strategies is developed.
4. Corrective strategies are evaluated.
5. Long term value of information on defect and correction is fed back to architects, draughtsmen, clients, contractors and building inspectors.

Enclosed within the building are the interior systems that provide the work environment. The building enclosure can accommodate or conceal HVAC systems, therefore, the design decision in isolation can reduce unintentionally the effectiveness/efficiency of an interior system in accommodating a work environment requirement. In an existing building the question must also be posed of whether or not corrective action can be taken at all and still be cost effective for the client. The range of critical problems identified in existing buildings can be organised into:

1. The gap between designed space and 'as built' space.
2. The gap between empty built space and occupied space.
3. The comparison between design brief and final result.

Consequently, within government as well as private industry, there is an increasing need to evaluate both the thermal effectiveness and the ability to maintain an interior environment satisfactory to the occupants. The compilation of this technical information into a useful and accessible compendium is critical to assist in improving the design and use of buildings and would ensure more efficient use of all advanced and current technology options in the operation and maintenance of our advanced technologically performing buildings. However, improved building performance requires both building science and occupational science to reflect a substantial increase in knowledge and it must be ensured that the underlying principles are applied to a much greater extent in the construction process. It is believed that one way of attaining this need is by the establishment of transdisciplinary building diagnostic centres (Mill, 1981).

2.4 BENEFITS OF USER CONTROLLED ENVIRONMENTS

There are many reasons why individual control of environmental quality is proving to be important to productivity - some newly discovered, but many longstanding. In examining the control of air quality, for example, there is growing evidence that occupants are much healthier in naturally ventilated buildings (occupant control), than in sealed, mechanically conditioned buildings. Research reveals that only a fraction of the office workers in naturally ventilated buildings are affected by major air quality related illnesses (see Table 2.7) (Keenlyside, 1981).

Attempting to set the limits of acceptable air quality, thermal quality, acoustic quality, or visual quality for the central management and control system, one has to fall back on code minimums set within the limits of survival or health. However, ideal environmental conditions for productivity may not be contained neatly within these boundaries of physiological comfort. Research by Markus and Morris (1980) suggests that stimulating environments must allow the occupant the occasional choice to create conditions outside of the comfort zone. On the other hand, excursions outside of the comfort zone that are dictated by a centrally controlled system will most always be resented by building occupants.

Adopting code limits for setting control systems is also inadequate because there are no 'typical' users, activities, or exterior environments. In defining the typical user, present codes and standards are intended to provide satisfactory conditions for 80% of the occupancy. It is not clear what is to be expected of the remaining 20%, or how effectively this approach copes with recent records of increased occupant sensitivities. In defining the typical activity, the widespread introduction of office automation and new office machinery has created conditions where two different activities, requiring two different environmental conditions, may occur side by side. Finally, the overlay of dynamic exterior environments on these interior dynamics creates an excessive stress on an exclusively technically controlled conditioning system.

These code limits for design and operation standards also assume that building occupants respond independently to their thermal, air quality, acoustic, visual and special environments. In fact, occupants are complex sensors of environmental conditions, often severely affected by combined stressors (the 'sick building syndrome'), which independently do not exceed acceptable limits. User-oriented controls can allow changes that reflect the occupants' environmental needs in an integrated fashion.

Most conclusively, the chance to affect productivity outweighs building construction and operation costs so significantly (92% in salaries over the building's life cycle to 2% in construction and 6% in maintenance and operation) that user involvement and user control is a major building strategy for today.

SICK BUILDING SYNDROME				
		MECHANICAL VENTILATION		
			HUMIDIFICATION	
	NATURAL VENTILATION	NO HUMIDIFICATION	NO RECIRCULATION	HUMIDIFICATION RECIRCULATORY
SYMPTOMS				
Nasal	6	14	22	17
Eye	6	8	28	18
Mucous Membranes	8	13	38	33
Chest Tightness	2	1	10	8
Shortness of Breath	2		4	3
Headaches	16	37	35	40
Dry Skin	6	6	16	15
Lethargy	14	45	50	52

Table 2.7: Study of air quality related illnesses

2.5 THE CONCEPT OF TASK AND AMBIENT SYSTEMS

Six different scales of environments must be managed by these technical, environmental or user control systems, each to be considered in design:

1. The environment immediately surrounding the individual (including occupant sensitivities, clothing and activity).
2. The environment created within the individual workstation.
3. The environment created by a closed or partially closed group of workstations.
4. The environment of an entire building floor (or coarse mechanical zones within that floor).
5. The whole building environment (including imbalances and inefficiencies).
6. The environment surrounding the building.

Field studies at Public Works between 1980 and 1985, which involved extensive surveys of these previous six environmental scales, concluded that the occupants of these surveyed public buildings indicated that a lack of visual and aural privacy in the work environment was the number one problem in government offices.   This requirement, that is critical to the first three environmental scales (1, 2, 3), is also influenced by aural, thermal, visual, functional and air quality characteristics of the remaining (4, 5, 6) work environment scales.

These surveys indicated that the most significant health issue was eye strain and headaches with as much as 65% of the respondents rating the quality of the visual environment as inadequate. This survey incorporated a diversity of workstation types.

The second most significant health issue was air quality with respect to its distribution near the workstation. In most instances, approximately 10 c.f.m. of outside air was being delivered to the overall floor although this level was less at the environment created within the individual workstation. Public Works, in response to this problem, developed a CO_2 test method in conjunction with McGill University to ensure that 20 c.f.m. minimum of outside air is delivered at each workstation. However, it was found that once an average air exchange rate of 20 AC/hr. was reached, additional air circulation did not improve air quality but simply caused thermal comfort problems at the workstation level.

The third most significant environmental problem was thermal comfort associated with both excessive and insufficient levels of temperature.

In 1980, Public Works developed the concept of a mobile diagnostic work enclosure to assist in the identification of ergonomic, productivity and environmental requirements associated with office automation. To co-ordinate the need identified with 'sick buildings' for work environment studies, the FUNctional Diagnostic Unit I (FUNDI) was developed to relate user response more effectively with the six different scales of work environment. A pilot study which was initiated in conjunction with the Department of Communications in a field trial on office automation has underscored the urgency for improved quality control at the mini-environmental level of the work environment. FUNDI II was developed for these field tests by Public Works and the private sector in order to achieve such a quality control.

The subsequent and current FUNDI III was designed to establish work environment requirements of office users who had moved into new offices or were situated in problem buildings, by providing them with local environmental controls. A bubble memory which had been developed previously for Public Works thermographic programmes can monitor these user-selected settings to enhance understanding of the relationship between user requirements and the total performance of the building.

Energy efficiency, comfort and user choice, as shown in the previous FUNDI project, was an approach which extended the traditional workstation concept to include controls of the work environment, yet operating separately from background environmental systems that now could be set at much lower levels, since the FUNDI 'fine tuned' each individual's needs. Alternatively, user needs can also be served by creating a centralised technically controlled ambient environment, and a localised user controlled task environment, with local environmental (climate) input in both cases. This concept extends far beyond the provision of ambient lighting for circulation and individually controlled task lighting to cover: ambient and task heating, cooling, and fresh air; ambient and task sound masking; even ambient and task spatial definition.

In each case a marginally acceptable ambient environment would be optimised by a central building management system with environmental input (and possibly user input) for health, safety and economy. User acceptable task environments would then be optimised by individual controls with sensory environmental input (and possibly central management input) for welfare, satisfaction and eventually productivity.

Another example is the Colonia Insurance building in Koln, West Germany (Kaplan, 1985b) which also illustrates this split between central control of ambient environments and individual control of task environments, to improve user satisfaction and productivity.

When the Colonia Insurance Company was confronted with the task of consolidating its many separately housed components into a single headquarters' facility, a user survey was conducted. The aim was to uncover the expectations that employees had when envisaging a newly designed computerised office. The most important concerns that surfaced centered on indoor air quality, natural light, and user control of individual environments (air, light and heat). In particular, users wished to sit close to operable windows. Along with corporate goals and macro-environmental concerns, the results of the user survey were incorporated into performance specifications for the entire building delivery process.

An extensive perimeter allows for maximum inside-outside contact, daylighting, and natural ventilation. Interdepartmental communication requires leaving one building and entering the other through the courtyard, allowing the changing climate and landscape to provide physical stimulation.

The layout of the individual office buildings incorporates four major wings, around an atrium that houses vertical circulation. The distribution of the workstations in each wing ensures that no station is further than one desk away from the window. A maximum of 32 workstations are placed within one wing. Not only is cross-ventilation possible, but also effective daylighting. The somewhat increased floor to floor height allows the innovative integration of both a hung ceiling for acoustics, ambient heating and ambient lighting, and a raised floor for individual fresh air supply and cabling. The acoustical ceiling is of panels of varying heights to liven the space visually, while acoustically helping to keep background levels at 35 dB. The air diffuser in the raised floor allows for flexible desk arrangements, and easy changes in cabling for power and information transfer. The operable windows are configured to minimise high speed air movement that would otherwise cause 'paper blowing', but they still ensure natural ventilation for both physiological and psychological satisfaction. Retractable venetian blinds are installed outside the window to allow user control against glare and solar overheating.

A lit control panel shows when user modification of cooling, ventilation or lighting is appropriate. Ventilation can be reduced when windows are open, and ambient light need only be provided when daylight is inadequate. When leaving the building, the night-time worker can check to see which systems are still on and where, including ventilation, lighting and security as the need arises. In all cases the central management system controls the ambient levels of heat, light and air, providing information to the user for the individual control of task environments; in other words, building intelligence for user requirements.

2.6 USER INVOLVEMENT IN INTELLIGENT BUILDING DESIGN

User controlled building intelligence is not created at occupancy. It is conceived and developed with the eventual occupants during the planning and

design stages, allowing intervention through such techniques as full scale mock-ups. Information updates, walkthroughs and decision making involvement continues through the construction and commissioning stages. Finally, the ongoing maintenance and operation procedures are inseparably integrated with local use patterns and individual environmental control systems. The new TRW building in Cleveland, Ohio illustrates this user involvement in the design of the user-intelligent building for work satisfaction and productivity.

The TRW headquarters were designed to provide a superior working environment capable of attracting, motivating and retaining the very best professionals. To achieve this, the building was to be designed from the inside out to be completely user and function oriented. Front-end investments were to be increased by 25% to thoroughly determine individual and organisational needs, technical change and innovation, and to evaluate the state-of-the-art options for each building system and sub-system. A 'four-legged team' was established with division of responsibility and decision making authority: the interior/architectural design team; the exterior/architectural design team; the construction manager; and the corporate representatives.

Team decision making was ensured through a shared initiative programme, where each firm received a negotiated fee, plus or minus 25%, based on their ability to complete their contracted tasks on time and on budget and to support the other team members in completing their contracted tasks on time and on budget. The team concept employed in this project is directed at achieving supportive, constructive and productive working relationships within and between all team members, fundamental to achieving the primary objectives.

The result is the integrated office, providing individual choice in workstation type, in task environmental systems and in detail. Not unlike the Colonia building in configuration, each occupant is within sight of a window offering daylight and a view into the landscaped setting. Raised floors and carpet tiles allow effective wire management and flexible cabling for power, lighting, electronics and communication systems. Drop ceilings accommodate adaptable heating, cooling and ventilation units to be keyed to changing workstation layouts. Centrally controlled ambient lighting is accompanied by individually controlled and placed task lights at each workstation. Demountable partitions and modular furniture allow for changes in workstation and workgroup layout, as well as changes in job type or activity. The curtain wall has also been redesigned from the inside to avoid poor mean radiant temperature conditions in winter; to provide individually managed sunshades to control glare and overheating; and to allow flexible space changes with the modularised workstation furniture. Again user building intelligence has been achieved.

2.7 CONCLUSIONS

The paper has outlined the argument for user-intelligent building design, construction, and operation to provide continuously satisfactory working environments for all occupants. To this end, a combination of centralised control systems for ambient environments and localised user controls for task environments might best ensure comfort, energy efficiency and related job satisfaction. To accommodate the dynamics of changing occupancies, functions, and environmental conditions, intelligent building design must affect envelope and interior control systems in addition to the mechanical control systems (see Table 2.8).

	spatial	thermal	air quality	acoustic	visual	building integrity
Structural & Envelope	●	●	○	○	○	●
Structural & Mechanical	●	○	○	●	●	
Structural & Interior	●			●		
Envelope & Mechanical	●	●	○	○	●	●
Envelope & Interior	●	●	●	●		
Mechanical & Interior	●	●	●	●	●	●

KEY
●: Critical implications for the delivery of this performance mandate.

○: Some implications for the delivery of this performance mandate.

Table 2.8: Critical two system integration for performance

In order to be responsive to changing environmental and occupancy conditions, buildings have to be conceived as totally dynamic systems. Also, since the designer wishes to make buildings more durable for building intelligence purposes, he/she must give more consideration to the effect of the environment on building systems, components and materials, as well as the effect of the enclosure on the interior environment. This includes the way that materials, systems or elements of the building are arranged and respond to each other. In particular, information about intelligent building performance must increase substantially in the next several years. What new knowledge has been gained in recent years in general has not been widely disseminated. Unfortunately, such information has too often been based on observed failures rather than developmental achievements.

The significant intellectual effort that established existing building diagnostics in the late 1970s has also initiated the discussion of workplace design in relation to interior environmental quality, in Whole Building Performance committees at ASTM, CIB, ISO, and NIBS/BTECC. However, much less professional effort has gone into the application of this growing understanding about interior environmental conditions in relation to job satisfaction and productivity. The recently completed FUNDI III Project, the

Colonia Building and the TRW Building demonstrate a promise of field evaluation, innovative team decision making, inside-out design, with continuous use involvement, towards the creation of better work environments for satisfaction and productivity.

2.8 ACKNOWLEDGEMENT

Significant sections of this paper were prepared for discussion at the Architectural Research Centre's Consortium Workshop on the 'Impact of the Work Environment on Productivity', 17-19 April, 1985 at the AIA in Washington D.C.

2.9 REFERENCES

Blanchere, G. (1972), *The Notion of Performance in Building: Building Requirements, Proceedings of Performance Concept in Buildings,* National Bureau of Standards, NBS 361.
Brill, M., Margulis, S. and Konar, E. (1984), *Using Office Design to Increase Productivity,* BOSTI, Buffalo, N.Y.
Harris, Louis and Associates (1980), *The Steelcase National Study of Office Environments: Comfort and Productivity in the Office of the 80's,* Louis Harris and Associates, Inc., copyright Steelcase Inc.
Hartkopf, V., Loftness, V. and Mill, P.A.D. (1983), *The Concept of Total Building Performance and Building Diagnostics,* ASTM E6.24 Conference Proceedings, Bal Harbor, Florida.
Hartkopf, V., Loftness, V. and Mill, P.A.D. (1985), *Integration for Performance, in The Building Systems Integrated Handbook,* Rush, R. (ed), Wiley, New York.
Honeywell (1985), *The Integrated Building - Greater Than the Sum of Its Systems,* Honeywell Techanalysis.
Kaplan, A. (1985), *Impact Assessment - Office Environments DOC/OCS Field Trials,* Architectural Diagnostics, Ottawa.
Kaplan, A. (1985b), *FUNDI Field Trial DOC/OCS,* Public Works Canada.
Keenlyside, R.A. (1981), *NIOSH air quality research,* unpublished presentation to American Physical Health Association Conference, San Francisco, California.
Markus, T.A. and Morris, E.N. (1980), *Buildings, Climate and Energy - Peoples' Response to the Thermal Environment,* Pitman Publishing, London, 30-45.
Mill, P.A.D. (1981), *Thermography & Diagnostics Centres,* Thermosense IV, Ottawa, 238-243.
Osborne, D.J. and Gruneberg, M.M. (1983), *The Physical Environment at Work, The Environment and Productivity: An Introduction,* Wiley, New York, 1-10.
Public Works Canada (1981), *Architectural and Building Science Directorate publication on New Brunswick Taxation Buildings,* Public Works Canada Design and Construction.
Woods J S. (1982), *Do Buildings Make you Sick?,* Proceedings of the Third Canadian Buildings Congress on Achievements and Challenges in Building, National Research Council No. 21158.

Chapter 3
What building users want

A. RUBIN

3.1 INTRODUCTION

The intelligent building has received a great deal of attention concerning its technological features, but a case can be made that its potential impact on the user is just as great. Yet, this issue has not received the attention that it deserves. In many ways the office workplace is becoming qualitatively different from its predecessors from the standpoint of the work being performed and the tools available to accomplish it.

As more electronic systems are integrated, decisions are required concerning the staffing of monitoring and control stations for such systems, for example, energy management and security. Because of the multitude of subject matter and the complexity of the issues, it is often neither desirable nor feasible to pre-programme responses to cover all contingencies, that is, to automate fully such facilities. Rather the systems include manual and automated features, with a knowledgeable person in the decision making loop. A person who fills this job must be highly trained and knowledgeable, not a passive monitor. Such systems should be designed with this division of responsibilities in mind. For example, information must be available to facilitate appropriate decision making and timely control of actions. 'Off the shelf' energy management and security systems used in intelligent buildings should be evaluated from this standpoint.

Even when systems are fully automated, manual override is often needed to account for unforeseen contingencies. The Three Mile Island Nuclear Facility accident pointed to the importance of proper ergonomic design and practices. In this case, operators acted in a way that intensified problems because the displays, controls and procedures were inappropriately designed for operators who had to cope with unforeseen emergencies.

The building and all of its 'intelligent features' can be viewed as a complex system comprised of a range of sub-systems. The particular sub-system component neglected by too many planners and designers is the human one. The intelligent building provides opportunities for attracting and keeping new personnel and organising their efforts for greater effectiveness.

The old acceptance of poor working conditions, badly designed equipment and inappropriate environments is disappearing, especially among younger workers. The upgrading of existing offices is a valuable part of organisational change and represents a vehicle for changing attitudes and making a new corporate culture visible and meaningful to the staff (Stewart, 1985). Naisbitt (author of Megatrends) makes the further point, ''the more technology around us, the more the need for human touch, the more we'll be looking for ways to reconnect as human beings''.

3.2 POTENTIAL INTELLIGENT BUILDING PROBLEMS

A case can be made that when problems arise in high technology buildings, with substantial system integration, the problems can escalate rapidly into major ones. The interdependence of building, information and communication systems in some instances may have this result. To offset this possibility, building diagnostic systems are required which have the same requirements as those for energy management and security. Automated systems must provide information, in a manner which facilitates the location and diagnosis of problems, to those responsible for dealing with them. Similarly, manual systems should be considered for circumstances where the automated ones are not available or are not yet cost effective.

A problem receiving increasing attention is the use of automated systems to monitor work performance. These systems are often used because of their technological capabilities but without a careful examination of their implications. Such systems can have a detrimental effect on the perceived quality of working life (QWL). The tradeoff is one of values, not technology.

The experience of many users with office systems, whether word processing, information management or communication, is quite similar. 'Black boxes' and/or software packages are placed on the desks of people with virtually no training or experience, with the expectation that this action will improve productivity. The reverse is likely to be the case, at least initially. A game of 'catch-up' has to be played by workers who now are faced with performing their regular jobs while simultaneously trying to learn new systems, languages and technology. The traditional methods are no longer at hand, and the information typically available to explain the new technology is likely to be written in a language that only computer programmers find to their taste. End users are rarely part of the process used to select systems, hardware and software.

3.3 SOME COMMON ASSUMPTIONS

What do we mean by an 'intelligent building'? A National Academy of Science committee in the US with this title spent the better part of two years on the project and changed the working definition many times. However, in formulating any definition it is difficult to avoid making a number of assumptions:

1. Is intelligence to be equated with automation?
2. Is pre-planning for automated responses to contingencies considered more efficient and/or effective than alternative approaches, for example, a combination of manual and automated responses?
3. Is the ability to automate a function economically sufficient reason to do so?
4. What planning process is employed to identify and evaluate tradeoffs between automation and the desires and/or requirements of users?

These questions include value judgements regarding issues basic to the acceptability of buildings by their users. Perhaps the most fundamental one is the extent to which the individual employee exercises independent judgment and control over the work performed and its setting. For example, should control of lighting or thermal environments be done automatically?

In examining the requirements of building users, we must first determine who we mean by 'users'. Unfortunately, this question is often not raised explicitly, leading to many problems associated with buildings, intelligent or otherwise. One operating premise in these instances is that individuals in the management hierarchy can readily speak for all users and the architect and his team can fill in the gaps based on previous experience and information collected during initial planning. Typically, the resources and time available for this activity is insufficient for the task (Rubin, 1986).

As a result, a broad range of suppositions are made about individual requirements which may not be suitable for a particular building designed for a given organisation. The substitution of these conjectures for carefully collected information from appropriate sources can make the difference between a building that works and one that fails from the standpoint of organisational effectiveness.

Another popular assumption is that user information defining appropriate technology for a given building/organisation is objective in nature, that is, a 'value free' determination of organisational activities is possible, resulting in technically-based objective decisions suitable for all circumstances. This formulation disregards a variety of potential conflicts among the objectives and cultural outlooks of organisations and the individual and social needs, characteristics and desires of employees (Dainoff and Dainoff, 1986). Furthermore, as we examine a variety of building users, it becomes evident that these contrasting viewpoints and values are not limited to the organisation and the end user, but with others, for example, facility management, maintenance or visitors.

3.4 OFFICE BUILDING USERS - WHO ARE THEY?

The office workforce is being dominated by knowledge workers, whose desires, expectations, actions and needs are quite different from their clerical counterparts. They are trained to make decisions and often balk at systems and environments which are imposed on them. They expect and often demand to be placed in the decision making loop. They resist the need to adapt to technology. Instead they want tools that support them in jobs they can help define. They want and expect a high quality environment; one not merely functional but pleasant and comfortable. These factors, formerly considered tangential to the central importance of salary and professional growth in making job decisions are now important determinants of whether to stay with or leave one's job (Kaplan, 1982).

Office buildings have many other major users with requirements that sometimes differ from those of knowledge workers. In the case of intelligent buildings, these users merit even more detailed consideration. Among those whose requirements should be understood are people who engage in the following:

1. Maintenance. Those who respond to new classes of technology which change rapidly. They also respond to users working in time frames markedly different than those of the past, for example, accelerated computer-based operations.

2. Monitoring. Those who have duties and requirements that are rapidly evolving with new technology.

3. Facility management. Those who work with new equipment and systems and maintain detailed records of changes as they occur.

4. Information management. Those who maintain operational databases and must be sensitive to particular organisational needs.

5. Visiting. Those who function in new and strange surrounds.

3.5 ORGANISATION

Organisational culture is a primary determinant in workspace design and planning office systems. A highly centralised structure is typically based on a uniformity of spaces and furnishings and top-down planning with limited user involvement in decision making. A decentralised approach is more tolerant of differences among technology, furnishings, working styles and organisational practices. Distributed databases and decision making at all levels of the organisation are more likely to occur, and even encouraged as a form of job enrichment.

Fast changing technology and competitive environment makes organisational flexibility important. Groupings of people and activities change rapidly and the environment must accommodate these needs. Many projects are large scale: groups of people are often called upon to work on a single activity.

One problem is the need for the individual to feel that he or she is an integral part of an organisation. There is a tendency among professionals and managers to identify and maintain contact with peer groups performing similar activities in other organisations. Loyalty then becomes associated with these peer groups and their technical and professional societies, at the expense of the organisation where they happen to work. As jobs get more technical and specialised, there is a greater tendency to seek out colleagues who 'talk the same language' wherever they are to be found. The work performed by the National Bureau of Standards and other research has indicated that automation has fostered a variety of new needs in the office (Rubin, 1983). Among these needs are:

1. Exchanging information by informal networking in contrast to formal organisational structures.
2. Places to encourage chance encounters to offset technology.
3. Conference rooms, large and small for meetings requiring privacy and to get away from the computer display dominated work floor.
4. A greater dependency on work groups for intangible benefits such as work satisfaction and job fulfilment.

3.6 PLANNING

Planning starts with the formation of a team responsible for making planning decisions. The team should be well represented by end users throughout the process, including a feedback system which permits ongoing evaluations of operational and building activities during the lifetime of the building.

People planning is vital. Recruitment, training, motivation and other user issues are intimately involved in facility planning. In the past, the delivery of a facility has been a technological and design problem, that is, space needed to house people. The intelligent building is created to support the organisation and individual user. It provides working conditions that can produce stress, discomfort and distractions or alteratively, to enhance satisfaction, productivity and communication. The facility, the people and technology require more integration into a single system than ever before. Planning must accommodate this need.

While changes are planned, the entire staff should be kept informed to ensure that the technology is not perceived as a threat to job security or a means to downgrade the importance of the work of the individual. Technology can be used for job enrichment as well as routine work; the choice is open (Frazelle, 1984).

Recommended steps in the planning process are (Anon., 1982):

1. Identify the objectives of the office.
2. Determine the specific functions critical to accomplish objectives.
3. Define the space and equipment requirements for each office function.
4. Define the inter-relationships among office functions with the help of the staff.
5. Determine the office facility location.
6. Generate alternative space plans.
7. Evaluate alternative plans by identifying critical criteria and weighting them accordingly.
8. Implement the plan chosen.
9. Maintain and adapt the plan as changes require; employee involvement is critical to identifying equipment needs and provide feedback information.

3.6.1 Training

A frequently overlooked aspect of automation is the need to ensure that its potential users have the capabilities to make best use of the systems. For those building and operational sub-systems requiring manual intervention of different kinds, training should be planned for users. This training ranges from the need to make furniture adjustments to connecting equipment using hardware and software to perform work activities. Just as office automation should be considered to be an ongoing process, training should not be thought of as a one time activity. The availability of appropriate training facilities are an essential feature of high technology buildings.

There are many instances where equipment is in place but not used effectively. For example, in a study performed for the National Academy of Sciences, it was found that most of the advanced features of newly installed telephone systems were not used because the users were not trained properly.

They had high technology systems, with a variety of capabilities that were being paid for, but the telephones were being used in the 'old fashioned' way.

3.6.2 Introducing automation

The introduction of technology into the workplace should be undertaken with care since it can profoundly affect the ultimate success of such systems. The end user of technology should be an active participant in planning the automated office by being an integral part of the decision making processes affecting the technology and workplace design. This approach has many benefits:

1. It draws upon the detailed knowledge possessed by the end user in defining system requirements.

2. It provides the user with a stake in the outcome not available when systems are imposed from above.

3. It offsets the uncertainty, fear of loss of job, and the hostility which often accompanies the introduction of new technology and other
important organisational changes.

3.7 WORKSTATION

The electronic workstation is the central building block of the high technology office. It is where all technological advances must be available at the fingertips of all staff members: clerical, administrative and professional.

The workstation setting should include a consideration of individual controls for the environment, for example, task lighting. Similar considerations should apply to furniture, especially chairs which accommodate individual dimensions and preferences. Components should be capable of being readily modified with little or no need for tools. People must be informed of the possibilities of adjustment. Furnishings made to be modified tend to be kept in a fixed configuration unless an effort is made to inform people about these capabilities.

Workstation design must reflect a range of human needs:

1. *Anthropometric:* body dimensions, physical capabilities such as sitting and standing height, reach lengths. The best design reflects economy of effort, minimising fatigue.

2. *Sensory:* visual, auditory and thermal comfort needs.

3. *Social:* interpersonal relationships among colleagues and others.

4. *Privacy:* the ability to regulate and control social interactions and

avoid interruptions.

5. *Territory:* an area with boundaries under control.

6. *Status:* workstation design is commensurate with organisational role.

3.8 SOME SPECIFIC ISSUES: IMPLICATIONS FOR USERS

3.8.1 System Modification

1. Who is responsible for making the changes?

2. To what extent are particular skills needed?

3. Are changes made by internal staff members or those on contract?

4. How do these decisions affect down-time of ongoing operations and the time it takes to institute new technology?

5. What provision is there for recording changes in a centralised database concerned with providing current facility features?

3.8.2 Fire safety

1. How much of the system is automated?

2. Who mans the fire safety system?

3. How is the the system monitored?

4. What actions and decisions are required by the system monitor?

5. What kind of training and/or experience is needed to perform this activity?

6. What information is given to the people affected?

7. What contacts are possible between building occupiers and police and fire departments?

8. What messages are given to people affected?

9. What types of alarm systems are used, for example, auditory alarms and voice messages?

10.   Are the messages pre-recorded?

11.   Is there a manual override system of pre-recordings to provide specific information?

12.   Is there a capability for two-way communication, for example, can affected people initiate calls to provide information, ask for feedback etc.?

13.   What provisions are made to train people concerning emergency behaviour?

14.   How familiar are building occupants with egress routes to safe areas or to the outside?

15.   What provisions are there for visitors in emergencies; are actions supposed to be self-evident?

16.   Is there an evaluation procedure to assess results of emergencies to ensure that errors are identified and mistakes corrected?

3.8.3 Servicing the intelligent building

1. Are staff equipped to perform the work?

2. What, if any, training or documentation is needed to ensure that the system works effectively?

3. Is there a need for 'on the job' training?

4. How will this be accomplished?

5. Are the staff resources available?

6. How long will it take?

7. Can problem areas be pinpointed?

8. Is it readily accessible?

9. What periodic maintenance schedules are appropriate, for example, cleaning ducts and replacing lamps?

3.8.4 Diagnostic systems

1. What types of diagnostics are available?

2. What information is provided?

3. Who monitors and acts upon diagnostic information?

4. What expertise and training is needed for system operators?

5. What actions are to be taken by the operator, for example, to what extent is the system exclusively a monitoring activity?

6. Are action priorities built in as part of the system?

3.8.5 Expert systems

1. What expert system will be used?

- What criteria will determine its use?

2. Who designs the system?

3. Who operates the system?

- What level of expertise is needed by the operator?

- What flexibility does the operator have in making decisions, choices, etc.?

- What data resources are available to the operator?

4. Is the system designed for periodic updating?

- If so, who provides input information?

- What is the role of the system operator in this process?

5. What training or experience is needed to operate the system?

3.8.6 Ergonomic issues

Organisational, design and personal needs are integrated at the workstation, which must therefore be designed to meet a variety of requirements differing from person to person: physical, sensory, and cognitive. Flexibility is essential for workstation furnishings and equipment. For example, selecting and placing objects serving the worker requires considerations of physical comfort, body movement, and individual preferences and needs. Employees at workstations must have ready access to the tools and materials needed to do their jobs. Size of components, clearances, allowances for free body movement are integral to the proper fit of person to workstation.

'Humanising' the workplace can lessen the frustration of the job and the increasing technological emphasis. People need the feeling that they are controlling the system and not being controlled by it (Brill *et al.* 1984).

1. Before purchasing equipment, a realistic needs assessment should be performed.

2. A systems approach to design is essential; components must be compatible.

3. Operators must be trained to operate new systems and software.

4. Equipment, systems and software should be selected on the basis of performance and ease of use.

Workstation design should enable individual expression and personalisation to offset the stark environment associated with automated workplaces. A survey of architects indicated the importance of a 'high quality' environment and 'control' (Malcolm, 1986). Other issues were visual and acoustical privacy, freedom from intrusions, noise and glare-free lighting.

An office should reflect the working style of the user. It should permit the worker autonomy within a range of possibilities; re-arranging furnishings, using a task light that can be positioned at the user's discretion. Stewart (1985) suggests the planning approach outlined in Table 3.1 for improving productivity, based on a study of what people require to do their jobs.

Stages of life cycle	Ergonomic input
Analysis	User needs analysis
Planning	User profiles, allocation of functions
Design	User interface design, office design
Implementation	Management of change, ergonomic quality control
Operation	Ergonomic evaluation, user feedback

Table 3.1: Ergonomics inputs to office system design

3.8.7 Design factors

Factors to be considered in design are:

1. The integration of different technology in existing organisations and their assimilation by users in their daily work.

2. How to include technological factors in the design process.

3. Office design based on system concepts rather than focusing on micro issues such as individual hardware components.

4. More new and small firms are being formed; they often are more innovative than larger ones and more likely to employ the latest technology.

5. Larger organisations are delegating more decision making to subordinate groups; technology is fostering decentralisation.

6. Building designers are being asked to provide support such as health and athletics centres, baby sitting facilities, etc..

7. The ratio of professional to staff members is changing; fewer support personnel are employed.

8. Advanced telecommunications has enabled companies to disperse operations geographically; small suburban centres are becoming popular in contrast to large centralised operations.

(a) Workstation needs

1. Flexibility to accommodate the range of tasks performed and the individuals performing them.

2. Vertical and horizontal surfaces for materials use and storage; place for continuous paper supply and output.

3. Power and communication capabilities consistent with performing required activities.

4. Ready access to work materials.

5. Workstation layout to facilitate performing activities.

6. Individual controls for equipment and selected environmental features, for example, task lighting.

7. Capability for personalising workspace.

8. Easily reached controls; easily read displays.

9. Sufficient space to facilitate comfortable movement.

10. Capability for rapid changes and moves.

(b) Workstation flexibility checklist

1. It should be capable of change with minimum disruption to staff or activities.

2. Adjustments should not require special skills or tools.

3. Systems should be simple and made of standardised components

and be cost effective.

4. Dimensions and heights of work surfaces should be adjustable and accommodate a range of activity and individual requirements.

5. New component configurations should accommodate changing requirements.

6. Furnishings should be responsive to individual differences, for example, left and right handed people.

7. Adjustable seating with firm back and neck support is vital.

8. Components and design should be cost effective.

(c) Workstation environment/design checklist

1. Acoustic privacy.
2. Freedom from auditory and visual distractions.
3. Glare-free lighting.
4. Physical separation of unrelated activities.
5. Ease of power and communication changes and additions.
6. Non-disruptive traffic patterns.
7. Clearly defined personal boundaries.

3.9 CONCLUSIONS

The planning of electronic systems and workspace design should be based on the premise of the central importance of the end user. The supposition is that the overall goal of these activities is to improve organisational effectiveness. Productivity is thought to be directly or indirectly influenced by the quality of the physical surrounds and the intrinsic features of the job - fostering professional growth.

The design challenge is for a well integrated planning process to enhance productivity and not diminish environmental quality or productivity. End users should be well represented in the design team. By being team members, the planning process can be used to resolve potential conflicts among management, office workers and others with differing requirements.

The technology used should not be visible to the user. A model to be emulated is the traditional telephone, which immediately places the world at your disposal for contact. All capabilities are available with minimal training. Another appropriate model is the one being pursued by some software designers. The systems accommodate expert and novice users in different ways, for example, menu or icon systems for the untrained, and more elaborate and 'elegant' input methods for experts, which make more extensive use of the system and enable it to respond faster. Finally, a novice can learn new features at his own pace, migrating from basic usages to more inclusive ones.

The effective workplace is one which responds to the whole person, including the needs for self-esteem, motivation, autonomy, self-expression, growth and control. In the high technology workplace it is particularly important to ensure that the worker is the master, not the servant of technology.

A reflection of the importance of working conditions is the increased interest expressed by many organisations and researchers in the QWL. This is a general formulation including management, design and ergonomic issues. A rationale for improving environmental conditions as a means of increasing productivity is that improved conditions can lead to greater satisfaction and more motivation, which can result in improved productivity (Walton, 1973). However, successful programmes have certain pre-requisites:

1. Management must be committed to a participative style, inviting employee involvement.

2. Employees should be given opportunities for career advancements.

3. Traditional status barriers between management and workers must be overcome.

4. Supervisors require training in participatory management.

5. Employees should receive feedback on results and recognition for improved performance.

6. Positive and negative results should be analysed and evaluated with the results used toward further improvement of the system.

The assumptions for a QWL orientation to improved productivity are:

1. Workers are regarded as good sources of ideas for methods of increasing productivity. Job enrichment is a viable method.

2. Work should be a rewarding activity in terms of satisfaction. Workers should and do take pride in their work.

3. Greater job satisfaction results in increased productivity.

4. Employers should show more concern for the welfare of employees.

5. Improved feedback to workers as to performance is needed, resulting in improved attitudes and motivation.

6. An improved work environment will result in greater satisfaction, leading to improved performance.

3.10 REFERENCES

Anonymous (1982), *Frustration in the Workplace: Its Effect on productivity*, Journal of Micrographics, 15, (3), March.
Brill, M., Margulis, S. and Konar, E. (1984), *Using Office Design to Increase Productivity*,

BOSTI, Buffalo, N.Y.

Dainoff, M. and Dainoff, M. (1986), *People and Productivity,* Holt, Reinhart and Winston, Toronto.

Frazelle, E. (1984), *Worker participation in office space planning and design process pays large dividends,* Industrial Engineering, 16, (12).

Kaplan, A. (1982), *The Ergonomics of Office Automation, Modern Office Procedures,* May.

Malcolm, C. (1986), *Paradox in the Office: Fitting the Workplace for People,* National Productivity Review, 5, (2).

Rubin, A. (1983), *The Automated Office - An Environment for Productive Work, or an Information Factory?: A Report on the State-of-Art,* NBSIR 83-2784-1, National Bureau of Standards, Washington, D.C.

Rubin, A. (1986), *Revised Interim Design Guidelines for Automated Offices,* National Bureau of Standards, Washington, D.C..

Stewart, T. (1985), *Ergonomics of the office,* Ergonomics, 28, (8), 1165-1177.

Walton, R. (1973), *Quality of Working Life: What is it?,* Sloan Management Review, 15, (1).

Chapter 4
Intelligent buildings:
their implications for design
and construction

T. CORNICK

4.1 INTRODUCTION

In order to consider the concept of intelligent buildings it is first necessary
to define what is meant by building and intelligence, and then to see if the
reality of the implied concept is both possible and desirable. Although many
definitions could be found for both terms, the following should suffice for the
purposes of this paper.

First, a definition of building:

"...building is a system of physical materials and components
which go to make an environment of a form of space...is a process
of total cycle of activities associated with a particular environment
from its inception to its demolition...is a character from the aggre-
gate of characteristics required to describe everything to do with a
building environment..." (Martin, 1971)

"...building is a set of conceptual systems of order which can be
perceived through spatial organization, functional organization,
circulation systems, physical imagery and context...these are reinforced by physical systems of construction that range from structure
to services..." (Ching, 1975)

From these definitions it can be seen that the nature of building is such that
it is both a process of conception (design) and realisation (construction) and a
product of physical systems that enclose and control an environment in order
to create a particular, desired effect.

Secondly, a definition of intelligence:

> "...intelligence is a sensory-motor adaption...in an organism it supports life which is a continuous creation of increasingly complex forms and a progressive balancing of these forms with the environment..." (Piaget, 1977)

Although this definition is limiting in psychological terms, in that it precludes the aspect of 'creative thought', it is the only definition that could possibly be applied to an inanimate object such as a building.

As a result of combining these definitions, it can be seen that for a building to be considered in any way 'intelligent', it must be able to respond to changes, by its own efforts, in its internal and external environment. It is then necessary to consider if this 'intelligence' is being applied in parts of the building, in a combination of parts or in the building as a whole system.

The use of the term 'intelligent building' has evolved because information technology - electronic data processing - and automatic services control have grown in importance in modern buildings, with once diverse systems now becoming increasingly integrated. However, the mere automation of any particular services system would hardly seem to constitute intelligence in a mechanical or electrical component: for example, the ball-cock cistern, the thermostat, or even vacuum communication tubes could hardly be described as intelligent systems (Eley, 1986). Even the integration of very sophisticated communication and control in other modern man-made artifacts, such as planes and ships, does not seem to attract the attribute or description of intelligent. So why should buildings?

It is likely that the term has evolved more for pure commercial marketing objectives in selling or letting built facilities than for the purposes of describing what any building is possible of achieving by its own efforts. It is interesting to note in this context that, in a recent survey of modern office accommodation needs (reported elsewhere in this volume by Worthington), some of the characteristics of a 'smart' project were considered to be such items as adequate car parking, room for expansion and capacity to install machines. The question to be addressed, therefore, is what really should constitute an intelligent building: why not 'smart concrete' as well as 'intelligent environments' (Cross, 1987)? How can they be created and what is the ultimate financial incentive for doing so?

4.2 ARTIFICIAL INTELLIGENCE APPLIED TO BUILDINGS

In recent years, artificial intelligence (AI) techniques have been experimentally applied to various aspects of the building design and construction process. These computer techniques have particular advantages over conventional computer programs (Cornick, 1986), the most significant of which is that they can model human reasoning. This means that knowledge-based 'expert systems' can be applied to every knowledge domain that is utilised in the building process; from the design of fabric systems (Cornick and Bull, 1987) to the creation and guidance of building regulations (Stone and Wilcox, 1987), and through to the control of services' systems of buildings in use (Birnie, 1987).

Their ability to model reasoning stems not so much from an imitation of the way people think - both creatively and with systematic analysis - but more from the way that the computer programs themselves can be developed by adding new information, gained from experience of practice, and still maintain their original integrity. This is because the data is kept separate from the 'inference mechanism'. Such an approach also permits questioning and answering through the use of natural language in the processing and presentation of conventional CAD graphical and textual data based on automatic calculation, retrieval and representation. This is an important innovation if the use of computers is to reduce and not increase the incidence of error in human decision making.

Ultimately, by integrating CAD graphics and knowledge-based systems (Gero and Maher, 1987), the modelling of the implications of design proposals for production resources and 'performance in use' can be achieved (Cornick and Bull, 1987).

Once this capacity has been reached through developments in hardware and software, it will be quite possible to produce a computer model of a building which encapsulates all the information on its conception, realisation and requirements for maintenance and operation. The development of sophisticated CAD graphics with databases is already allowing one major US architectural practice to extend into offering a facilities management service (Byles, 1987). All that remains to be added to such a computer system is a range of 'expert modules'. Once achieved, a complete information-base for a whole building can become a knowledge-base, with graphics and natural language processors creating an extremely user friendly interface.

4.3 ROBOTICS APPLIED TO BUILDINGS

The application of robotics to building is comparatively new and is being essentially considered, both in practice and research, for the physical construction process. The motivation for applying robotics to construction has been primarily to improve safety, quality, productivity and to compensate for a growing shortage of manpower coming into the industry: Japan has led the way in its introduction (Koskela, 1985). But of particular interest in the context of intelligent buildings, with respect to robotics, is the aspect of automatic reaction to changing conditions through sensors. The major problem to be overcome, in the design of sensor architecture for construction robotics, is creating the ability to detect location as, unlike the factory, the construction site is a dynamic environment. However, image processing and electro-optics are capable of meeting this need given enough cost incentive for application development (Yavni, 1987).

The application of robotic sensing in the completed environment would be, to all intents and purposes, static rather than dynamic. The reporting of an increase in design load on structure, design joint movement in element junctions or design circulation pattern on the corridor floor system would simply require the detection of movement. The in-service monitoring of structural performance, for such things as deflection under wind-loading, is already a reality in the UK through experiments being carried out by the Building Research Establishment. In addition, monitoring 'construction in use' is being advocated as part of a maintenance management system to be developed for local authority housing in Hong Kong (Bates, 1987).

4.4 COMBINING AI AND ROBOTICS IN BUILDING

The means exist already to develop an intelligent building. In a practical sense this could mean that the building would:

1. Begin its life with a knowledge-base that contained not only a resource record of its composition but also all the reasoning of why it was designed and constructed in a particular way.

2. Continue its life with robotic sensing that would monitor and demand correction as necessary against the knowledge-base of every elemental part of the building in use (and not only the services elements, which is the case with the current concept of intelligent building).

However a very strong cost incentive and management determination must exist for this to be applied in practice. This is because the briefing, design and construction phases of the total project process must be carried out in a far more rigorous and continuous way than is currently practised (Cornick *et al*, 1987). Moreover, this process should ideally begin with a 'maintenance policy'.

The continual reviews and confirmation of decisions all the way through every phase of the process, the employment of reasonably sophisticated computer systems, the addition of sensing systems to all elemental parts of the building and the degree of communication required between all the project participants - including the client - might not be possible with current forms of contract used in procuring buildings. But the very fact that many buildings may be required for a much shorter span of time than in the past, because of rapid social and economic change, might mean that all this effort is not really worth making. On the other hand, if it is decided that for resource conservation reasons buildings should be designed and built to last, but be capable of adaption in use, such an effort is well worth making as an aid to economic facilities management.

4.5 CONCLUSIONS

It can be seen that the technology is, or very soon will be, available to create reasonably intelligent buildings, in terms of a much truer definition than is currently being promoted. The incentive, however, for doing so has to be a very strong one because of the management commitment required. That incentive is likely to exist only if buildings are still to be considered as a reasonably long term investment and that their facilities management should be carried out in a much more rigorous and systematic activity than it is currently practised.

4.6 REFERENCES

Bates, R.A. (1987), *A Maintenance Information System,* in Spedding, A. (ed), Building Maintenance Economics and Management, Spon, London.
Birnie, W. (1987), *Expert systems are here to stay,* Controlled Systems Journal.
Byles, C. (1987), *Practical aspects of CAD,* CIB Working Group, W-78, London.
Cornick, T. (1986), *ESCAD '86 Workshop Report,* University of Reading, Reading.
Cornick, T. and Bull, S. (1987), *Expert Systems for Detail Design in Building,* Proceedings of the CAAD Futures Conference, Eindhoven, University of Technology, Eindhoven, Netherlands.
Cornick, T., Biggs, W.D., Broomfield, J. and Grover, R. (1987), *A Quality Management Model for Buildings,* Proceedings of the European Organisation for Quality Fifth Seminar, London.
Ching, D.K. (1975), *Building Construction Illustrated,* Van Nostrand Reinhold, New York.
Cross, T. (1987), *Intelligent Buildings - Business Opportunities,* Intelligent Buildings Corporation, Denver, Colorado.
Eley, J. (1986), *Intelligent Buildings,* Facilities , 4, (4).
Gero, J. and Maher, M. (1987), *A future role for knowledge-based systems in the design process,* Proceedings of the CAAD Futures Conference, Eindhoven, University of Technology, Eindhoven, Netherlands.
Koskela, L. (1985), *Construction industry towards the information society - the Japanese example,* FACE Report No.7, Technical Research Centre of Finland, Helsinki, Finland.
Martin, B. (1971), *Standards and Building,* RIBA Publications, London.

Piaget, J. (1977), *The Origin of Intelligence in the Child*, Penguin, London.

Stone, D. and Wilcox, D. (1987), *Intelligent Systems for the Formulation of Building Regulations*, Proceedings of the Fourth International Symposium on Robotics and Artificial Intelligence in Building Construction, Haifa, Israel.

Worthington, J. (undated), *Smart Parks - Accommodating the Needs of Information Users - A European Perspective*, DEGW, London.

Yavni, A. (1987), *Sensor Architecture for Mobile Construction Robots*, Proceedings of the Fourth International Symposium on Robotics and Artificial Intelligence in Building Construction, Haifa, Israel.

Chapter 5
Design for new technology

M. DAVIES

5.1 INTRODUCTION

The last twenty years have seen the emergence of a second Industrial Revolution, where the results of fundamental new scientific research in solid state chemistry have radically changed habits, life styles and operational systems in modern industrialised countries.

One of the largest growth sectors in the industrialised world has been the field of information technology and its hardware and software support. Methods of organising and processing data of all descriptions have taken several quantum jumps, each of which has been catalysed by break throughs in micro-chip chemistry and in miniaturised assembly processes.

In fifteen years, the computer has shrunk thousands of times in volume and has achieved colossal increases in processing power whilst dropping to a fraction of its original cost. Development is still continuing rapidly towards the transputer, a complete computer system on a single chip.

The science fiction of the 1930s has become a reality. The ray gun of Flash Gordon is here in the form of the laser, and the universal spy data banks of the despots are present as minicomputers. But rather than ruling the world, the laser and the spy data banks are now printing the letters, reading the discs and doing the accounts, as useful tools serving man's needs.

The information revolution has changed our life styles and working methods and is placing new demands on our built environment, particularly in the world of trade and commerce. Our modern buildings are now being affected by three powerful influences:

1. The growth of information technology and its infrastructure requirements.

2. Greater expectation and demand for increased quality of the human environment.

3. Demand for better building performance, maximum economy of building operations, maintenance, growth and change.

It is these three influences which are shaping our new buildings into a high technology profile. It is also possible to identify an increasing demand for more individual and identifiable buildings. This is simply a market realisation that individual distinction, quality, character and identity are preferable, more saleable, and better liked than the uniform office acreages of the 1960s. This is an important demand but is not fundamentally affecting the evolution of high technology building.

5.2 GROWTH IN INFORMATION TECHNOLOGY

The first major influence, the growth of information technology, is forcing the building design team to allow for new technical requirements and to study and incorporate new elements. Key elements and requirements stemming from the impact of new information technology include:

1. Major data distribution networks integrated within the building fabric.
2. Communications input and output systems for the building including satellite dishes, microwave antennae, radio, television, laser and other aerial relay systems on roof tops and hard-wired below-ground links such as cable TV and dedicated data line systems in addition to normal telephone links.
3. Ease of access to all building data-ways and reservations without major disruption to the working environment.
4. Exponential growth in numbers of local and individual data processing and terminal points.
5. Significant growth in power requirements in high terminal usage areas.
6. Significant growth in density of power, telephone and data connection points.
7. Artificial lighting, glare and anti-veiling reflection control in relation to data display terminals.
8. Growth in thermal loads in the typical office environment despite increases in efficiency of equipment.
9. Growth of 'black box' parks, secure data storage areas, remote CPU rooms etc..
10. Growth of technical services support for information systems: uninterrupted power supplies, stable current generators and power smoothing equipment, emergency generators, battery rooms etc..
11. Growth of computing support personnel areas and maintenance zones.

12. Growth in thermal loads in 'black box' and technical service support areas.

The overall information technology demand is essentially for well integrated, accessible information networks with adequate reserve and back up support in a flexible building fabric incorporating realistic servicing space allowances.

5.3 INCREASED QUALITY OF ENVIRONMENT

The second influence on our building, greater expectation and demand for increased quality of environment, is characterised by:
1. Higher general design and ergonomic standards.
2. Greater expectation and demand from the thermal, luminous and acoustic performance of the general building environment.
3. Greater demand for local and individual control of personal space in terms of thermal, luminous and acoustic parameters.

There is a realisation that good design and the ability to express individual preferences within the general environment increase efficiency, quality of life and job satisfaction.

5.4 BETTER BUILDING PERFORMANCE

The third influence, the demand for better building performance, economy of operation, maintenance, growth and changes, brings in key design issues:
1. Appropriate design for the task.
2. Good planning and efficient net-to-gross usage.
3. Inherent energy economic design.
4. Good technical fabric specification in terms of structure and equipment, and in terms of skin performance, insulative and solar control properties.
5. Energy monitoring and management within the building, including daylight linked automated control of internal lighting systems, integrated as part of a building automation system.
6. Low running and maintenance costs of fabric and energy systems.

The demand here is for high performance, efficient and easily operable and maintainable buildings.

5.5 SPECIFYING HIGH TECHNOLOGY BUILDINGS

These three areas - the demands of the physical fabric, the demands of the new information technology and the environmental demands of the human users, when viewed together, specify the needs of the emerging high technology building.

The convergence of these demands obliges the design team to allow for the physical changes required in the building fabric, the sub-floor wire-way, the vertical data riser network, the satellite dish housing, the 'black box' park, and the locally controlled flexible air conditioning system. Design teams are now resolving these issues and the elements are already being incorporated in high technology buildings along with a related general improvement in new buildings of net-to-gross area ratios, multi-tenant divisibility and general flexibility of use. The demands for new spaces and places within buildings can be provided relatively easily as integral parts of high technology building.

The overlapping demands of high performance building fabric, increased user comfort, and integrated information systems are far more difficult to resolve when viewed from the point of view of the building services. It is the area of building services rather than in fabric or general building image that we can expect to see the greatest change and the strongest moves towards a true high technology environment.

Building services are beginning to undergo fundamental changes stemming from the spin-offs of information technology and the new chemical revolution.

The first pattern of change is from building services as generalised equipment systems, providing averaged environmental conditions in generalised spaces, to local area response systems providing particular conditions selected by individual users in particular spaces within the overall environment. Individual choice of environmental parameters is becoming necessary owing to the impact of information equipment in the local space. Systems with local heating, cooling conditioning, lighting and even acoustical control are emerging.

Building services are beginning to respond to the technology on the desk, at the desk. Floor-based lighting, air conditioning and fluids distribution systems are now emerging which are compatible with and run alongside the information distribution networks.

The new personalised workstation can be almost entirely serviced from the floor as an individually treated environmental zone. What is emerging is a more flexible, more locally responsive building services system. One can see building services in discreet form beginning to pervade the variable and soft interior spaces of the building as flexible and adaptive systems, rather than being fixed distribution trees tied to the structure.

The second pattern of changes of the building services in the high technology building leads to a more radical harvest, the seeds of which are nevertheless already in evidence.

Building services systems spend most of their working lives combating large thermal swings due to excessive solar gain or radiative thermal loss through inefficient building envelopes. The glass industry has moved from the single glazing of yesteryear to double glazing and to various forms of tinted, aluminised and, more recently, low emissivity coated glass, each with increased thermal performance. These building envelope products are, however, skins with fixed properties. Once chosen and installed as building cladding, fixed sets of skin properties pertain. The reflective glass that is good for reducing solar gain in the summer is not the glass one wants to help gain maximum energy penetration in winter conditions.

The building services work hard to compensate for inadequacies of the building skin at different times of the day and night, the week, and the year.

Several buildings have been constructed where the building envelope permits air circulation between glass leaves, allowing a certain amount of energy to be transported away from the facade to other parts of the building, or to heat exchange and storage systems. Energy can also be transported to the facade by the circulating air to be deliberately lost as radiation to the external environment. The concept is a crude example of a dynamic facade. But is such a facade a simple wrapper, or is it part of the building services system?

Advanced molecular chemistry has brought us the micro-chip and the solar cell, both originally prohibitively expensive but now universal in application and costing a matter of pence. The same chemistry has also brought us a new range of compounds, which have variable properties. Photo-chromism, the property of a product to darken or lighten depending upon incident light levels, is familiar to us as 'Reactolite' spectacles, a Pilkington development. This is a light controlled, variable property product. New electrically controlled surface darkening products, electro-chromic materials, have now emerged, which change their visual transparency levels by the application of a variable low voltage electrical current.

A fully reversible electro-reflective surface with properties variable between clear, highly reflective, or black surface states, would have a radical effect upon the thermal and luminous transmission performance of the building skin and would banish forever, the current concept of fixed building services inside a fixed property building envelope. For the first time, we would be in possession of a dynamically viable adaptive building skin material which would inevitably be an integral part of the services systems of our buildings.

A second generation range of multi-layer building skins, 'polyvalent walls' with dynamically variable properties may be developed, incorporating low voltage electrical distribution patterns and simple sensing, logic and control devices which would themselves be connected to the computers which would monitor other building services. We then have at our disposal an intelligent, integrated services system.

We would then add to this technically 'smart' network, the capability of remembering and responding to the habits of building users, via building automation and energy use monitoring systems. We can record which areas are used at regular times, which rooms are unoccupied, need pre-heating or mothballing for the rest of the day, how people's lighting level preferences vary depending on the weather, where people congregate in large numbers and increase thermal and humidity levels, when the night security system should cut in, allow for the late meeting or maintenance shutdown. The coupling of climatic environmental monitoring, active response, and control with awareness and response to the building users and their habits and needs creates the concept of the intelligent environment.

The molecular chemical nature and pattern configurations of the polyvalent wall are such that it will be able to exhibit selective area darkening or colour change. The polyvalent wall can therefore carry display information and imagery. Combining this capability with the communication and data transfer infrastructure of the new building will make the building come alive visually as well as technically, enabling it to be used in part as a live information screen. We now have a thinking and communicating building.

5.6 CONCLUSIONS

A vast range of simple solid state products of the second Industrial Revolution are developing around us and are at our disposal. If the truly high technology building is to come about and provide a more responsive and adaptable working environment, our task as architects, developers, scientists, engineers and manufacturers is to elaborate the dynamically interactive building, that is, the design of the intelligent environment.

The proposal here is a form of unified field theory of building services where the building shell, the building services and its information systems become one intelligent organism. The theory is still in its early evolution but happily most of the operational elements required to bring this theory to practical fruition as a working concept exist already. In the next decades, advanced buildings will come alive.

Look up at a spectrum-washed envelope whose surface is a map of its instantaneous performance, stealing energy from the air with an irridescent shrug, rippling its photogrids as a cloud runs across the sun; a wall which, as the night chill falls, fluffs up its feathers and turning white on its north face and blue on the south, closes its eyes but not without remembering to pump a little glow down to the night porter, clear a view-patch for the lovers on the south side of level 22 and to turn 12 per cent silver just after dawn.

Chapter 6
Retaining flexibility for future occupancy changes

J. WORTHINGTON

6.1 THE CHANGED WORKING ENVIRONMENT

The assimilation of automation is having a profound effect on working environments and the specification of the building they are housed in. The building environments of the mass data processing operations of the financial institutions are hard to distinguish from the assembly functions of an electronics manufacturer; whilst the managerial, professional, and analytical roles of many office functions reflect an environment more akin to the home or the 'club'.

Advances in microcomputer technology have meant:

1. Increased computing power in a smaller amount of space, so that complex workings can be crammed into smaller products.

2. Miniaturised 'intelligent' chips which now turn the computer into a component that can be embedded in an increasing number of end user devices that can perform or control a variety of functions.

3. Increasingly sophisticated international, national and local building communication networking systems.

4. Greater freedom for the individual to become a manager and a strategist.

The last fifteen years, stimulated by the increased ease of communication afforded by information technology, have seen a change in organisations from:

1. Being corporate, hierarchical and centralised to being more individualistic, breaking down into small autonomous profit or cost centres, and decentralised.

2. Being composed of clerical and supervisory staff to having a greater proportion of managers, professionals and analysts.

Research by EOSYS in the UK ORBIT 1 study - also involving DEGW - identified that by the end of the decade about four million of the roughly ten million UK office workplaces will accommodate some kind of electrical device. This is approximately half the rate of take-up being experienced in the US and yet quite enough to put enormous strain on our stock of existing office space.

The impact of these changes on the built environment will result in:

1. More sophisticated equipment requiring more space at the workplace as well as specialised rooms and servicing.

2. More professionals requiring more and better quality space and a reduction in the number of clerical functions.

3. The allocation of space to tasks rather than people.

4. More demand for ancilliary space such as meeting rooms.

5. More demand for privacy and individual offices.

6. Longer opening hours and shift work to maximise the expensive equipment.

The direct physical consequences will be more wires, larger ducts, smaller spaces and a greater diversity of environmental standards to reflect the wider range of functions.

Most of the technology which will have greatest impact on office design over the next ten years already exists and is being used by organisations at the leading edge. The current problems which organisations are experiencing are not short term. The popular conception that information technology equipment can operate in the conventional office environment is optimistic and misleading. The computer has escaped from the computer room. Information technology is wild and likely to occur randomly in more or less problematical concentrations anywhere within a building. Developments in technology such as more powerful, thinner cables and smaller, less environmentally demanding equipment will not unluckily, at least until the end of the decade, cure the building problems generated by information technology.

Problems will continue to exist as:

1. New equipment only partially replaces models in current usage.

2. Machines become more powerful relative to size.

3. Cables become more powerful and elegant, although equipment will proliferate and require interconnections.

4. Increased density of equipment generates the demand for power and other connections.

Computer technology is developing at a frightening speed, but buildings take a long time to change. Most of our office building stock already exists, as we replace only about 3% per year. Much of this stock is of the 1960s and early

1970s and has inadequate floor to floor heights, is underserviced and has poor insulation. The result is that many of these buildings are quite unable to cope with the impact of information technology.

6.2 REDUCING THE LIKELIHOOD OF BUILDING OBSOLESCENCE

ORBIT 1, a multi-client study mentioned already, concluded that upgrading typical 1960s speculative office blocks could cost in the region of £15-£35 per sq. ft. (1983 prices). The implications of this for many 20 year old office buildings with inadequate floor to floor heights, poor cladding and minimal environmental systems is that it would probably be cheaper to demolish and rebuild. In the City of London the prognostication has been proved correct with the demolition of Lee House on London Wall.

One of the immediately useful products of ORBIT was the building appraisal. The objective was to devise a means for assessing the potential of any given office building new or old, or on the drawing board, to accommodate information technology. Criteria were assembled under four main headings, building on the case studies and the team's professional experience:

1. *Capacity:* how easily can the demands of information technology be physically accommodated, that is, space for vertical and horizontal ducts, and cellularisation?

2. *Adaptability:* assuming the building has sufficient capacity, how easy is it for the occupier to effect later changes?

3. *Buildability:* how easy is it for the contractor to carry out changes?

4. *Manageability:* how much effort and cost must be put into running and adapting the building?

The main characteristics that continually asserted themselves were:

1. Effective planning, servicing and perimeter grids, which allowed for small individual offices, group spaces and ancilliary areas such as machine and meeting rooms.

2. The configuration of the floor plan (say up to 18 m width) which allowed for small offices for external aspect and a central internal zone for support areas.

3. Provision for cooling and zoning of air conditioning to cope with random concentrations of heat-producing equipment.

4. Space both vertical and horizontal for ducting, to allow for increasing interconnections of equipment by cables of various types.

5. Lighting which could be varied to cope with a wide range of tasks.

6. Adaptability of services both mechanical and electrical to cope with accelerating change.

The specification for the effective building included:

1. Good scope for partitioning: depth of floor plan 14-16 m wide; perimeter detail, window mullion space to provide effective width offices (2.5-3.0 m), a flush finish and reduced sound transference; servicing and lighting grid not in conflict with partition locations.

2. Ample ducting: adequate floor to floor height to accommodate a raised floor and ducting (minimum 3.0 m but in financial services and other high technology buildings, as much as 4.0 m); raised floors (150 mm clear) or high grade floor trunking (1.5 m spacing); dense outlet points; adequate risers (typically, 2% of office floor area).

3. Finely zoned ventilation system: individual control of identifiable areas; local thermostats and switches; zoned plant, decentralised systems; capacity for add-on local plant to meet specific functions; flexibility for adjusting systems.

4. Permeable structure and adaptable finishes: service voids easily accessible; finish easily changed.

Since the ORBIT study, DEGW have developed their approach to building appraisals in the realisation that just like any other product it should be possible to test building proposals against predicted user requirements, thereby improving the life expectancy of a building.

6.3 DESIGNING FOR TIME

Buildings are permanent whilst the organisations and activities within them are continuously changing. To reflect their different timescales the process of building briefing and design can be layered:

1. Building shells: the structure and enclosure of the building lasts at least 50-75 years, whilst the function within may change many times over. The robustness of a shell to allow for change is reflected in the:

- Depth of space, that is, the dimensions from a perimeter window or central core to perimeter: the choice of depth influencing the flexibility of servicing and environmental control; the percentage of enclosure possible; and the variety of size and configuration of

working groups.
- Location of cores, which influences spatial efficiency, zoning for security and sub-divisions, and ease of communication.
- Space for services, influenced by the floor to floor heights, to allow for horizontal duct space, distribution of vertical risers and easily accessible space for locally distributed add-on plant.
- Configuration of building blocks to allow continuity of space for flexibility of layouts and ease of interaction between working groups.
2. *Servicing:* the heating, ventilation, distribution and cabling infrastructure of a building, which may have a life span of 10 years or less before the technology becomes redundant. Specific servicing configurations may be added to adapt the building to special functional requirements, such as a training facility, mainframe computer or laboratory spaces.
3. *Scenery:* the fitting-out components of a building, such as ceilings, lighting, finishes, walls and furniture, which adapt a building to a specific organisation's requirements. In city centre offices where organisations tend to grow and change, the life span of a retro-fit may be in the region of 5-7 years.
4. *Settings:* the day to day and week by week adaptations of the building in use to the minor adjustments of the organisation and re-arrangement for varying activities. The facilities manager and individual members of staff have an important role in orchestrating the continuing adaptation of the building to reflect the dynamism of the organisation as it adapts to meet the demands of changes in the marketplace and technology.

6.4 ORGANISATION STRUCTURE

Organisations vary in their demands on buildings, depending upon their maturity, size and expectations. Research by DEGW has identified five stages in the growth of an organisation. At each stage, as the organisation matures, different accommodation demands are apparent. The five stages in the 'premises ladder' are:
1. *Embryo:* start up organisation often working in somebody else's premises, or part time and still employed by a large organisation.
2. *Infant:* own space within a larger building. The thrill of establishing the organisation precedes concern about the quality of the working environment.
3. *Youthful:* individual entrepreneurship is all important, systems

are established, real estate policies formed and a concern emerges for the quality of the external image.

4. Mature: the organisation has its own building, with an in-house premises specialist and the desire to project a distinct corporate style.

5. Established: the organisation owns land and buildings. Single functions tend to be located in individual buildings. Procedures and standards are well established.

Requirements may be further influenced depending on the expectations of the organisation, which may be craft-based, wishing to stay small, with the owner in control and undertaking the work, or opportunistic where the original owner will wish to grow by passing work down to others and by applying technology.

ORBIT 2 identified that the demands on a building to absorb information technology varied according to the type of organisation to be accommodated. The study concluded that organisations could be classified according to the speed at which they were changing (fast or slow) and the type of work they undertook (routine or non-routine). The profile of demand for a high change, non-routine organisation varied considerably from that for a slow change, routine organisation.

6.5 BUILDING LAYOUT AND ORGANISATION STYLE

The pattern of work undertaken by an organisation is reflected by the layout and strategy adopted for dealing with information technology. A professional firm of lawyers, working on a one to one basis with clients, tends to work in individual offices, with decentralised office automation, whilst a design office of a manufacturing company requires open planned easily changed project groups with centralised databases.

The interior layout of buildings may similarly reflect the management style an organisation wishes to adopt, depending upon the degree of enclosure, the distribution of space to individual or communal activities, the information technology strategy and the quality of finishes. The long term adaptability of a building will most likely depend upon the range of organisational demands that can be accommodated.

6.6 BUILDING APPRAISAL

With consumer products, the customer is provided with clear measures of attributes which show why one product might be better than another for specific market sectors. Consumer organisations publish comparative guides on the performance of anything from tin cans to radios. Why is the same vigour not applied to the assessment of buildings?

Eleven Buildings Compared, a comparative study of major buildings being built in the City of London, was undertaken by DEGW for Rosehaugh Stanhope. The study, which was guided by the requirements of the financial services sector, analysed the effectiveness of each of the buildings in meeting a typical organisation's requirements. The criteria used covered:

1. Location and accessibility.
2. Spatial efficiency.
3. Quality of space provided: depth of space; ability to meet varying layouts; potential for locating service areas and ducts; and space for trading floors.
4. Building services: air conditioning; electrical services; lighting and security systems; vertical access and lifts; and overall flexibility.

The optimum building form was medium depth, with large floor plates (15,000 sq. ft. or more), continuous space, adequate floor to floor heights and dispersed cores.

For the first time in London the choice of buildings could be compared and rated against common criteria.

The approach has been further refined at the building design stage allowing a building proposal to be tested against a series of tenant profiles, the location of cores, structural and planning grids, and depth and configuration of space adjusted to provide maximum efficiency. The results of these studies, having been used to enhance the design process, are then subsequently used to explain the building's potential to tenants.

6.7 DEALING WITH THE EXISTING BUILDING STOCK

A problem faced when adopting information technology is that it happens gradually: first, a word processor system is installed followed by, say, four microcomputers for professional use, and then a minicomputer for the accounts. The result is that four separate organisations (within the one organisation) have a stategic plan for dealing with the upgrade of the building to accommodate information technology, but are drip-feeding money out of revenue to pay for adaptations. In a study of the operating budgets of a cross-section of organisations, Bernard Williams Associates found that as much as £1.25 per sq. ft. of the annual maintenance budget could be spent upgrading to meet the needs of information technology.

Organisations, as their take-up of information technology increased, found:

1. Deterioration in their utilisation of space, as more individual offices are added in an ad hoc fashion; space is taken over for support machinery and equipment proliferates at the individual workplace.

2. Duplication or triplication of systems; increasing numbers of terminals, local area networks (LANs) and peripheral devices, and dedicated processor units becoming decentralised on to the office floor.

3. Deterioration of the working environment, with heat from the machines and peripheral devices, trailing wires, reflections on displays, and a cluttered visual environment.

4. Adaptation costs increasing, with the continuous need to reposition or add cabling, change partitions, and the addition of local air extractor systems to alleviate the heat build up. It is not unusual for organisations to be spending £2.50 per sq. ft. per annum on adaption costs and a further £2.50 per sq. ft. on energy costs to match the needs of information technology in inadequate buildings.

As the pressure on space increases, the quality of the workplace decreases, and the office population becomes more professional and demanding. More forward-looking organisations want to plan ahead for information technology and audit the ability of their building stock to cope with these demands. The outcome of such a review is to establish the speed of information take-up; the capacity of the building to handle information technology; the efficiencies of space usage; and future organisational demands.

To meet these pressures, organisations are looking for an incremental upgrading programme that can be integrated with an office automation policy and initiated over, say, a two to four year period, without disrupting the day-to-day pattern of work.

6.8 PROJECT PRIORITIES

On one recent project in Scotland, the priorities were to provide a flexible planning concept that restructured the space to allow for increased efficiency, and create a robust infrastructure of support services and standard sized offices around which change could occur. The principles for planning were to maximise the central zone of the building and reduce the width of the central corridor by establishing perimeter zones for offices, an offset corridor, a central mechancially ventilated zone for machine rooms, shared terminals and filing. The services infrastructure was upgraded by:

1. Establishing a central bulkhead with ducting for heat extraction and space for localised units to be installed as required.

2. Providing enclosed rooms in the central zone with heat extraction and adequate wiring capacity for noisy and heat generating machines.

3. Disengaging cable distribution from demountable partitions and installing a three compartment trunking system with adequate capacity, easy access with removable covers, and frequent outlet points. This system has been established at the perimeter and can be planted on partitions and furniture systems.

4. Improving the lighting, with the use of uplighters which reduce the reflection on screens, heat gain and ambient light levels while maintaining a sense of brightness and control over intensity.

6.9 CONCLUSIONS

As organisations rationalise and apply the latest information technology, they are becoming more aware of the shortcomings of their premises. In future they will be looking to improve the ways they use space so as to increasing its effectiveness. At the same time, they will be increasing organisational flexibility and upgrading the working environment to match the aspirations of a more enlightened workforce. Ways of reducing adaptation and maintenance costs will also receive attention.

Chapter 7
Communication infrastructures

D. LUSH

7.1 INTRODUCTION

Describing communication infrastructures, after papers on design and flexibility for intelligent buildings, may perhaps be seen as putting the cart before the horse - a more traditional description of failure to communicate. However, it may be a blessing in disguise as the range of elements encompassed by an infrastructure for communication impinges on all the features described in those other papers.

This volume deals with intelligent buildings, a title which in itself forms a classic example of a breakdown in communications as, currently, it may, and does, have quite different meanings to colleagues in the same office. Intelligent buildings, to the author, are those with a facade construction whose thermal and optical properties may be controlled automatically (and possibly directly by climate changes), and which can be integrated with the sophisticated and networked electronic and processor driven systems used for building services and office communication (information technology) tasks. A 'smart' building stops short of the variable parameter facade. There are others who reverse these definitions. At this point, which version is correct is less important than the fact that the definition is given.

The specific example is ideal for making a basic point. All communication systems or infrastructures are people dependent and technology is one of the tools used to make it easier, or so we are led to believe. The proper use of technology is to be welcomed, but in the construction industry it needs to be stressed that, from project conception to practical completion, professionals and technologists are involved and there are still problems of communication, at whatever level of technology is used. After practical completion, building occupants are expected to understand and operate the multiple systems designed into the building, all of which form part of the hierarchy of the communication infrastructure. It is fair to say that the capability of the majority of occupants falls short of the necessary standards. They can certainly be assisted by specialist organisations, but the technology of communication has outstripped the public's ability (and sometimes the equipment supplier's as well) to keep abreast of the changes. Education and greater awareness of the problems, whether during design, installation or operation, should alleviate the situation, but care is needed in the interim period.

The use of newly coined phrases or 'buzz words' to represent some novel facility or feature (or the repackaging of an existing system) is an area where a glossary of terms is essential. Without it, the most appalling mistakes can be made following a perfectly reasonable conversation between parties using the same words and phrases, but each meaning something different.

Before considering the logical sequence of a communication infrastructure, related to buildings, it would be helpful to take a look at another example of communication technology. It concerns the wholly numerical system for telephone numbers. For many years after it was introduced, telephone engineers much preferred to talk about, say, LANGHAM rather than 526 or REGENT instead of 734 for the adjacent London telephone exchanges. Words are still appreciated more than numerical codes by the majority of the population, whereas interpretation and transmission of data by technological means are better when using numerical forms. It may be the only realistic solution to the modern situation, but it has left most of us poorer in terms of certain geographical knowledge. We should welcome the reversion to the 'good old days' where, thanks to the progress in digital control, we are able to use optical character readers (OCR) and other forms of identification to scan and transmit written words cheaply and without error.

7.2 COMMUNICATIONS FROM BIRTH (THE BUILDING'S BRIEF)

It is reasonable to assume that the overall communication infrastructure will be correct only if it commences at the point where the brief for the building is being determined and then covers the requirements up to, and beyond, beneficial occupation. Figure 7.1 illustrates the communication infrastructure from concept to operation of the building.

There would be little argument with the statement that the problems are exacerbated with increasing sophistication in buildings and building services, although the potential problem should not be ignored in simpler situations. The area of intelligent buildings (however defined) implies a level of complexity starting almost certainly with the inclusion of air conditioning. Clients vary, like any other identified group or profession, in terms of how they define their requirements. Some will provide an extremely detailed brief which will still need refining and expanding, but captures most of the essential points. Others will provide only an outline brief, which requires development in basic terms

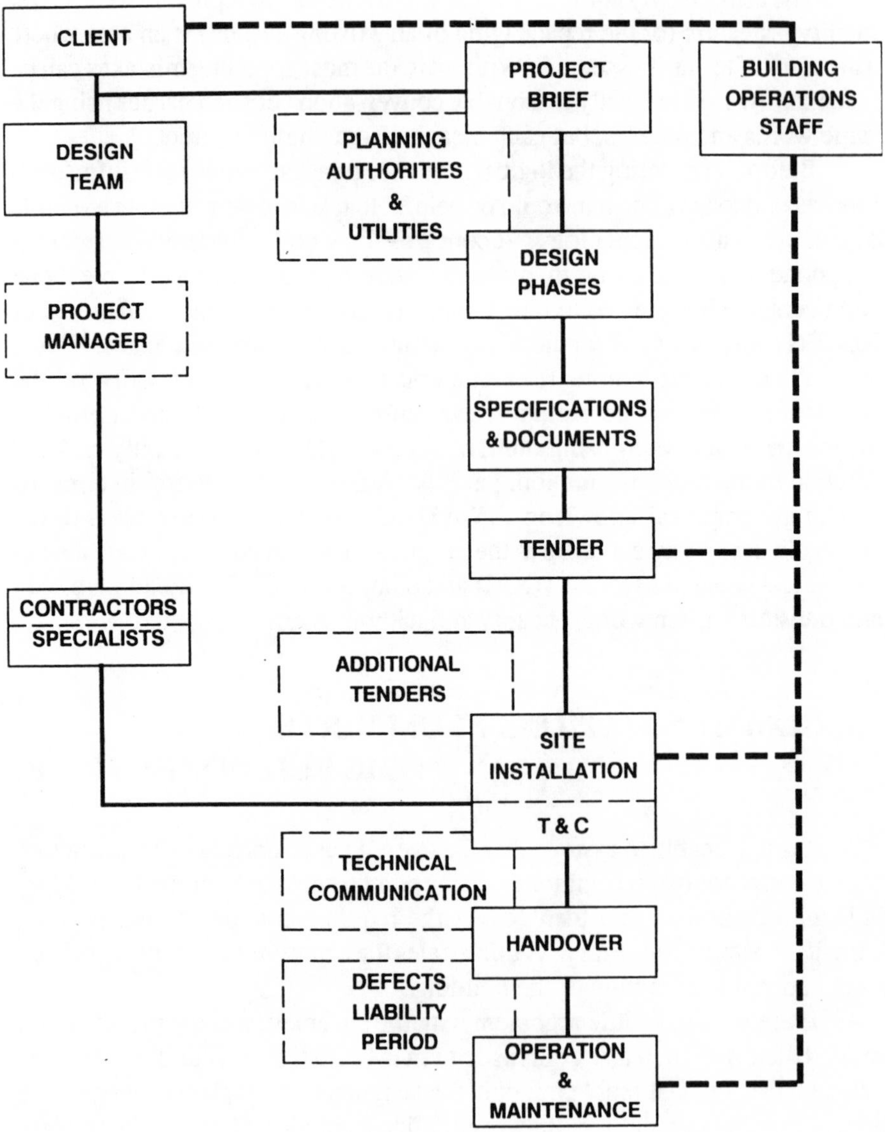

Figure 7.1: Communication infrastructure from concept to operation of the building

before approaching the detailed requirements. It can be difficult for owner/ occupier clients to clarify all the permutations for future use, changes in working practices, adoption of new technology and the flexibility to accommodate them (a subject addressed in another paper). The vast majority of clients for such buildings are providing speculative developments - however high the quality - and at the brief stage they normally do not know who the occupant is or whether it is a single or multiple tenant situation. It does not need much imagination to appreciate the additional problems for such cases, in completing the communications for the building brief 'loop' in the infrastructure.

A new dimension has been recently added in the context of communications and the brief (and in subsequent stages of the design, construction and operation of the building). It relates to the medically orientated elements that now have to be considered and which are outside the scope of the conventional designers' (architects and engineers) expertise. Irrespective of absolute importance, subjects such as legionnaires disease and the 'sick building syndrome' have to be included in the equation.

One element which needs to be clarified during any discussion on the brief is the quality of the necessary staff to operate and maintain the completed systems at the end of the project. Staff with suitable skills are always important and they are crucial to the success of high technology (intelligent) buildings. Agreement about matching skills to building services technology needs a fundamental link in the communication infrastructure which has far reaching implications, particularly if the final (unknown) occupier is responsible for employing such staff.

The status of the premises manager and maintenance engineers is still under-estimated by the majority of organisations involved in the financing, design and occupation/operation of buildings. Because the roles are undervalued, the staff employed tend to be underpaid and, as a consequence, are not educationally prepared for the tasks. There is a growing awareness among building occupiers of the need for facilities managers with suitable technical backgrounds, particularly where high technology office information systems are installed, but such managers are often short of the expertise for operating and maintaining conventional building services. This topic relates to communication in all its forms and warrants significant attention.

7.3 CO-OPERATION BETWEEN DESIGNERS

Traditionally, the client appointed an architect as the leader of the design team and consulting engineers of various disciplines were suggested by the client, for the architect's agreement, or the architect was given the freedom to recommend suitable consultants. The timescale and appointment of the professional advisers was such that the architect was entrenched and well down the design path before the other professionals were appointed and/or consulted. While the principles of appointment have not varied very much, the early involvement of the consulting engineers has become an essential feature of design for modern and, particularly, complex buildings.

Ideally, the consulting engineers should be involved in the discussion with the client on the content and development of the brief. So many elements of the internal environment for the occupants are dependent upon the correct development and design of the building services systems that the communication infrastructure should always encompass this common design approach. Joint professional briefing and development sessions with the client should be advantageous to both client and professionals. Mis-interpretation of needs and solutions should be minimised or, one might prefer to say, eliminated. At present the ACE consultants' agreements provide for this facility only as a 'time charge extra' rather than part of a normal service within the standard fee scales.

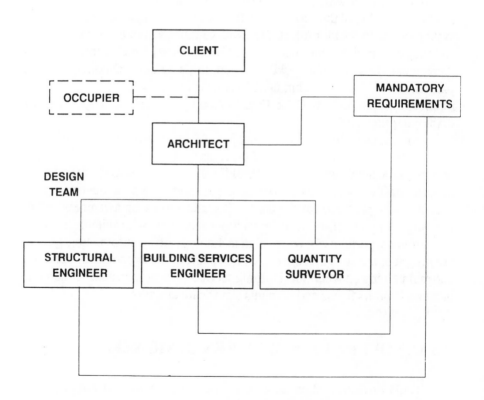

Figure 7.2: Conventional design arrangement

The conventional professional arrangement is shown in Figure 7.2, but for complex buildings (and possibly more generally) the multi-discipline design team (see Figure 7.3) should offer better results. The conventional system, with commitment from all the professions, can certainly provide wholly acceptable solutions. The multi-discipline approach may be a totally integrated professional team or a team of professionals from different organisations. Such arrangements should certainly offer advantages for better communication and more nearly ideal design solutions (the alternative view may be that there is less excuse for making poor design decisions).

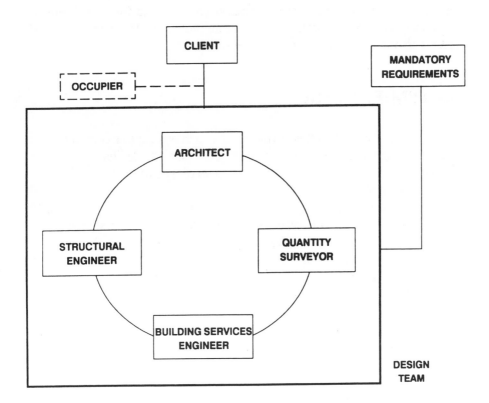

Figure 7.3: Multi-discipline design arrangement

Whatever form the design team takes, the process of design is an iterative procedure of communication between the various parties, limited by the physical resources available and the finite design fees. Thus informal communication to discuss and discard certain options is important to limit the more formal circulation of designs on paper and their subsequent amendment.

The designers also have to take into account the important communication network which covers local authorities, utilities, statutory requirements, and acceptable and accepted standards. Elements of this network may affect the brief either during design or at the conceptual stage.

The design work related to smart/intelligent buildings now encompasses a range of interfaces and boundary conditions between various elements of buildings and building services which were either unknown or unthinkable a decade or two ago. With the best will in the world, the total design and specification in such circumstances can only succeed where the individual design disciplines communicate about detailed requirements from a relatively early stage in the design process. Even then, changes in technology during the period from tender to installation can create problems. Holding one's cards closely to one's chest is not a recipe for success.

7.4 TENDER STAGE

It is generally at this stage in the construction process that contractors and sub-contractors become involved (there are forms of design and contract procedures which employ such organisations earlier in the process, but they are not included here).

The tendering process is important to the communication process in several ways. Fundamentally, it has to demonstrate that the design meets the financial constraints imposed by the client, as interpreted by the designers following the agreed brief. It also highlights, or should, any defects in communicating the brief, as a design, to the various contracting organisations, by virtue of their queries during the tender period or their qualifications submitted with the tender. One flaw in this viewpoint is to ask whether real or apparent defects in communicating the design intent on paper, for tender purposes, is seen by the tenderers as an opportunity for clarifying the intent, or driving a horse and cart through the holes at a later date (a slight variation on the horse and cart analogy used earlier). It is certainly the stage at which the designers have a final opportunity to check for potential problem areas, particularly at the boundary conditions between various complex high technology elements.

Buildings which have a potentially large high technology services and communication systems content suffer because the basic tenders have to be let well before the finalisation of many of the required systems. The communication infrastructure must be capable of identifying all the interface points for which solutions will have to be provided when the later systems are added. There is still a considerable learning curve to be climbed in this context. This area of uncertainty widens considerably when no tenant/occupier has been

identified at the tender stage. Recognition that such uncertainties do exist is the
essence of designing to minimise future problems.

7.5 CONSTRUCTION PERIOD

In the era of what is now called 'high technology buildings', the
construction period may be broken down, somewhat artificially, into several
stages. It is artificial only because there is little or no recognition as yet as to
the effect of complex building services and office automation systems on the
planning and site management of such projects. Where the fault lies is not for
discussion here, but the construction industry as a whole needs to rethink its
traditional practices (and communication infrastructure) on site - they are
rarely in tune with needs on modern sophisticated buildings.

7.5.1 Site installation

This covers the conventional period for the overall construction of the
building and building services, including testing and commissioning and up to
practical completion. Main contractors (or management contractors) are
responsible for planning the activities to achieve this, but the mechanical and
electrical (M & E) services are generally rarely defined in the necessary detail
for high technology buildings. Office automation systems, apart from telephones, are frequently part of separate fitting-out contracts, but where they are
included in the main contract they create the same problems as M & E services
and are not detailed to sufficient level in the construction plan.

One view of the present situation would be that a single block on the
network represents the installation of all the M & E services with, hopefully,
a period for testing and commissioning (which is always swallowed as float
time by all other activities in the network). Whilst this is a rather cynical
attitude, it is too often close to the truth. Somehow designers, contractors,
services sub-contractors and specialist suppliers need to improve their communications so that site planning for complex services becomes more realistic.

The bar chart in Figure 7.4 represents a simplified version of the activities
which have to be incorporated in the site planning network. It does not show
any of the office communication systems which could form an even more
complex, complementary network. Aspects of Figure 7.4 which relate to
testing and commissioning are dealt with below.

7.5.2 Testing and commissioning

The time required for these functions on a modern complex building may be two to ten times that commonly envisaged for sophisticated buildings of a decade ago. Testing and commissioning (T & C) does not cover the pre-commissioning checks such as pipe flushing and cleaning, all of which form part of the installation process. Figure 7.4 illustrates - apart from the cross-hatched area - a fairly conventional sequence of installation for an air conditioned building, either with or without a normal building management system (BMS) forming part of the controls and automation system. It is obvious from the diagram that the controls and automation testing and commissioning cannot commence until wiring is completed, and air and water balancing has been carried out. If these fundamental requirements are late, there is the tendency for practical completion and occupation to take place prior to such testing and commissioning. Without going into great detail, this situation highlights a basic misunderstanding of what a communication infra-structure is all about. The infrastructure is unsound, the technical elements of the controls communication system (and similar systems) are not validated and the occupants' environment will be unsatisfactory, creating other types of communication problems.

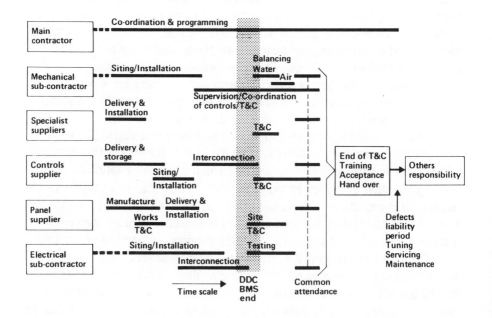

Figure 7.4: Site plan for M & E services, including testing and commissioning

Whilst beneficial occupation at the earliest possible opportunity is important to the tenant (because people have to be accommodated on a specific date) and to the developer (the generation of profit rental at the earliest date), does this outweigh the long term potential costs in utilising a building which does not meet the design intent and necessary environmental criteria?

Looking at Figure 7.4 in terms of the latest generation of BMS, with DDC (direct digital control), the new generation of sophisticated buildings will require an even greater change in traditional practices. DDC in building management systems replaces the conventional analogue controllers of traditional control systems. Since it is difficult, if not impossible, to run heating, ventilating and air conditioning plant without an operable control system, it will in future be necessary to commission part or all of the BMS using DDC, at a much earlier stage in the installation programme than is usual. It is not clear whether changes in attitudes or actions will be brought about by the slow process of education, pressure from clients or professional designers, contractors' realisation of the long term inefficiency or inappropriateness of the present system, or by some legal precedent initiated by a dissatisfied owner.

7.5.3 Practical completion and the defects liability period

At the end of the contractual site installation period, a certificate of practical completion is normally issued by the architect. This effectively signs off the contractor (and sub-contractors) as having completed the work they contracted to do (apart from clearly identified and listed snags which have to be corrected). Such a certificate, if signed before the testing and commissioning of systems worth seven figures has been completed, or even started, may be seen as either a breakdown in communication in its own right, or very risky. Contractually, no more work has to be carried out, other than correcting the listed snags and putting right defects which appear during the defects liability period - usually twelve months after practical completion.

This situation is potentially disastrous for specialist suppliers/sub-contractors, who are expected to complete their work, to the designer's satisfaction, often with the building already occupied. The consulting engineers are also in an invidious position as they have no contractual hold on such organisations. There is, of course, the retention of a small amount of money, but this is generally inadequate for the input often required. In fact, the engineers never have such control, but during the official contract period they can get the main/management contractor to exert pressure. In these circumstances, communication between parties has nothing to do with a formal infrastructure, it is based on commonsense, pride in completing one's own work and goodwill. It is nice when it works but it is not the correct way to complete projects and the goodwill is all too easily dissipated.

7.6 OPERATION AND MAINTENANCE

The need for staff with suitable technical training for the level of technology in a particular building was raised earlier, as a topic forming part of the brief for the building. It was acknowledged that even when defined, different situations arise with owner/occupier and speculatively developed buildings. In the former case, the staff should be selected and take up their role during the construction phase, so that they are fully conversant with the technical operation of the plant. In the latter case, tenants or lessees may or may not be identified in time to have staff on site prior to project completion. In both cases the infrastructure for communication must encompass the provision of comprehensive 'operating and maintenance' manuals for all the services and office automation systems in the building. They are a formal requirement of virtually every design specification and should be explicit in terms of detailed content.

Consistently, no matter how they are specified, they are difficult to obtain and often do not contain sufficient or even correct information. This is a perennial problem which becomes ever more important as systems become increasingly complex. Using specialists in the production of such manuals is an alternative solution but it still depends on obtaining 'as fitted' drawings from all the sub-contractors (having such drawings produced by the specialists would require site visits and measurements which would have serious cost implications). One means of applying pressure to obtain the manuals (draft versions must be available before testing and commissioning commences) is the declared opinion that it may be illegal under the 'Health & Safety at Work Act' to occupy and operate a building without such operation and maintenance manuals.

7.7 TECHNICAL COMMUNICATIONS INFRASTRUCTURE

The previous sections have covered communications infrastructure as it applies to the design, construction and operation of buildings and services within buildings, rather than to the technical communication infrastructure as it is, or may develop, in smart/intelligent buildings.

First, the main categories of information/communication systems in buildings need to be identified:

1. M & E Services: HVAC controls/automation; fire alarms; security alarms and facilities; lift controls; energy management; lighting controls; building management; public address/entertainment; closed circuit television (CCTV).

2. Office automation systems (information technology): telephones; telex; FAX; computers (mainframe with terminals and desk top machines); word processors/desk top publishing systems; audio-visual conference facilities; specialist requirements (for example, dealers' consoles).

The list itself gives some indication of the enormous spread of systems with elements of communication and information transfer, the majority of which have developed from different engineering sectors. The fact that most of these systems have embraced variants of microprocessor technology for communication purposes has not led to compatible data transmission systems, rather the reverse is true. Designers and users see some, perhaps many, advantages from compatible transmission systems and manufacturers concede that there is too much incompatibility. However, market forces tend to militate against compatible systems. It may require a large capital investment to redesign a system to meet a standard transmission protocol and a good system, with a unique protocol and a niche in a particular market sector, is some protection against competition.

There are initiatives towards information transmission standards, notably under the Alvey programme and latterly through the BEMS Centre set up with Department of Energy funding through the Building Services Research and Information Association (BSRIA). It will be some time before these efforts can be expected to produce agreed standards and in the meantime the design professions and users of buildings have to deal with the multiplicity of the building services and office systems.

The process towards networking of different systems and the reduction in multiple data transmission buses can only progress as fast as designers and users can assimilate the still rapidly changing technology and co-ordinate their efforts towards integrated systems. At the simplest level, experience has indicated that moving towards more complex building management systems, capable of performing an increasing range of operational and management functions, has not necessarily reduced the overall capital cost and has increased both the design time and site time during the testing and commissioning phase of the project. While this may be partly attributed to the learning curve and rapid changes in the equipment on offer (one generation not fully accepted before the next arrives), it provides a warning signal. The seductiveness of a totally integrated communication system can lead to an approach that creates problems and which the technology will solve. This tends to leave both designers and users finally hankering after what would have been perfectly suitable, simpler and an easier system in terms of both operation and maintenance.

There will be a time, not far distance, where such systems will be simple to design and co-ordinate. In the meantime, there will be increasing integration of existing systems and this is already taking place in the building services (M & E) field. Building management systems already provide control for HVAC systems, lighting control, plant automation and energy management, and are beginning to encompass fire and security alarm systems. In the past, fire, security and lighting were, and often still are, separate systems. Equally, the telecommunication elements of office automation systems are becoming more closely integrated. However, at present, the installation of specialist systems, such as dealers' room consoles, has been carried out at breakneck speed and has made total integration impossible. In some recent projects there have been as many as twenty-five separate specialist suppliers/contractors involved in the communication systems for such rooms. One is bound to ask if this is 'good' information technology?

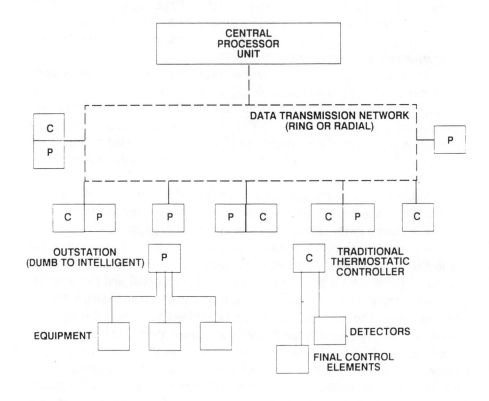

Figure 7.5a: BMS arrangements - obsolete form

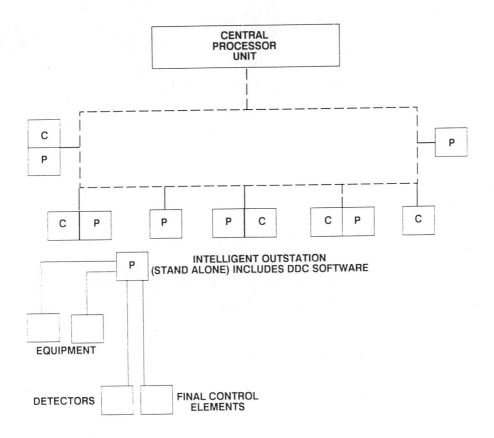

Figure 7.5b: BMS arrangements - current form

BMS arrangements are shown in Figures 7.5a and 7.5b. Some systems are still of the form shown in Figure 7.5a, although the move is towards the system outlined in Figure 7.5b. The intermediate stage of integrating a BMS with office automation systems could well be that shown in Figure 7.6, where there is a hierarchical network of independent systems monitored either by a superior version of the BMS processor or a separate supervisory processor. There will almost certainly be a need during this intermediate stage for transmission protocol transducers to allow data to be transferred from one data bus to another.

The real price of high technology communication solutions is still falling and users are steadily climbing the learning curve. This will lead to a continuing growth in sophisticated communication systems across a wide range of applications. The appearance of a new generation of equipment, while an earlier version is being installed for one's own system, does not necessarily

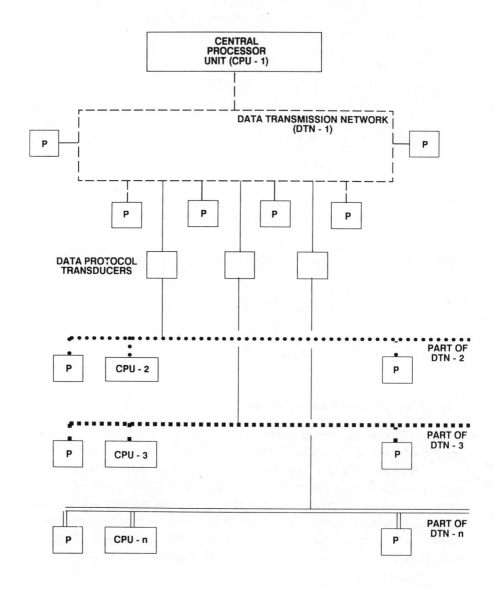

Figure 7.6: BMS arrangements - part of network hierarchy

make it obsolete, whatever the supplier may say. The most common claim for new systems is their ability to process data on a faster basis, which may be essential for one's own application. On the other hand, there are many applications where existing processing rates are already well in excess of what is needed: one should be aware of the need, or lack of it. While the ultimate communication infrastructure could be defined as one common data bus with all the related systems operating on the same transmission protocol, or through versions of the protocol transducers, there will always be a need for complementary data buses for normal standby purposes, for systems which are data secure for commercial secrecy reasons and for alternative routes for security alarm and fire alarm systems.

A good technical communication infrastructure is not necessarily the most sophisticated that can be devised or designed. It is one which satisfies the full design intent in accordance with the brief, in the simplest and most effective way to provide the user with a comprehensible, reliable and maintainable system.

Smart or intelligent buildings are those which use modern technology, and information transfer, to satisfy increasingly complex requirements in the simplest possible manner. This principle extends into the future when variable parameter facades will be available and the basis of the communication infrastructure will be 'keep it simple'.

7.8 CONCLUSIONS

Any communication infrastructure is composed of two elements: people and technology. Technology already permits the solution of any communication problem, at a cost, both in terms of equipment and the design and supervision effort needed to specify the system (and ensure that after installation it meets the design intent).

All forms of modern communication and information technology are well marketed and apparently attractive. Buyers and users do not always ask the questions most relevant to the needs of their system and suppliers are not always aware of, or forthcoming about, deficiencies in their own systems. In this field of endeavour, two points should be emphasised: the importance of people and *caveat emptor*. The success of high technology buildings is ultimately dependent on the people involved not the technology installed.

Chapter 8
Servicing the
intelligent building

R. PENGILLY

8.1 INTRODUCTION

Why is the question of servicing or maintaining the intelligent building a subject worthy of discussion at all? The answer is cost, in two senses of the word. The first, and probably the lesser of the two, is that intelligent buildings are more expensive to construct and require greater investment than 'conventional' buildings. Analysis carried out in the US indicates that the cost of putting up an intelligent building is somewhere between 7 and 10% greater than a conventional or traditional structure. It follows somewhat naturally that if you have spent more on your building, it is prudent to look after that extra investment by prolonging the life of the systems in it and getting the very best out of them.

The second sense, and the more significant, is that there is a quiet revolution going on in the way we use and run our buildings. For the first time, keeping a building running with all its systems operational has become crucial to many organisations' primary business activities. This applies whether or not they are tenants or owner/occupiers.

This recognition of the increase in strategic importance of keeping everything 'up and running' has itself been brought about by a change in attitude. That change reflects how we look at our buildings and what we expect from them.

The demands of today's business users is for immediate response. Their expectations of how their buildings will work for them has altered. Starting with the design on the drawing board, continuing right through the building's life, this shift can be focused in two quite distinct but related ways.

First, from the design aspect, the key word is 'flexibility'. Everyone wants a building that will be able to cope with change and meet the increasing demands of an expanding and changing world. There are many examples of where design considerations have had a major influence in this way.

However, once the building is up, the emphasis changes. Now the degree of flexibility is a finite quantity. You either have it or you do not have it. The new keyword emerges as 'functionality'. The need is to keep the building working; to keep all of the systems working; to cope with the changes going on all around without seriously impacting on the primary business activity on a day-to-day basis.

People, their businesses and even the machines they use, now demand sophisticated space envelopes in which to operate. Ignoring a system's supplier-driven influence, this customer-based demand has now taken over to some extent as the driving force and will continue to influence the speed at which intelligent buildings become part of our building stock.

8.2 OPERATIONAL, MAINTENANCE AND MANAGEMENT STRATEGIES

Clearly, if intelligent buildings are more complex and cost more to construct, there has to be a trade off somewhere. That trade off has to be in improved performance; either an improved performance from the systems and staff employed in the building or in reduced operating costs. These aspects of enhanced performance and operating cost savings are crucial to the intelligent building and emerge as important features in the definition of the Intelligent Building Institute. Broadly, they quote it as being one where the building management system is an integral part of the building and where these systems serve to enhance the well-being and productivity of the occupants. They also refer to the investment profile, operating cost savings and design flexibility as being specific attributes of an intelligent building.

It is evident that in the future all buildings will be intelligent to a varying degree, if only in terms of their energy efficiency, communications, data handling, fire and safety provisions and we will have to be able to cope with them.

There is a move towards intelligent buildings which can be seen world-wide. However, it is slower than the industry would like. Whilst this gives building owners, developers and facilities managers a breathing space, they must take this opportunity to formulate strategies to anticipate the consequences of this phenomenon rather than be left in its wake.

There have been instances where intelligent buildings have failed to live up to the initial hopes and expectations. The reasons for this are complex. However, two clear lessons have emerged from these cases. The first is that in order to succeed, a defined plan based on an integrated strategy of some kind must be followed. The second is that we must recruit and adequately train the right sort of people to operate and manage the buildings we are currently designing and constructing. In the recent past, when this has not been adequately done, we have ended up giving people buildings and systems for which they have no understanding of how the buildings will work or what they are supposed to do. At present, intelligent buildings rely on different forms of technology, albeit advanced. The sooner these can be brought together, and a management strategy established as to just how the building will be run in the long term, the better.

These different forms of technology are illustrated by the various systems serving an intelligent building and have been briefly referred to already:

1. An environmental system or building management system.
2. A business system or data handling system.
3. A communication system.

Each of these has an impact on the others at every stage of the building's development. Current practice is for these to be dealt with on an individual basis with very little reference or planned integration. Indeed, the level of skills and expertise is different in each case and, as a result, it is initially difficult to see how they could be brought together and combined under an umbrella of single source responsibility.

The technology involved, however, must be brought together somehow and managed efficiently to provide the owner/occupier with the necessary operational 'bottom line' performance if the additional capital investment in an intelligent building is to be considered worthwhile. The problem is that there are many new questions to be addressed before these elements can be successfully managed.

There have been attempts to achieve such an objective both in the US and here in the UK. The US has seen a variety of approaches:

1. The set-up of specialist companies to bring together different skills.
2. The large company offering a turnkey package addressing all areas within their own corporate structure.
3. The development of 'shared tenant services' giving a 'value added service' to the individually specified and installed services, throughout multi-tenanted buildings.

In the UK, developments have followed a less defined approach, with each element being designed separately and handled as an entity in its own right. Similarly, when the building passes from design to construction and on to occupancy, the manner in which these elements are treated reflects the fractional nature of the service industries. This leaves the responsibility and therefore the risk, with its associated costs, very much with the tenant or client organisation.

If the operation and maintenance of the services and systems within a high technology or intelligent building can be viewed in an integrated manner at the design stage, it would enable the building owner/developer to measure his requirements against the trade offs that might be gained by viewing the building as a whole throughout its expected life. In this way, the operational costs or overall 'cost in use' can be significantly reduced as a result of the economies of scale involved.

The problem that has to be resolved is one of how all these requirements can be accurately forecast at the outset and how they can be successfully integrated. To achieve this, it is necessary to take a longer term and broader view of the problem.

The total turnkey approach offered by a single company demands a very high level of control of the specification, which may well result in a degree of resentment or fear in closing off options too early. Indeed, it may well be difficult to see how one company alone can be a market leader in all of the necessary market skills and products.

8.3 AN INTEGRATED MANAGEMENT APPROACH

The increased capital incurred when producing intelligent buildings is linked to the expectation of reduced operating costs. In the UK, there are examples where owners and tenants are paying increased, even over the odds, premiums for such space. To date, often the only justification that can stand scrutiny for living in these types of buildings is that it either suits or boosts the corporate image.

This need not be so. Where an integrated approach is adopted to managing the systems in an intelligent building, the cost of residence need be no more than in a traditional building; indeed, it may well be less. To achieve this, a broader view of the services and their functions must be taken. This broader view has to take account of all the systems and the impact they make on each other. Although not specifically mentioned previously, this would have to include cable management as a significant component of either the building management or communication system. If the prospect of managing and operating intelligent buildings indicates that it is too broad for a single company to handle successfully, then it follows that it is similarly going to be difficult for traditional facilities management techniques to be successful. In this connection, it is worth considering how much is involved in terms of engineering knowledge alone.

Most organisations are not in themselves sophisticated energy users and therefore they need to look outside of their primary business expertise to find the more specialised resource they need. Similarly, in terms of communications management, how many organisations can truly claim to be abreast of all the current developments and changes that are taking place? Properly managed communications can have an impact on the success of a business enterprise and are of such strategic importance that they should be treated as part of the corporate plan. Generally, business system management is directly related to an organisation's primary activity and as such is to the fore of the previously mentioned areas; as a result, it is better served. However, the recent emergence of third party maintenance companies dealing in hardware and software maintenance indicates that perhaps all was not too well before, even in this area. Although just by being there, they create another headache. The choice becomes even wider than before and performance can vary tremendously. Selection demands insight and care, and consumes valuable management time as another factor is added to the equation.

So, if it is logical to adopt an integrated approach to managing these new buildings, does it make financial sense? It has already been suggested that many organisations are not sophisticated energy users. They do not have within themselves the financial and technical skills to maximise the current technological advantages, and this is in spite of the fact that, in many instances, their energy bill represents a very large proportion of their controllable costs. However, in endeavouring to get the energy usage under control, what criteria is used to judge whether the current performance is good or bad?

If the base figure is twice what it should be, then saving 20% or 30% is not really a major achievement - it is little more than the identification of obvious waste. Similarly, if by saving energy the equilibrium in terms of space comfort conditions is disturbed, the resulting interruption and dissatisfaction will soon eliminate the benefit of any expected savings. Energy costs, although important, cannot be viewed in isolation. It is a sad reflection that even now after the publicity that finite energy resources have had many architects, letting agents and property managers do not view energy efficiency as a factor in the marketing of properties. Whilst rental values move towards £50 and £60 per sq. ft., energy costs of £1.50 or £1.60 per sq. ft. are bound to have little effect on the overall equation.

It must be said that the unimaginitive approach taken by the Department of Energy and the Energy Efficiency Office to promote their ideas over the last twelve years has not really had a lot of style. First of all there was the 'Save it Approach', then the little lamented 'Lift a Finger Campaign' and now the more recent 'Monergy Programme': all have failed to convince. As a result of this, there is some comment that 1986's 'Energy Efficiency Year' was not as successful as it could or, indeed, should have been, as far as the overall property market was concerned. This is in spite of all the ministerial 'ballyhoo' and money that was spent.

What has changed is our view of the overall equation. If buildings are to be kept functional and save the purpose for which they were intended, then we have to take a broader, less fractional view of how we should run, operate and manage them. This indicates an opportunity for organisations with the requisite individual skills to work together under a single umbrella to provide single source (one stop) shopping that the market is currently seeking. This equation now invokes all of the support services in the service operations' budget:

1. Energy.
2. Repair and Maintenance.
3. Building Management.
4. Cleaning.
5. Security.
6. Lifts.

When these are included, the integrated management approach addresses a cost of nearer £6.00 per sq. ft. and the resultant cost savings become more significant. However, it is not just the cost of the equation that alters, but the very way we now look at it. The demand for instant response and constant availability demanded by organisations from their modern buildings or space envelopes means that it is not just enough to be able to keep one part working, the whole must be kept functional.

To cope with the change for which they were designed, today's buildings are often expected to remain up and working free from failure throughout their life. In many cases, this now means 24 hours a day, 365 days a year. It should also be noted that many energy management strategies are expensive in terms of the life of the mechanical plant serving the environmental services. Where this is not recognised and the energy management is not linked or integrated into the maintenance programme, the direct impact each has on the other can mean that money hopefully saved in one area is lost in another.

Moreover, where these functions are not closely linked under a common responsibility in the form of a performance contract, it is the client who picks up the extra costs. This is usually as a result of the well known phenomenon that when something goes wrong everyone tends to blame everyone else and with no common or single source responsibility the client very quickly becomes 'piggy in the middle'.

Within intelligent or high technology buildings, the level of performance of the environmental systems is greater than has been traditionally expected and so the likelihood of problems must be greater.

8.4 WHERE ARE THE SKILLS?

Generally, the need for an adequate supply of skilled labour is well recognised as being a national problem and there are signs that this awareness is stimulating action. However, if we are to cope with the increasing demands of operating and managing high technology or intelligent buildings, we need a much broader education for building designers. If we just go on educating ourselves as engineers and architects, instead of considering building design on the basis of benefiting other people, then it seems we are ignoring the real reason for the building, which is to seek and provide the technical, social and economic solutions.

Taking up the view that an intelligent building should be flexible and able to adapt to the changing needs of the occupants rather than the other way round serves to support this view. Therefore, we must turn away from the perceived requirement that building design is the vocation of the architect alone, with some help from structural engineers and surveyors, and move to the more integrated approach at the earliest possible opportunity. This must incorporate a wide spread of engineering, operational and general management skills.

Parents, school leavers and career masters do not take into account the prospects offered by building environmental engineering and in most cases are wholly unaware of the broader spread of opportunities that go to make up what is now beginning to be recognised as facilities management. Unfortunately the same could be said of our academic institutions, for the number of them offering full-time undergraduate courses is very small. Even more pitiful is the number of suitable applicants they are able to attract between them.

This lack of skilled staff is not just restricted to the professional level. In earlier years, the major manufacturing companies and contractors offered craft and technician apprenticeships and it was from these that the bulk of the industry's current workforce emanated. However, with the effect of the recession in the early 1970s, many of these training programmes were curtailed, the result being that the workforce was stabilised almost to the point of stagnation in the ensuing years. Today, many organisations in our industry can look to their staff to see that the average age of those they employ is considerably higher than it was ten years ago. Fortunately, steps have been taken to redress this imbalance and a number of worthwhile training schemes, at the undergraduate and apprentice ends of the scale, are again under way. However, it will be some years before their full effect will be felt by the industry.

Another area which affects the availability of skilled staff reflects the change in operation of many of the intelligent buildings that will serve the financial services market. These are now envisaging 24 hour operation to keep in touch with world markets and therefore require a full shift operation. Many organisations within the financial services sector have recognised this potential need and are gearing up to attract their share of suitable people. Unfortunately, they draw these people from the existing pool of industry-trained staff and offer no direct contribution themselves to future replenishment. This is especially sad when one considers that in most cases they could well afford to support their own or nationally recognised training schemes.

Moving on from the specific areas of engineering into the broader field of facilities management, it is clear that whatever career background a facilities manager may have - be it data processing, communications or whatever - he does need to understand the strategic implications of support services. It is the facilities manager's responsibility to not only install the equipment and see that it works, but also be responsible to look after the user's comfort in terms of the layout and environment. It is necessary to be able to communicate with architects and contractors, environmental, hardware and software engineers.

At the moment, the need for facilities managers is being recognised but little is being done to provide the necessary training and education. More often than not, the development of these skills is left to occur on an ad hoc basis. But things are beginning to change. The information technology revolution that has occurred is having an effect on the way we look at how buildings are designed and run. Today's information technology planner or systems manager may still be an engineer or technologist, but his responsibility is already seen as vital to business life. As a result, when his job is specified or advertised, it is often indicated that he will find himself reporting directly to the financial director, and rightly so.

For too long the cost of occupying buildings has been impossible to evaluate and measure. Technology can now allow us to do this and the new breed of facilities managers can demand and expect cost performance reports on how their buildings compare. £1.55 per sq.ft. for energy may not seem important when you are paying £55 per sq. ft. for space, but when you know your competitors are paying just £1.10 per sq.ft., then the £0.45 differential in prime energy costs will gather its own significance.

As skills develop and are recognised, the market will find its own answer to finding the people. Clearly, there is a need to provide the right recruitment and training prospects across the range of technology involved if we are to attract the right sort of people to operate and manage the buildings we are currently designing and constructing. If we do not, we will end up giving people buildings and systems which they cannot operate or even understand.

8.5 CONCLUSIONS

A secure business plan involving, at the outset, the building's operational requirements will enhance the chances of success for an intelligent building in the medium to long term. If a turnkey operation offered by a single organisation seems too restrictive or the breadth of experience demanded is too great for traditional facilities management to cope with, what other options exist?

It is entirely possible that we shall see a development of the 'specially set-up company' which originated in the US, but not as a single source organisation in terms of expertise. Instead, it is likely to be a group of expert organisations coming together as a consortium to meet the needs of the intelligent building's owner or occupier. Such a grouping would encompass the communication, environmental and business system skills, and offer the depth of experience and breadth of resource necessary to make it happen for the building owner. Similarly such a grouping can, by the economy of scale it would encompass, minimise the skill shortages that are now apparent. This would give the building owner a workable single source responsibility for negotiating his design specification and ongoing operational strategy, but allowing him the freedom to keep his individual options open.

In this context, the future of intelligent buildings is very much dependent upon our having the skills and management resources to operate them successfully. Without this structured capability to service the intelligent building, there are many potential pitfalls and increased operating costs awaiting the unwary owner/tenant.

Chapter 9
The intelligent building in practice

D.S. BROOKFIELD

9.1 INTRODUCTION

Although the term intelligent building has become a 'buzz word' of the 1980s, the first 'smart' buildings - those equipped with building automation systems - have actually been around for nearly 25 years. Over time, what has changed more than the technology itself has been the manner in which this intelligence has been showcased. Seen in the 1960s as a labour saving device, intelligence by the 1970s had become associated with energy conservation and crime prevention. Today, stemming from technology which permits shared, but secure access of computers, intelligence has taken on still another meaning. The newest evolutionary models pair building automation systems with sophisticated telecommunications and data processing capabilities, translating into a new angle on a building's marketability and an organisation's efficiency.

Once upon a time, buildings were simple structures. They had lights, air conditioning, plumbing, heating, a few stand-alone amenities and that was about it. Today, prospective office owners and occupiers are looking for more sophisticated features to be supplied as part of the original office shell. They are now looking for flexibility and rationalisation of network wiring, complex lighting arrangements, energy management systems, integrated fire and security, and access to wide area networking services.

Developers and architects are beginning to respond to this new demand by starting to build a completely new type of pre-wired and automated building - the new generation of intelligent buildings. The building may not look any different from the outside. But inside it will contain sophisticated electronics to revolutionise not only the way information is handled, but also the way in which a building's environment and services are managed, and indeed the way those services can contribute to an organisation's efficiency.

9.1.1 Defining the building's function

If we are to consider the role of building service applications in a smart building, or integrating building systems as a whole, there are a number of basic questions to be continually addressed:

1. What goes on in the building?
2. What role does the building play within the total organisation (worldwide)?
3. How best can the building, the environment and the services support and improve the business performance?

If we can answer the first question we are a long way towards understanding what makes a building work for an organisation. By considering what goes on in the building, not just the functions of the mechanical and electrical services but the specific services required to match the business function, the organisation can call upon those services to support the operations of employees and the environment. Clearly, with a speculative development the user has not been identified and the building can be equipped to meet the goals of the developer only. It is significant in the evolution of the smart building that the developer and the architect recognise the importance of information technology to the building occupiers' business performance. It can be assumed that he will require at least a safe, secure and comfortable environment in which to carry out his business and that he will need a telephone system, data processing, and telex facilities. However, more and more services and facilities are becoming essential in a building.

9.2 ACCOMMODATING INFORMATION TECHNOLOGY

The Department of Trade and Industry together with the British Institute of Management are continually encouraging UK organisations to implement information technology as a tool for improved efficiency and competitiveness. Most major organisations will now develop an information technology strategy in support of their operational business plan. Those organisations who extend their information technology strategy further to include their buildings and environments are in effect developing and supporting the smart building evolution.

So, what goes on in a building?

9.2.1 Applications spectrum

It is possible to consider the total information technology installation as an applications spectrum covering the three distinct areas of controls, communications and computers. At one end of this spectrum, we have the control systems which provide and manage security, safety and comfort. There will be a need for a considerable amount of interaction and integration within the control systems segment.

At the other end of the spectrum we have the information systems providing data and word processing, electronic mail, filing, text retrieval and specific business applications. The middle area of the spectrum is occupied by communication systems for voice, data and video, with transportation over LANs, WANs, microwave and satellite links.

It is here in the communication's segment of the spectrum that we can provide the lower layers of integration between sub-systems and also the means for flexible cable management and rationalisation. The smart building will embrace the integration of these three segments of the application spectrum to provide:

1. Lower installed costs resulting from shared communication paths, less cable and containment, and shared distributed processing across sub-systems.
2. Increased operating efficiency and faster, more accurate management for better decision making.
3. Lower operating costs due to improved network resilience, more effective staff utilisation and reduced maintenance costs.

To illustrate these points, it is helpful to consider an example integrated building management system and to consider firstly how it performs and secondly how it relates to the overall applications spectrum of a smart building system.

9.3 EXAMPLE INTEGRATED MANAGEMENT SYSTEM

Industry is continually striving to provide new and efficient products and systems for the management and control of security, safety and comfort within premises. Features of these systems include:
1. Distributed intelligence.
2. Increased security.
3. Reduction of false alarms.
4. More information for the operator.
5. Interaction and integration between systems.

However, it would be foolish to ignore the fact that the implementation of sophisticated systems may also:

1. Limit the choice of functionality to a single supplier's systems.
2. Create the need for higher grade operations' staff.
3. Involve complicated administrative routines.
4. Create islands of information.
5. Increase paperwork.

This situation is unacceptable for a smart building. It encourages additional problems for the organisation and contributes nothing other than primary functionality. In other words, it is a matter of how the various services and systems perform secondary functions that determines their place within a fully integrated smart building.

So, how should the various integrated sub-systems of security, access control, CCTV, fire detection, energy management etc. perform within the environment of a smart building? Or more importantly, how can they contribute to the efficiency of the organisation as a whole?

9.4 OPERATION OF INTEGRATED SYSTEMS

A typical system's architecture may include intelligent addressable sensors capable of transmitting analogue information via a LAN to distributed processors for alarm processing and verification, access card authorisation or output initiation. A number of distributed processors may communicate on a common token ring or bus for added resilience. This network may also be shared, with data serving many PCs and host computers.

Software to enable input and output events between disparate systems would be resident at the distributed processor as would the ability to self-test, verify and run diagnostic routines. Indeed, in order to minimise the operator interface, the main system's functions are delegated to distributed processors. The system operator would be given information on a predetermined need-to-know basis or when it has been decided that he is required to make a decision that the system cannot make on its own.

9.4.1 An example integrated system

A possible scenario may be where a security guard patrols a building and its grounds at night. He would use his access card at patrol points and card readers, thereby unsetting areas of protection before him and automatically resetting them behind him. Corridor lighting could be enabled to follow his route with lifts, for instance, made available for his sole use. CCTV cameras would be used to sequence his progress. Whilst there is constant data flowing between sub-systems, and inputs/outputs are automatically co-ordinated, no manual functions are required from the centre. However, should he, for example, be compromised on his route the situation would clearly require intervention. This level of integration is applied in many instances today and satisfies some of the primary needs of an integrated security system. This example may be taken further...

The security system may also require access to a database, for the generation of graphics, reporting and the presentation of activation messages. It is at this point that a gateway can be created from the controls system environment into the information systems to transfer data throughout the organisation for increased functionality and improved efficiency. Alarm data listings with graphics can be transferred into word processing files for report generation or standard letter formation and then sent automatically through the internal electronic mail lists or over wide area networks to other locations. A logical development of this capability could be that...

Comprehensive reports in the form of a screen full of data with graphics could be transmitted instantaneously with alarms to the police or fire services via open networks, should such a facility ever be needed. But keeping with administrative routines...

Service and maintenance manager files can be automatically updated with activation details of device, zone, network node etc. to provide incident recording for common fault analysis. Parts listings with serial numbers would assist in component tracking. Preventative maintenance schedules can be planned and cost controlled in conjunction with resource and revenue programmes.

The precise configuration for all installed systems including the specification, cabling and wiring can be held on shared databases to identify areas of protection, system loading, cable or bandwith usage, spare capacity etc., essential in assisting with prompt fault finding and accurate systems expansion or modification.

The overhead for these administrative routines is not carried by one system alone, yet the benefits are common to all sub-systems of fire, security, energy management etc. by using communications as the integrator and thereby eliminating islands of information.

9.5 CABLING - THE MEANS FOR COMMUNICATING

In order to achieve this level of integration across the spectrum, many intelligent buildings will encompass a cable management system. This also minimises the initial installation cost and provides for flexibility. Future modifications, additions and deletions could then be handled simply with minimal cost. This would be true for any device from a PC to a telephone or security sensor.

A cable management system comprises the cables, adapters and other supporting equipment that connect telephones, data terminals, sensors and communications devices, allowing them to talk to one another. As such, a distribution system is an assemblance of standard component parts. But a distribution system also provides a basis for arranging these components within a building or on a campus in a logical, coherent and economical fashion. After all, equipment alone does not make a system any more than building materials make a building.

9.5.1 Cabling standards

One noteworthy cable management system is PDS, Premises Distribution System, which is made up of a number of sub-systems that collectively support a wide range of communication applications in almost any physical configuration.

At the simplest level, PDS begins with a set of standard connectors and adapters for workstations (typically PCs), telephones and sensors. These are cabled back to a horizontal sub-system administration panel where they can be cross-connected to the required services being supplied over the backbone riser sub-system. It is at this point that the electronics interfaces such as MIUs, fibre optic multiplexers or cluster controllers are used to gain access to LANs and host systems.

In effect, this means that moves and changes of equipment, people and services can be made efficiently by simply re-patching at the secure administration frame. Furthermore, security devices can be added to the monitored network without the need for major re-cabling.

When it comes to voice and high speed data, the PDS supports multiple manufacturers equipment so that the end user is never locked into one particular product line simply because of the cabling requirements. The user can ensure support for any BABT approved PABX as well as computer equipment, whether it is IBM, DEC, Wang or Honeywell.

All systems run over the balanced unshielded twisted pair cabling of PDS which eliminates the need for expensive coaxial or twin axial cable. PDS also supports interactive circuit switched and packet switched environments.

As the building occupiers' data needs increase, data transmission can be off-loaded to a fibre optic backbone using a LAN. Yet, the connection and interface to the terminal or sensor remains the same. As the cost of electronic interfaces drops, so we will see more fibre optics in the smart building adding to the speed, accuracy and security of all communications.

9.5.2 Accommodating future expansion

The cabling systems should also allow provision for future communication technology such as Integrated Services Digital Networks, ISDN. The communication systems of the future will enable the information technology strategies of the organisation to be pursued by ensuring compatible standards through Open Systems Interconnection, OSI. Different computer and control systems will eventually communicate directly with each other, opening up many new opportunities for efficiency improvements, freedom of choice for the customer and flexibility.

The capability of the PABX to handle voice and data communications provides further opportunities for integration of shared services over common communication paths. This configuration is widely used in the US where 'shared tenant services' are provided through the PABX in large multi-tenanted buildings. The PDS also supports this configuration.

The total integrated services within a smart building will form part of the organisation's overall information technology strategy and would be planned somewhat differently by senior management. They would be supportive of an adaptive business posture that would enable additions and changes to be made with minimum cost and disruption. For example, should the organisation decide to implement a flexible hours management system, say, four years into the building services life cycle, then it should be possible to utilise existing security access cards into new registration terminals and communicate over the common network. Administration facilities would be provided from a variety of existing workstations or PCs, thereby minimising the cost of cabling or redundant equipment. A further example will illustrate these important points.

One particular organisation is known to have made a significant investment to ensure that its integrated building systems are a strategic part of its operation. They are installing two private remote, central stations for the management and control of security and building services for 1,150 premises over their existing X.25 data communication network. Precise analogue data on every sensor is available to the central station which can also set, unset and re-programme each individual system or sensor on the network. No additional BT lines are required and the organisation will have immediate and accurate information from every system with comparison reports. The total installation will be complete at the end of 1988 and will have taken three years. The cost of the installation represents 7% of the organisation's total information technology expenditure over the same period.

9.6 CONCLUSIONS

Smart or intelligent buildings are rare in the UK, but there are numerous examples of integrated control systems that satisfy specific primary objectives and which gain from the benefits of integration. For the market to mature there will need to be a genuine acceptance of these systems by a wider base of organisations. This is unlikely to be achieved by mere 'carrot dangling' of advanced systems features by suppliers/manufacturers. Furthermore, information technology strategies will need to incorporate some means of measuring return on investment if they are to be willingly endorsed by the organisation.

Chapter 10
Sensing and control systems

D. UTTON

10.1 THE PAST

The past 20 years have seen dramatic changes in the manner in which controls have been applied to the commercial building or site. In the 1960s the preferred means for control in the large building was by use of pneumatics for both the primary plant and the secondary control for the floor space.

These systems consisted of a central air compressor with the associated levels of drying and oil filtration delivering compressed air via dedicated air lines to the associated pneumatic devices for sensing, controlling and driving the associated actuators to obtain the required comfort levels in the space. They worked on the principle of the sensor bleeding off or increasing the air pressure to a specific level and thereby passing the resultant air signal direct, or via a controller, to the required position. The concept was simple, reliable and more cost effective to install on the majority of medium to large installations than the larger electronic valve amplifier control systems of their time.

Centralised monitoring and control, was very much in its infancy and consisted of a separate electro-mechanical system with its own range of sensors overseeing the control systems. These incorporated manual and limited centralised time clock control of the air handling plant primary drives and associated services.

The most significant advances in the industry came about not just in response to the demands of the end user, but in the evolution of the silicon chip which provided the vehicle to supply cost effective solutions for the modern building. Its initial impact was primarily in central monitoring and control due to the demand to conserve energy in the 1970s and the need to provide a more extensive and accurate means of monitoring and controlling the associated primary elements and services in the building. They introduced to the HVAC control market not only the first applications of the microprocessor, but the means to multiplex data down a twisted pair cable and offer a software-based solution. This gave the specifier and the user the opportunity to review the ways and means for economising on the running of the primary services with minimal detriment to comfort conditions within the occupied space. Being software-based, it also introduced a level of flexibility which was not necessarily available with the previous generation concept of centralised monitoring and control.

The intelligence of the early monitoring systems was centralised at the primary central processing unit with the sensing and commands to switch plant via remote non-intelligent data gathering panels located at the vicinity of the plant or process being monitored and controlled. These panels incorporated their own sensing devices and as with the electro-mechanical systems, they oversaw the control systems operating the plant.

Transmission of data between the central processor and data gathering panels was multiplexed over a twisted pair cable in a digital format allowing for fast transfer of data and the ability to monitor and control a considerable number of devices and elements. Their primary purpose was to centralise the information in respect of alarms, status of plant and variables, such as temperature and humidity and electrical consumption. From the various ranges of inputs they provided the means to centralise the automatic and manual control of the plant against variables such as time, outdoor temperature and energy saving programs.

As the cost of the processor decreased, and computing power increased, so the viability of decentralising the intelligence of the central controller became a reality. Its effect was to merge the growing prominence of electronic control with the monitoring system and set the microprocessor as the natural selection for today's primary plant control, namely, Direct Digital Control (DDC).

10.2 THE CONTROLLER

Conventional analogue control systems, be they pneumatic or electronic, incorporate a central loop which consists of one or more sensors, the logic function and the output signal. The logic function determines what type of action to take on the basis of the sensor signals and other control parameters, such as the setpoint and throttling range adjustments. The output signal drives the output device to provide whatever control correction is required. The output device could be an electric motor, relay, an electric heater control or any other device for directly controlling the medium.

A wide range of control strategies are required for achieving optimum control of the system and with analogue controls this necessitates a wide range of devices to achieve the solution. Microprocessor- and software-based Direct Digital Control Systems allow for multiple logic functions for several control loops to be contained in one single device. The sensor signals now form the various control loops within the vicinity of one controller and are fed into a common microprocessor which performs the logic functions for each control loop. This provides the relevant outputs to the valve and damper actuators etc. for the process. If the same input, such as outdoor air temperature, is used for more than one control loop, then only one sensor is required and the microprocessor will use the signal with the appropriate control logic functions.

The basic unit in the Direct Digital Control system is the controller which is responsible for a number of control loops, these being dependent on the number of sensors and output devices per control loop. The controller has two elements: input/output processing and the central processor. The sensors and output devices connect to the input/output processing board which continually scans the sensors and stores information. When the central processor is ready to look at a control loop, it calls up the sensor information from the input/output processor and feeds it into the appropriate program for the control loop. The central processor then determines what control action is required and sends the appropriate signal back to the input/output processing board to drive the output device to the necessary position.

There could be as many as 32 sensors - 16 analogue and 16 digital output devices - connected to a single controller. The function of the input/output processor is to read each sensor periodically, convert the analogue sensor reading from, say, a temperature resistance element into a digital format of typically a 12 bit pulse word, then store the information for access as and when required by the CPU. The same processor must also store the output signals from the CPU, convert them from digital to analogue and then route each control signal to the correct output device. The input/output processor handles one input signal only, at a time. This is achieved by an electronic switching device called a multiplexer which connects each sensor in sequence for conversion and reading by the processor.

10.3 INPUTS AND OUTPUTS

The sensors themselves are either digital or analogue. Digital sensors are termed 'clean contact devices', giving a two state signal of either on or off. Analogue sensors operate on the basis of a variable input, from a range of industry standards such as platinum or similar temperature resistance elements, of 4-20 mA and 0-10 V for meters etc.. The input/output processor normally allows the inputs to be configured in any combination or mix of digital and analogue sensors to maximise on the point count of the controller in the vicinity it is located. This provides for point processing and calibration, providing accurate interpretation of the data received. Typically, this would include the ability to define for each analogue input, the overall range the controller-should take for the sensor. For example, the sensor range is 0-50 degrees centigrade and the control setting is 20 degrees. The processor could be set to look at a range of 10-30 degrees. To this would be added the ability to linearise and compensate for offset in the reading and with 'analogue to digital' conversion provide for accurate sensing of the variable. To compensate for possible noise interference on the sensor lines or malfunction of the sensor, the processor can also provide for a 'reasonability check' to be carried out on each input. This allows each input to be viewed as to the accepted change to be expected on each scan of the sensor, which if exceeded is typically automatically reprocessed five times for validation.

Today's controllers also provide the ability, with digital inputs, to supervise the cabling between the controller and the contact device being monitored. It brings the ability to provide the facility of supervising critical M & E functions such as smoke alarms for air handling units and similar critical life-safety interlocks with, say, the primary fire system for the building.

The output signals again are divided into analogue or digital format, the latter being two position control of fan drives and pumps. Motors are either electric or pneumatic, depending on the size of device being driven. With pneumatic outputs, suitable 'electric to pneumatic' transducers are used to convert the original signal to give the correct air signal to drive the motor.

The processing of input/output variables on the controller is continuously scanned at a rate of usually once per second, which allows for very accurate and fast response to system changes. Being software-based they also allow for predetermined reactions to take place in the event of a detected failure. For example, sensor failure will drive all dampers and valves to a set position or if the application allowed, revert the control from, say, discharge to return air control.

10.4 CONTROL

With the introduction of the microprocessor into the local loop came a new level of intelligence. Not only is the control processor able to adjust to the information inputs received from valves and dampers, but it is also able to check the performance of each loop.

The control processor first reacts to a change in temperature and the greater the change, the greater the reaction. This is called 'proportional control', and was the basis of most older 'control 32' systems. However, the level of change is often undesirable when comparing the required and actual temperatures for the loop. These deviations are monitored by the control processor to initiate further reactions as required to eliminate it. This is called 'integral control', which tends to provide a practically constant temperature at all load conditions. The frequency at which the 'integral' calculation and reaction is executed is quite critical, and is dependent upon the time it takes for the reaction of, say, a valve moving to be detected by the control loop monitoring input sensor.

If calculations/reactions are executed too frequently, excessive reactions cause over-corrections which create negative changes and reactions, and the loop then goes into an excessive cycle or hunting mode. If calculations/reactions are executed too infrequently, inadequate reactions cause the change to be eliminated at an unsatisfactorily slow rate, leaving the deviation present for an undesirably long period.

Technicians with experience of their software, the characteristics of the sensors (thermal lag) and the dynamics of the thermodynamic loop (space, discharge air and hot water control) can tune the execution interval of the integral calculation/reaction for optimum loop performance, provided that the loop dynamics are constant. This tuning provides the full benefits of the digital control processor with precise and responsive control for which the user paid.

But what about loops where the dynamics are not constant, such as variable air and water flows, which are common in HVAC systems? Here, calculation intervals must be set slow enough to avoid the 'berserk situation', which in turn would compromise the preciseness required during heavier loads (faster dynamics). To provide optimum control of these variable processes necessitates the contol processor having the ability to self-learn, which is termed Adaptive Direct Digital Control.

Adaptive DDC works on the principle of the control processor detecting the proportional changes and correcting them, then determining the actual and varying thermodynamic rates of the loop, that is, it executes a reaction and monitors the time duration of the resultant temperature change. With the control processor monitoring this dynamic response rate, it can automatically and continually adapt the integral calculation/reaction interval to match the varying loop dynamics. Whilst it further burdens the processor and requires additional memory, it does provide the expected digital computer response and precision to all control loops within today's buildings.

It should be noted that even on constant dynamic loops, the use of the Adaptive DDC algorithm will automatically and optimally tune the calculation intervals, thus minimising technician and user time in setting up these control strategies.

10.5 PLANT INTERLOCKING

The power of the microprocessor gives flexibility to the specifier and designer of the control system in being able to apply the necessary range of electrical interlocks within the same processor. This helps to eliminate the need for extensive hard-wired interlocks with relay logic, previously found in analogue control systems. It has meant the starter control equipment specified is now of a more standard concept with the necessary hand-off auto switch and run/trip status indicators for local control of drives. All other interlocks associated with starting and stopping the equipment can now reside in software. It enables interlocks to be checked and certified before the commissioning stage, reduced wiring costs both inside and external to the panel and greatly simplified building of the panel.

10.6 ENERGY MANAGEMENT

A range of 'energy management programs' are available today. These are integral with the controller and provide Direct Digital Control optimum performance of the plant at minimum energy usage. Such programs include:
1. Optimum start - time program.
2. Optimum stop.
3. Night cycle.
4. Night purge.
5. Duty cycle.
6. Zero energy band.
7. Load reset.
8. Enthalpy control.
9. Power demand.

The software allows common energy management programs to be applied to several plants or processes being controlled by the device. These programs can, however, be very complicated and require a higher order of processing time compared with the normal control of the plant. In order to perform all the energy management functions without delaying control, the energy management functions can be broken up into parts and interdispersed between the control cycle/update. Normally energy management programs do not require to be updated as frequently as control and so dividing these programs into segments does not penalise the overall strategy of the system.

Briefly, the energy management programs most commonly used within commercial buildings are straightforward time switch control, self-learning optimum start/stop and night cycle programs for the primary services. These programs provide for self-learning techniques, based on past building performance, to be accumulated within the processor in order to calculate the latest possible time that equipment can be started to achieve the required comfort levels at occupancy. Normally, the calculations are based on outdoor against indoor conditions and the required comfort range for occupancy. Similarly the processors are able to self-learn to provide early stopping of plant and still maintain comfort conditions within the space.

During plant shutdown periods, the processor reverts to night cycle which maintains the building at a lower setting to protect the building environment against extremes in outdoor temperature/humidity conditions and at the same time provide a base temperature condition to provide for optimum boost periods to reach occupancy levels. Whilst not necessarily applicable in the UK, programs such as night purge are available which optimise on opening the fresh air and exhaust dampers to utilise the outdooor air to pre-cool the building space prior to occupancy and so reduce the refrigeration cooling load.

During normal occupancy, zero energy band, load reset and enthalpy control can be applied. By using a command priority structure, the programs can be intermixed to provide optimum energy saving performance of the plant. Zero energy band aims at running the plants with both heating and cooling loads off within specified comfort limits. Load reset compensates for varying outdoor design conditions to set discharge conditions from the primary plant to minimise on heating and cooling load requirements. Enthalpy control is primarily designed to look at the most effective means of cooling the space by either selecting outdoor or return air enthalpy conditions to minimise on the amount of mechanical cooling needed.

Other programs such as duty cycle and power demand optimise on electrical energy usage by switching plant on or off to conserve energy, without detriment to the space or area being served by the plant. However, care has to be applied when using these programs to ensure the number of start/stops per hour does not exceed the design characteristics of the drive and starter equipment to the extent that maintenance and repair costs exceed the envisaged saving on energy usage.

10.7 COMMUNICATIONS

So far, we have reviewed the typical characteristics of one controller and highlighted its benefits in providing a single device capable through software of monitoring and controlling multiple disciplines (or functions). Not only does it reduce the type of hardware to a single device, but it combines the monitoring and control sensors into one and so reduces cabling costs for the installation. Also, it reduces field commissioning time to a minimum as all programming and verification can be carried out at the system supplier's premises prior to installation of the controller.

In a typical installation there would be several controllers located throughout the building and the need to communicate between them becomes a preferred requirement for sharing of information received from common sensors and programs for optimum plant performance and minimal installation costs. For example, in refrigeration control, the primary machine could be in the basement and the cooling tower fans and condenser water control could be at roof level. By utilising the communication bus, the respective sensors at both levels would be fed into the nearest controller and data transferred between controllers to achieve the required control. The result is reduced installation cost and optimum use of point count on the controllers. The sharing of information is not restricted to sensor inputs and can cover any program resident in the controllers. For example, all controllers could share the same optimum start/stop program. Any event occurrence or sequential start up of plant could be carried out over the network, even distributed loading shedding of plant could be achieved without the need for a central controller.

To provide this level of processing and communication necessitates a high level of integrity of the system, whereby communication between controllers should not be reliant upon any central computer or master controller having to send messages. All controllers should be true equals allowing for communication to continue between them while the transmission line is connected. If broken, the transmission of data should continue between controllers on either side of the break. Where the break prevents transmission of data, the controllers should default to the last received signal and automatically re-initialise on re-connection.

There could be as many as 29 controllers on one bus alone handling 1,500 points. It is essential, therefore, that the highest level of error checking such as 'Manchester Encoding' is employed to match the required speed and reliability of the system.

To ensure that the speed and response of the system is retained regardless of the number of inputs and outputs configured, today's systems utilise a token bus network. This provides a means of direct access to the device rather than polling each outstation individually to find the controller with the required information. This provides for very fast execution of commands in the order of 3 to 5 seconds, and similar alarm response regardless of the point count for the system.

Another beneficial feature of this form of network is the ability to run the transmission cable in any form of star or 'tee tap' layout to suit the building or site being monitored and controlled.

10.8 CENTRAL ARCHITECTURE

With intelligence now available at the outstation, the central computer is free to perform the functions of true computing. Today's systems can either deploy a central minicomputer or a network of PCs. They provide an easy means of communicating and reporting at a central location on all the activities occuring within the system. They incorporate both menu penetration and direct screen access techniques to match the operator's experience, with dynamic data shown in logical group formats for accessing system operation.

PCs allow the use of proven third party software to be run concurrently with the BMS control software. It allows data from various sensors to be stored and transferred with variables to spreadsheet packages, allowing the operator/ user to manipulate and display data in a wide range of formats for analysing building and plant performance. Colour graphics present the operator/user with real-time data in a pictorial form and maintenance management programs allow automatic issue of work orders based on accumulated run time, alarm or fixed time occurrence. Also included in this type of package are the relevant budget and inventory controls, labour rates and projected work load programs to monitor and control maintenance of the building.

10.9 CONCLUSIONS

This paper has reported on the 'state-of-play' in sensing and control systems. The next major advancment to emerge will be intelligent room control, giving access at a central point to view/analyse and change the conditions within a specified room. At present, the cost is high when compared with standard electronic and pneumatic control, but no doubt this will change quite quickly, with advancements in communications and premises distribution cabling techniques making it a viable alternative to the conventional systems of today.

Chapter 11
Fire and security protection

J.D. WALTER

11.1 INTRODUCTION

The first part of this paper deals with the basic theory of fire and security systems with a review of typical products available in the marketplace. The second part deals with the needs of fire and security as independent systems and discusses the implications of integration with particular reference to standards, approvals, reliability and serviceability. The advantages and disadvantages of the integrated approach are discussed with reference to the benefits for the client, designer, installer, building user/owner and maintenance organisation.

11.2 FIRE DETECTION

The human being is the most efficient fire detector, provided that he is actually there at the time. The combination of his eyes, ears and nose allows him to differentiate between various phenomena. He can smell the difference between cigarette smoke, burning toast and something more sinister such as burning paper. He can see smoke and flames and will often hear a fire before he has noticed either the flames or the smoke. Sometimes, the first thing he notices is heat, for example, a hot partition wall. It is these phenomena that fire detector designers measure to detect the onset of fire. It is the onset of fire that is crucial; very small fires can be put out quickly and safely with portable fire extinguishers, or even a cup of coffee if detected soon enough. Obviously, the smaller the fire, the less it may be observed. Fire detectors must, therefore, be designed without the risk of false alarms. So what technology is used today to detect these phenomena?

11.2.1 Smoke detection

Two techniques are used for the detection of smoke: photo-electric smoke detectors and ionisation smoke detectors. Photo-electric detectors are arranged so that, although visible light cannot enter, smoke can enter freely. This type of detector is based on a matt black chamber about the size of a coffee cup. A dividing wall is placed in the middle of the chamber on either side of which is located a light transmitter and a light receiver. Under normal circumstances, light from the transmitter is not received by the receiver, as the chamber is not reflective. When smoke particles enter the chamber, light bounces off these particles which results in a signal being received. A similar effect can be observed when sunshine enters a smokey room. These photo-electric detectors are highly sensitive and reliable, so long as the smoke particles are visible.

Certain classes of fire, however, emit invisible smoke particles long before the fire is actually alight and in these cases an ionisation smoke detector must be present. Although the design of these detectors is slightly more complicated than in the case of photo-electric detectors, the basic principle is very simple. Two metal plates are separated by several millimetres and a voltage is applied across them. Since air does not conduct electricity, no current flows. If an ionising radioactive source is brought close to the plates then the air itself is ionised, that is, electrically charged particles are present between the plates and these allow a tiny current to flow. Any particles entering the chamber, either visible or invisible, tend to neutralise the ions, thus decreasing the current flow. It is this reduction in current which is monitored in measuring the amount of smoke that is present.

11.2.2 Heat detectors

Two types of technology are used. First, mechanical heat detectors rely on expanding solids, liquids and gases to close a switch; secondly, electronic detectors use a thermistor to measure the actual temperature. Furthermore, there are two variants: fixed temperature detectors which simply produce an output when the temperature exceeds a predetermined level and rate of rise detectors that provide an output when the rate of rise in temperature exceeds a pre-defined limit. However, rate of rise detectors invariably have an upper temperature limit at which they will provide output regardless of the rate of rise function.

11.2.3 Flame detectors

Flame detectors look for characteristic emissions of either infra-red or ultra-violet light from the flames. This type of detection is particularly useful for fires caused by volatile fuels, for example, gas and petroleum spirit. With the aid of these detectors the fire detection industry is able to move some way towards simulating the ability of the human to detect a fire. It may not be as good as the human, but it is available 24 hours a day and 365 days a year, at a very reasonable cost.

11.3 INTRUDER DETECTION

There is a far wider range of intruder detectors available than is the case for fire detectors. It is necessary to thwart the intelligent criminal whose ingenuity knows no bounds: if they can get round it, they will.

The simplest intruder detectors are basically switches operated from such disturbances as opening doors, walking on pressure mats, cutting essential wires etc.. In these detectors, the skill is in the mechanical design. For obvious reasons, it is not possible to discuss the operation of intruder detectors in great detail here.

In addition to simple contacts a wide range of movement/presence detectors are avilable. The most common of these is the passive infra-red (PIR) detector which can detect the heat of a human body against the natural ambient temperature. This is no mean feat considering the human body is at 37 degrees Centigrade and that is the internal body temperature, let alone skin temperature. With outdoor clothing the target may only be some 0.5-1 degrees above the ambient. Other active sysetms are available, such as microwave and ultra-sonic. Both of these techniques depend upon the transmission of a signal which is reflected from any moving object in range. Movement alters the frequency of the received signal (the Doppler effect) and it is the difference between the transmitted and received signals which indicates the speed of movement.

11.4 INTEGRATION

When one talks about intelligent builings perhaps this is intended to refer to buildings designed as an entity, a complete system with all parts working in harmony to provide a comfortable, efficient and safe environment. We can draw an analogy to the human body where virtually every part is a highly desirable, if not an essential, part of the whole. However, in the same way that the legs of an Olympic runner are not needed by an average typist, high speed data communications may not be needed by a diamond merchant. It could be argued that all of the components systems comprising even the simplest low technology building are already integrated; the light switch is close to the door, a time switch turns the heating on in the morning, the PA microphone is close to the switchboard in reception. Generally, everything is chosen and installed to make life easier.

It is technically possible to integrate or interface any electronic building service; for example, digital data communication, voice communication, FAX, intruder alarms systems, fire detection and energy management systems. The list grows year by year as technology marches on. But is it logical to integrate these services and, indeed, what does one mean by integration?

For many years these systems have been interfaced to one another; for example, the fire controller may send a signal to shut down the ventilation system or be interfaced to the telephone system to signal an alarm to a remote manned central station. But this is not integration. The individual systems are totally independent and usually only a very small number of dedicated hard-wired links are made between those individual systems.

By integration, it is implied that components in the system are shared, such that individual sub-systems may share a common database in order that the operating characteristics of one system are dependent upon the status of another. For instance, an intelligent fire detection system could be integrated with an energy management system so that signals being received from smoke detectors could be compared with signals being received from room tempera-ture sensors. With appropriate software, this might help to confirm a genuine fire condition.

Electronic building systems can be split into two main categories. First, there are the foreground activities such as telephone, telex, FAX and computer data communication. The requirement for these foreground activities is dependent upon the degree of activity in the user's business. During busy periods these services are stretched to a maximum and during slack periods they may be under-used.

Also, as the user's business evolves over the years his requirement for these foreground services may well change. Furthermore, there are the background functions such as fire detection, security and environmental control. When all is well, these services work away quietly in the background, but when something goes wrong they must spring into action in an instance. No delays can be tolerated, particularly in a fire system where seconds count if a small fire is not to get out of control.

These background services have one very important thing in common: they need prompt response by a human and they need to be monitored by a human. It is logical, therefore, to consider the integration of these services at least at a level which permits all alarm messages to be displayed on one device. So why not integrate the foreground services as well? After all, one central computer working on a single communication bus must be more cost effective.

Unfortunately, this is likely to occur only where there are enough buildings with exactly the same requirements. In practice, the needs of each building are usually quite different. There would be considerable difficulty in getting one fully integrated system to handle all of the electronic building services. Furthermore, what would be the benefit?

The cost of computing continues to fall, although hardware savings are more than likely to be offset by the system's engineering and software requirements. It is, therefore, no more logical to integrate the telephone system with the energy management system than it would be to integrate one's tongue with one's big toe. Both have equally different functions and the condition in one is not dependent upon the condition in the other. It is, however, logical to integrate fire, security and energy management systems because they can benefit by sharing a common database and can in many cases share at least the same technology, if not the same components. Also, engineers from these three disciplines usually have a similar background and can appreciate the problems and design solutions across those disciplines. ˜

From the user's or owner's point of view, it is unlikely that highly skilled personnel would be employed to monitor the building 24 hours a day. A great benefit of the integrated system is the ability to prioritise multiple alarms. In a large and complex building, considerable thought and planning is required to determine the procedures to be taken in the event of alarms being raised. Usually, these procedures are written in the Building Operation Manual, but how often are these strictly adhered to after the building has been occupied for some time and the staff have changed? By integrating fire, security and energy management systems, these complex procedures are stored in a central processor so that simple instructions can be given to the guard or operator on duty. He is presented with one instruction at a time and so is less likely to make a mistake in an emergency.

In small buildings, multiple alarms are a very rare occurrence, but in larger buildings, as the number of input points to a system is greater, the probability of multiple alarms rises considerably especially in an emergency such as a fire. The skilled operator or service engineer can monitor the entire system, diagnose faults and in some cases effect a temporary repair from the central station. This permits faster and more efficient maintenance and, most significantly, reduces nuisance to the user.

The latest systems are capable of detecting and indicating incipient faults within their own components. This permits the service engineer to be called before the system malfunctions and he can be told in advance which spare parts are needed. If the integrated system is interfaced to the telephone network via a modem, the supplier's service department can assess and control all parts of the system. Safeguards have to be incorporated in fire and security systems; for example, certain changes to the systems must be followed by a walk test to check the correct operation of the devices which have been re-programmed or altered in some way. Nevertheless, this is a great benefit to the user who can enjoy a much faster response.

Since the integrated system will normally be provided by a single supplier one call only need be made regardless of which system requires attention. In a conventional system, interfacing is often required between the sub-systems and where several different suppliers are involved there are often arguments as to whose equipment is defective.

Intelligent systems invariably keep a record of all alarms, faults and action taken, together with the time and date. This is very useful in helping to determine troublesome areas quickly and with the minimum of nuisance. For example, clogged grease filters over a kitchen range may result in cooking fumes leaving the kitchen and triggering a spate of false or unwanted alarms. A print out of the exact time and location of these alarms helps to identify the real cause of the problem.

11.5 HOW SHOULD SYSTEMS BE INTEGRATED?

With the introduction of less expensive, smaller and yet more powerful microcomputers, the trend throughout industry is to distribute intelligence further and further into the field, away from the central computer. The microprocessor has now become the preferred tool for even the simplest function. They perfom better, they are more flexible and they permit a degree of intelligence to reside in the field where the action is. Even relatively humble components can now be given autonomy, that is, they are capable of making decisions locally and taking action locally. It may be that these components or sub-systems are permitted autonomy only in the event of a loss of communication with a higher authority, for example, a local outstation or central computer. Alternatively, this autonomy may be used to reduce the amount of information that needs to be transmitted regularly between that component and the central computer.

In the introduction, the intelligent building was likened to the human body, with all parts working in harmony to make the whole. Perhaps autonomy stretches this analogy to breaking point; for instance, what would be the point of autonomous legs? It is essential to ensure that the decision making process and the output control capability is not delegated to a component which cannot be trusted to make the right decision.

The system specifier (or designer) is wise to select systems which are constructed from a number of stand-alone systems. Provided that the sub-systems have been genuinely designed to operate on their own, without supervision, they will always be able to perform intelligent control in the event of a loss of communication. In addition, stand-alone systems will have been designed to meet the relevant standards and may have, therefore, been approved by an independent test house.

If stand-alone systems are constructed from standard products, the supplier's engineers will have greater familiarity and access to better support than would be likely with custom-designed products. Therefore, the integrated system should consist of a number of standard products designed to be interfaced to one another and which are connected to a central computer, again using a standard product where possible. The precise tailoring or configuration of the system to meet the individual requirements of the building should be accomplished by the central software. As far as the central display is concerned, more than one consul needs to be interfaced to the system. For example, there may be a need for displays in a number of different locations such as guardrooms, reception and financial services section. The requirements for each of these consuls may be different and often the degree of control from any one consul will need to change either according to the time of day or change of shift. Therefore, the system should be flexible enough to permit a wide range of operating modes which can be easily changed by the user.

11.6 ELECTRONICS FOR DIFFERENT DISCIPLINES

The main differences between the electronic requirements for the disciplines are data communication (that is, the amount, speed and accuracy) and the integrity of the data (that is, the likelihood of accidental or deliberate corruption). Since each discipline in an integrated system shares a common communication path, the performance of that communication path must be adequate for the worst case in any of the disciplines involved.

In an energy management system, large numbers of accurate analogue signals need to be constantly transmitted from the sensors to local control panels and from the panels to field components such as valves. The communication path is therefore very busy. In a security system a smaller number of random digital events are transmitted from the security sensors to the local controller whilst the building is occupied. The communication path is quite busy although less so than in the energy management system. In a conventional fire system few, if any, signals are sent from the detector to the local controller, therefore, the communication path is rarely used.

It is very unlikely that any deliberate attempt will be made to intefere with either the energy management system or the fire system (other than crude vandalism). The security system is, however, a target for the ingenious criminal. If the system has been constructed form stand-alone standard products, a high degree of security will have been designed into the basic system. Integrated systems should be designed to withstand the worst conditions of each discipline. For example, a system designed primarily for energy management, whilst perfectly able to transmit security alarms, may not incorporate the necessary safeguards to thwart the criminal. It follows therefore that the supplier of the integrated system must not only design the stand-alone products to meet the requirements of each discipline, they must also be designed to meet the requirements of the other discipline with which they will be integrated.

11.7 STANDARDS

11.7.1 Intruder systems

In the UK, nearly all security systems are installed either at the express request of an insurance company or to obtain a reduction in insurance premiums. The insurer is therefore concerned that the products and the installation meet acceptable standards. The insurance company is also likely to insist upon a supplier who is a member of the National Supervisory Council for Intruder Alarms (NSCIA). In order for a security supplier to become a member of the NSCIA, he must satisfy certain minimum requirements and give an undertaking that his systems will be installed in accordance with BS 4737. Member companies then issue NSCIA certificates provided that the system has been installed in accordance with the British Standard. Although adherence to these standards is not enforceable by law, it is clearly preferable for them to be adopted.

11.7.2 Fire systems

In the UK, most buildings are required to have a fire certificate before they can be opened to the public and this is enforceable through law. The Fire Officers Committee (FOC), which is now part of the Loss Prevention Council (LPC), is the body responsible for ensuring that fire systems are designed, installed and serviced in accordance with recognised standards. The FOC are primarily concerned with the insurance risk. In order for a supplier to satisfy the requirements of the FOC, both his products and engineering services must be approved.

Fire certificates are issued by Fire Officers who are concerned with the safety of the building rather than its insurance risk and they consider all fire safety matters such as evacuation routes, emergency lighting, exit signs and adequate alarms. In terms of the automatic fire detection system, Fire Officers seek the same basic standards as the FOC although they do not necessarily require an FOC certificate. As far as FOC are concerned, they are quite happy to accept integrated systems, provided that no defect in the other system could possibly result in a fault in the fire system. In addition, they require that the alarm path is an approved system and this includes all components from fire detectors through to bells and signalling equipment.

11.7.3 Service

Once integrated, the fire, security and energy management systems have to continue to operate for many years to come. When the integrated system was put together in the first place, the supplier probably had a team of engineers dedicated to design, installation and commissioning of that one system. Once the system has been installed that team is usually disbanded or, at the very least, employees leave. But the system has still to be serviced and maintained. Therefore, any such system must be built from standard products so that the supplier's service engineers have familiarity and an adequate range of spares. Even so, a multi-discipline service organisation is needed with service engineers having experience across the disciplines. In the case of the fire and security elements of integrated systems, a round-the-clock response is required of the service organisation.

There are 'lots of eggs' in the 'intelligent building basket' and there is much at stake when that building is not operating at peak efficiency or in the extreme case of being evacuated. Therefore, the speed of response from the service organisation is crucial. The supplier of the integrated system should be prepared to guarantee service call out within an agreed time.

11.8 CONCLUSIONS

Anyone who has ever been caught up in the arguments between different suppliers of equipment to the same building will understand the potential problems. The cynic might argue that these problems are mainly 'buck-passing', but in the vast majority of cases such arguments are due to misunderstandings in the scope of supply, the type of interface etc.. This is a common problem in conventional buildings and the situation becomes even worse as the building becomes more sophisticated. With today's fast building programmes, increasing sophistication and the intelligent building, it is becoming increasingly important for designers to look for a single competent supplier for the fire security and energy management systems: one supplier means one contract and one service call means one commissioning team. And one supplier means no arguments about whose responsibility it is to ensure that the complete system works to the client's satisfaction.

The integrated system also provides one integrated display and control unit. Any number of display terminals can usually be added to the integrated system as appropriate, but the principal advantage is that display and control is available for all three systems at one single point, at the same time. All alarm messages can be correctly prioritised under computer control to provide a correct response regardless of how complicated the emergency might be. In the same way that any number of terminals can be added to the integrated system, buildings can also be networked to provide a central monitoring point at a remote location. Examples of networked buildings would include hospitals, universities, shopping malls, banks, leisure centres, retail headquarters, defence establishments and schools.

A further benefit of integrating fire, security and energy management systems is the obvious reduction in cabling. By sharing the same data communication bus, the number of individual cores can be reduced and because the integrated system philosophy is usually coupled with distributed intelligence, the number of signals that need to be transmitted may often be reduced. In spite of the reduction in cable, the amount of information available to pinpoint the source of any alarms or problems accurately is greatly improved by the use of digital communication. By integrating fire, security and energy management systems, truly intelligent systems for intelligent buildings are now available.

Chapter 12
Developments in workstation technology and the impact on building design

J. LANE

12.1 INTRODUCTION

In this paper, the term 'workstation' has been taken to mean either a personal computer (PC) or a computer terminal (display) and the surrounding furniture that makes up an office worker's accommodation. The information technology industry has recently adopted the term workstation to embrace a type of high performance PC typically used for computer aided design (CAD) and similar tasks involving the manipulation of graphic images. Whilst these CAD workstations provide an indication of the performance of the next generation of PCs, they remain for the present a specialist device.

The first part of this paper reviews the requirements of existing workstations in terms of the furniture, cooling, lighting and noise levels appropriate for staff who spend a considerable proportion of the working day looking at a display screen.

The second part considers developments in office automation and computer technology that can be expected to have an impact on the demands placed upon an office building. The trend towards the integration of voice, data, text and image functions into one system will be examined. Finally, the increasing demands of information technology for space, power, cooling and improved lighting will be considered over the medium term.

12.2 THE PHYSICAL ENVIRONMENT

The environmental requirements for the use of information technology equipment in offices are complex but well understood. New technology will be equally as demanding. With the more widespread use of PCs and computer terminals, it will be necessary to consider the majority of the office space rather than particular areas. For example, in a Ford motor company design office draughtsmen used to be positioned near windows but were moved away from this natural light source when CAD equipment was introduced. Engineering staff took their place but now they too have problems with their new colour graphic terminals.

It is important to recognise the widely varying intensities of use of PCs. Staff who are involved in word processing, order entry or enquiry activities may be required to use the equipment for more or less all of the working day, perhaps 70-90% of the time. In contrast, a recent survey of PC use in professional offices gave a surprisingly low average utilisation of twenty minutes per week, that is, less than 1%. Even though this may rise with the introduction of applications like electronic mail and so on, users can accept a less than optimum environment if use is relatively low. In this connection, it is worth reviewing the requirements of current systems before considering the impact of new technology. The following sections apply to the 'intensive use' workstation.

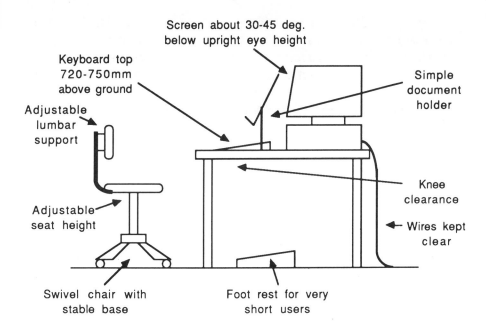

Figure 12.1: Comfortably seated working position

12.3 THE WORKPLACE

There are four main requirements for a comfortably seated working position, and these are illustrated in Figure 12.1:

1. Some physical movement is essential to maintain or restore proper circulation of the blood. This movement can be provided by installing flexible and adjustable equipment and by ensuring that adequate work surfaces are available for spreading out work items. To avoid fatigue, sufficient leg room is required so that the operator can change posture.

2. The seat should have a back support that maintains the inward curve of the lower spine.

3. The chair seat should be firm (only slightly padded), angled back a few degrees and curved at the front so that it does not cut into the thighs.

4. The height of the seat should allow the feet to be placed squarely on the floor, with the angles between the spine and the thighs, and between the thigh and the lower leg, each at approximately 90 degrees.

Many manufacturers now supply terminals that have desirable ergonomic characteristics such as integrated turntables, screen-tilting mechanisms and thin detachable keyboards: such terminals can be used on a conventional desk. The ergonomic limitations of earlier terminal designs can be overcome by using adjustable desks. However, many of the adjustable desks now available provide excessive scope for adjustment that is neither helpful nor usable.

In most cases, mechanical ventilation will be necessary and conventional ceiling-mounted supply and extraction is acceptable. In the most demanding situations, however, it is desirable to supply cooling air from under the floor and for part of this to be directed at removing heat from the equipment. Good examples of this are the Lloyd's underwriters' boxes and the Midland Montague dealing room. In both cases, a simple, manually variable outlet has been provided to control the air volume passing up through the equipment in and on the desk.

The cooling effect of air movement is well known and, if excessive, people undertaking sedentary tasks will complain of draughts. Approximate acceptable air velocities over the skin within the comfortable working temperature range of 20 degrees Centigrade to 26 degrees are 0.1 m/sec and 0.5 m/sec respectively (CCTA, 1983). In practice, office temperatures should be towards the lower end of this range at 20 degrees to 22 degrees, so that air velocities will be limited to about 0.2 m/sec.

The cost and complication of humidity control sometimes prohibits its consideration for conventional office space. Whilst a range of 40% to 70% relative humidity (RH) may be acceptable for most people, there are special considerations where there is intensive use of information technology equipment. In applications where the screen is viewed for long periods, it is desirable that relative humidity should not fall below 40%.

One reason is the effect on the eyes of the electrostatic field which carries a stream of dust particles from the display screen. There is excellent evidence of this on Victoria station where, as Figures 12.2 and 12.3 illustrate, displays mounted behind glass in the ticket office have become almost invisible behind a layer of dust discharged onto the inside of the glass. In the office, the operator's eyes become the target for this dust. Maintaining the RH above 40% reduces the strength of the field and also tends to reduce the evaporation of the film of protective liquid from the surface of the eyes.

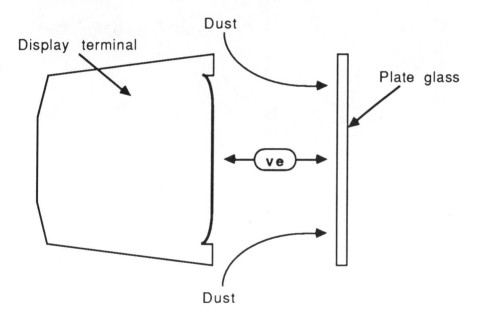

ve = electrostatic field between front of
display and plate glass

Figure 12.2: Dust build up in station ticket office - side view

The second reason for controlling the humidity is the risk of electrostatic discharge. The increasing use of plastic for equipment housings, makes equipment more vulnerable. This is especially true in the case of keyboards which now contain several integrated circuits. Moist air provides a conductive path for the electrostatic charge, preventing high voltages being generated as people walk across carpets.

The electrical resistance between the top of the floor surface and the electrical earth for the building should be kept below 2,000 Mega Ohms to minimise the risk of electrostatic discharge. This must be considered when selecting floor finishes.

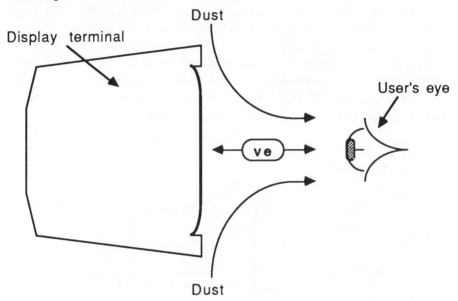

ve = electrostatic field between front of
terminal and user's eye

Figure 12.3: Electrostatic dust stream - side view

12.4 LIGHTING

When people use displays, they are likely to suffer from glare for two reasons. First, a typical display has a dark screen and so the eyes adjust themselves to the low light level. Secondly, the line of sight is higher than is usual for conventional paperwork, and this means that the sources of light (windows or light fittings) are more likely to be in the terminal user's field of vision.

Both causes of glare can be overcome if the terminals are positioned so that the user's line of sight is at right angles to the sources of light, provided the light fittings have proper glare shielding and there is an ambient level of illumination of about 350 lux. For applications where much of the time is spent reading from documents, the lighting level should be increased towards 500 lux. For some applications where the operator reads from the screen only, a lighting level below 350 lux may be preferred. For mixed applications, 'task' lights may be required.

Windows provide visual access to the outside world and are useful when people need a distant view to rest their eyes. When visual display terminals are used near windows, however, some form of control over the amount of daylight that comes through the windows is usually necessary. This may be achieved by installing solar control films, blinds, curtains or shutters.

The floor and walls of an office in which displays are used should ideally reflect about 30% and 50% respectively of the light that strikes them. The desktop should also reflect as little light as possible; matt black is better than light coloured laminates or polished wood, for example.

12.5 NOISE

A frequent problem in offices is the adverse effect that the noise of impact printers has on human communication and concentration. Impact printers typically produce noise levels of between 75 and 80 decibels, and concentration begins to suffer at noise levels between 55 and 65 decibels. However, noise problems are beginning to disappear with the introduction of quieter non-impact printers using Laser/Xerographic technology.

12.6 COOLING

It is very difficult to predict the amount of additional cooling needed for information technology equipment in an office. Typically, modern offices allow the following:

1. 20 W/m2 for lighting.
2. 20 W/m2 for small power.

Additionally, there are allowances for people, solar gain, conduction etc.. The 'small power' figure is primarily intended for information technology equipment.

It is essential to know the maximum occupation density that is likely to occur. In the UK, the space allowed per person is rising. This is partly due to the shift in the office population from clerical to professional work and partly to provide space for information technology equipment. Averages of 150 sq.

ft. (14 m2) per person are common now compared to the 85 sq. ft. (8 m2) of a few years ago. This increase in space provides a corresponding increase from 160 W to 270 W per user for cooling information technology equipment (at 20 W/m2).

12.7 TRENDS IN INFORMATION TECHNOLOGY

In order to determine whether today's standards of provision of space, power, cooling and lighting are going to be adequate in the future, it is necessary to consider trends in information technology. Whilst there has been remarkable improvement in the performance of computers per unit of space or power consumed, the demand for more processing power and information storage is growing much faster. For the last five to ten years, most large organisations have experienced a growth in demand for processing power and on-line storage of 40-45% per annum (compounded) (Butler Cox Foundation, 1987). The rate of technical improvement in terms of reducing electrical power and space requirements has been only 10-15% over the same period. The result is a net increase of about 30% per annum (compounded) in space, power and cooling requirements.

12.8 WORKSTATIONS

At the workstation level, the space and electrical power requirements are more closely related to the ergonomics of the keyboard and the display rather than processing power of an integrated circuit. The idea of a workstation that is capable of all office functions was a popular one but is now seen to be flawed.

The advent of multi-function office workstations, that is, terminals handling text, data, voice and images, in an integrated way, is proving a much slower process than was envisaged just a few years ago. Such workstations are not yet in widespread commercial use, though in theory, they would appear to offer significant benefits to users in flexibility and convenience. In many respects, what the manufacturers are offering does not match the real needs of the user.

The starting point in the argument for multi-function equipment is the fact that, with few exceptions, office workers tend to perform not one task but many concurrently. Attempts to increase productivity by automating or otherwise improving only one of the tasks, whether for managers, professionals, secretaries or other clerical staff, can have a limited impact only. Compared with the use of single function products to achieve the same overall purpose, multi-function terminals are in principle more compact, less expensive and more convenient. Slow growth in the use of multi-function office products is accounted for by three main causes: the difficulty of cost justification, the high cost of products, and the lack of maturity in the products.

There is evidence that suppliers have tended to design terminals with more functions than are needed by most users, and hence the available machines are unnecessarily expensive. Users' experience also shows that it is not sufficient to implement systems which provide a general set of office tools; an organisation's specific requirements and current practices should be investigated fully before deciding which products are appropriate.

Many user organisations find that current integrated products fail to match their particular needs. Suppliers have expended much effort on the ergonomics of terminal design, but have failed to ensure that their products address the real needs of the users.

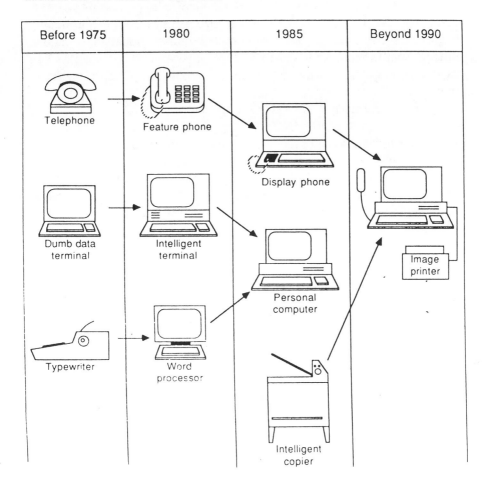

Figure 12.4: Evolution of an integrated workstation

Figure 12.4 shows a possible integration of telephone, personal computer, computer terminal and eventually FAX into an integrated workstation which provides:

1. Text and image creation and editing.
2. Internal and external communication of voice, text and image.
3. Input (scanning) and output of text and images.
4. Integrated functions such as voice annotation of text, automated dialling from an electronic directory and automated answering with voice response from an electronic diary.

Many manufacturers have tried to develop hardware-based products to meet these requirements. Early examples include products emerging from telephone equipment manufacturers such as Northern Telecom's Display Phone. Simple display-phone terminals do, however, have a number of disadvantages. Functionality is limited and there is no processing power to manipulate data locally. Also, the screen size is restricted if the terminal is small. This may cause problems with high definition graphic applications, although small screens are adequate for displaying bar charts, graphs etc.. PTT regulations may constrain the opportunities for combining data and telephone units.

More recent products such as Mitel's 'Tonto' and the ICL 'One-per-desk' terminal based on Sinclair's QL technology have sufficient local processing power to overcome some of the disadvantages mentioned above. However, these products, for apparently mainly commercial reasons, are not in widespread use. It is obviously difficult to justify the investment in new equipment if all staff already have a telephone and either a PC or a computer terminal. Many organisations are not able to afford a comprehensive workstation for every member of staff. However, if a group of staff need a particular facility then this can often be provided by a separate add-on device. This 'mix-and-match' approach provides the clue to the future of integration in the office environment. The system must allow the flexibility for facilities to be added only when they are needed and expensive equipment, such as laser printers, should be available on a sharing basis.

Typical data processing applications are those developed for specific tasks such as sales accounting or management accounting. These are self-contained applications, tailored to the specific needs of a particular activity within an organisation. Figure 12.5 illustrates these typical data processing applications as vertical shaded bars in sales accounting and management accounting, for example. In contrast, office automation provides a basic set of tools to process, retrieve, store, transcribe and communicate information. These are illustrated as horizontal bars in Figure 12.5 as they span the whole range of an organisation's business activities.

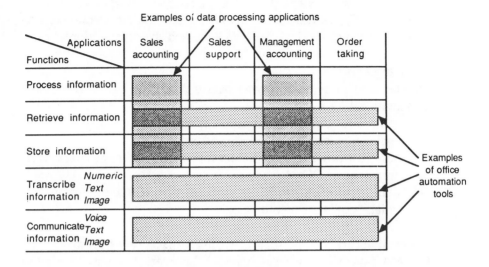

Figure 12.5: Data processing versus office automation

Office automation exploits the parallels between the activities in each department and provides a unified system covering all departments and activities in an organisation. Here again, we find the level of investment required to introduce broad universal office systems is too high for most organisations. At present, only computer companies using their own equipment at cost price have been able to adopt large scale automation. It is perhaps no surprise to learn that both IBM and DEC have more than one computer terminal/PC per employee and that they have global networks with desk-to-desk electronic mail throughout the organisation. For example, you can type in your name in California and read the letters accumulating for you at your office in Lyons.

The PC has now become the driving force in the adoption of office technology. Its low cost and accessibility have resulted in widespread, if rather unmanageable, use. Until recently, many have been purchased on the stationery budget.

By adopting 'open standards' for its PC, using the established MS.DOS operating system and publishing full details of the internal bus, IBM enabled a huge cottage industry of software writers and add-on component manufacturers to identify what users really wanted. This has been a novel experience for the computer industry which has previously tried to sell a complete system based on its own ideas of what is required and frequently designed to lock-in customers to its product range.

Whilst PCs were stand-alone devices, a de facto standard in terms of operating system, disc format, display, and so on, was acceptable. Now, as more staff have PCs, there are many pressures to provide intercommunication (or, more strictly, networking) between them and the organisation's mainframe.

These pressures arise from:

1. The need to avoid re-keying data that already exists in the corporate database.

2. The need to combine the function of mainframe terminal with personal computer to save desktop and office space.

3. The need to provide secure storage for text and images generated or reformatted on PCs.

4. The desire to automate more internal functions such as electronic mail, diaries and time recording.

Networking has been slower to arrive than expected and has proved more difficult and expensive than was hoped. However, it is now the fastest expanding market sector with a growth of 77% last year, for example. The PC has been the enabling mechanism because it is relatively simple to upgrade a PC with a plug-in card and a special version of the operating software. IBM's latest announcement, the Personal System/2 (PS/2), will provide a strong influence in the networking direction because the new operating system OS/2 has the multi-tasking capability that was missing from MS.DOS. Multi-tasking is the capability of the operating system to do two or more things at once, for example, to receive and store an electronic mail message without interrupting a user who is creating a piece of text or graphic image. Multi-tasking is a pre-requisite of acceptable network operation.

12.9 PERSONAL COMPUTERS AND LOCAL AREA NETWORKS

PCs and Local Area Networks (LANs) are the building blocks of the integrated workstation of the future. LANs provide high speed data communication between computers of all types over limited distances, usually within a building or part of a building. The significant point here is that integration will be provided at the group level only, rather than for each individual.

Figure 12.6 shows a typical departmental network. The workstations are standard PCs with a multi-tasking operating system and a LAN interface card. The LAN could be Ethernet or IBM's token ring and, although shown as a ring here, would most probably be physically wired as a star from a wiring closet or local equipment room. All other facilities are shared between the users.

They include a scanner and laserprinter for hard copy input and output respectively, and a number of external network interfaces for FAX, and public/ private wide area data networks (WANs). The important point is that expensive equipment and telecommunication facilities are shared between group members and are supplied only to those groups who need them.

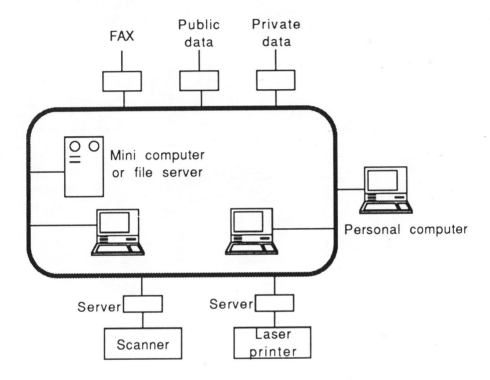

Figure 12.6: Integrated departmental network

At present, neither LANs nor WANs lend themselves to voice and data integration. However, even with separate networks one can, for instance, telephone somebody to discuss the electronic mail message or FAX that has just been sent. It is possible that voice annotation of text or image will be adopted (see Figure 12.7), provided that national or international agreement can be reached on the standards to be used for encoding speech and storing it compactly in digital format. The cost of a microphone and plug-in card for a standard PC could be in the region of £60 to £100.

Another development with significant potential is the use of a PC for telephone directory functions. Data modems for sending data over ordinary telephone lines have been available, with autodialling, for some time. The autodialling equipment can be used for setting up ordinary telephone calls using a directory of frequently used numbers stored in the PC (see Figure 12.8). Here again, this is not voice/data integration at the network level but a simple and practical way of providing the user with what is needed with add-on boxes or cards.

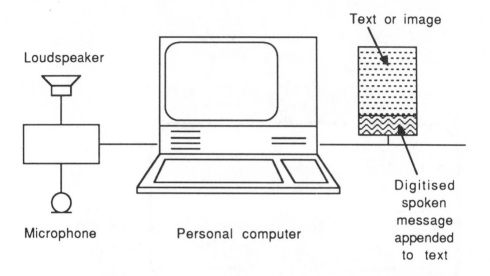

Figure 12.7: Voice annotation of text

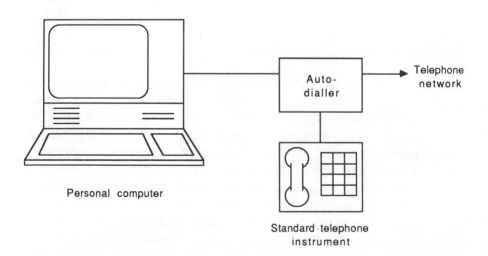

Figure 12.8: Automatic dialling/answering

12.10 DISPLAY TECHNOLOGY

High resolution colour graphic displays for the office environment are at present most economically provided by cathode ray tube (CRT) technology. The introduction of windowing techniques, where more than one page of information can be displayed at once, is encouraging the introduction of larger displays. A major US bank has several hundred dealers and analysts using 19 inch screens showing four 80 column, 25 line pages simultaneously: some screens can be as much as 2 ft (600 mm) deep. Power consumption is approximately proportional to screen area, as shown in Table 12.1.

Colour display size	Power (W)
12 inch	72
14 inch	98
19 inch	180

Table 12.1: Relationship between size of screen and power consumption

Plasma displays offer considerably improved size with depths of only two to four inches and are being adopted. They are at present more expensive and dissipate more power than a conventional CRT. They are, of course, available in monochrome (orange/red) only and cannot match the resolution of the best CRT displays.

Liquid crystal technology and particularly the new 'super twist' displays provide very thin screens at very low power consumption. 720 x 400 element displays are now available, providing good character definition and adequate business graphics. However, they too are only monochrome at present. Considerable research effort is being put into liquid crystal colour television displays but it will probably be five to eight years before products are commercially available. One must remember that even if the display requires significantly less power, this will account for no more than one third of the total used by today's workstations.

It is likely that power and cooling requirements will increase in the medium term. Table 12.2 compares the power requirements of today's workstation, the IBM PC AT incorporating a 12 inch colour display, with a powerful Sun Microsystems workstation with a 19 inch display.

A word of caution is necessary in view of these alarmingly high figures. First, many manufacturers quote peak or worst case figures: the average consumption of most equipment is only a half or one third of the quoted figure. Secondly, as products mature, more functions are carried out by fewer integrated circuits. When products as powerful as Sun are in widespread use, the power consumption will have fallen to 300-400 W for the CPU.

Approx year	Model	Power dissipation (W) CPU	Screen	Total
1981	IBM PC Mono	65	45	110
1987	PC AT Colour	110	68	178
1989	Sun 3/260	987	205	1,192

Table 12.2: Workstation power dissipation

In addition to individual equipment, there will be a requirement to accommodate central equipment such as departmental minicomputers, file servers, communication interfaces and patch panels. For a typical office floor of about 6,500 sq. ft. (600 m2) accommodating, say, 45 people, one should allow approximately 10 KW of power/cooling and 215 sq. ft. (20 m2) of floor space.

If it is assumed that 70% of the staff will have an IBM PC AT colour type of workstation (70 x 45 x 178 W = 5,607 W), plus task lighting for each member of staff (45 x 60 W = 2,700 W), and we allow a further 5,000 W for laserprinter(s), FAX machine, telex, and photocopier, we have a total 'small power' requirement of 13,307 W or 22 W/m2 for the office areas. This is not out of line with typical planning figures of 20 W/m2 being used today. In addition to the office areas the equipment room would require supplementary cooling of 10,000 W and this would need to operate 24 hours a day.

12.11 CONCLUSIONS

The individual multi-function workstation has been superseded by the PC and LAN which combined are capable of providing similar functions at the work group rather than individual level. Users will demand larger colour displays and more individual processing power in the future.

However it is possible to achieve a satisfactory environment, including task lighting, with a small power allowance of 20 W/m2 up to a terminal penetration of 70% (1992 estimate), provided that staff are given reasonably generous accommodation in the order of 150 sq. ft. (14 m2) per person.

It is now vital that workstation manufacturers do everything possible to reduce the power dissipation of their products and for those involved in the design of buildings to obtain accurate data on the cooling requirements for each assignment.

12.12 REFERENCES

Butler Cox (1987), *Planning the corporate data centre,* Butler Cox Foundation Research Report 55, April, 10-14.
CCTA (1983), *Accommodation for computer and office systems,* IT Series No. 4, HMSO, August, 45-49.

Chapter 13
Local area networks and office automation

I. PALMER

13.1 INTRODUCTION

The personal computer (PC) is a processor in its own right and has, until recently, been used as a stand-alone unit, with communication between PCs accomplished mostly by handing disks around. With the advent of local area networks (LANs), communication can now occur across the network, that is, between many different users. The growth in LANs has been stimulated by the increasing power of individual computers (processors) to support more and more terminals. This paper discusses the 'coming of age' of LANs and the benefits that they offer building users today. Moves towards the paperless office are also discussed.

13.2 THE NEED FOR LANs

Many organisations have already installed information systems on their computer systems and the number is growing daily. A consequence is that it has become essential for personnel be given the facility of attaching to such resources. These resources have also been growing as more sophisticated software becomes available, with most software houses writing programs for several types of processor. The requirements for resilience, that is, not keeping all your 'eggs in one basket', demand that the user be able to switch from one resource to another. So, if a costing program is on Host 1, but the user is attached to Host 2, it should be possible to switch to that resource and execute the program. This eliminates the need to have more than one terminal per user and also allows the user to switch to other resources, such as printers, plotters, modems, telex and X25, which may be attached to the network. Users do not normally require the use of a computer port or service for 100% of its available time and, therefore, some form of sharing is sensible. Most LANs offer queuing or contention eliminating multiplexer type equipment to enable competition for services to be managed.

Typically, a service is put into a group and given a name, that is, a 'hunt group'. This enables the user to execute a service by attaching to that name. The system will look through the group and try to attach to the first available port or report back that the service is unavailable. This works in much the same way as a hunt group works on the telephone system. This facility is not restricted to one's own computer, but can be used for any service that may be required.

This approach to networking works well provided the organisation has one type of processor and one type of display. However, if several different processors are being used or changes to their specification are envisaged, this can mean a totally different story. Multiple hosts with different protocols and connections will mean that a LAN purchased from one computer manufacturer will not 'talk' to a LAN from another manufacturer.

13.3 LAN PROTOCOLS - THE OPTIONS

There are two main protocols for LANs: synchronous and asynchronous. The type of protocol depends on whether or not the LAN can handle the clocking on the computer. In some cases, it is possible to profile the node access point to handle both synchronous and asynchronous, but satisfactory results are by no means guaranteed.

Two of the largest computer companies, namely IBM and DEC, have adopted different protocols and connections: DEC use V24/RS232 and IBM use cluster controllers and coaxial cabling. There is, therefore, no possibility of effecting an external connection between such different hosts, other than by a protocol conversion or a MAP interface. This incompatibility problem is compounded as most users select their computer systems on the basis of what is best for individual applications. The result is that either a compromise is needed or the user ends up with two or more terminals.

One of the ways that users have been able communicate when faced with different hosts (with different protocols and/or connections) is via a PC, which is capable of emulating the required display device. However, this tends to involve additional software and hardware (typically a printed circuit board, PCB) at extra cost. This protocol conversion option has its advantages, but may have significant disadvantages owing to loss of functionality and the overhead of the protocol converter. Alternatively, users might prefer to standardise on one protocol and one type of connection. This will probably be the least cost option, but will limit future expansion plans.

A further option is to use a PC with emulation package, involving additional software and PCBs for each PC. However, it is possible that the PC may not have sufficient room left within it to fit a new PCB, necessitating an external card cage.

All options have their advantages and disadvantages, but one thing is certain: if there were a standard, life would be a lot easier. Unfortunately, there is no standard, that is, a single protocol and connection type. Instead, several 'standards' are beginning to emerge on the more commonly available LANs.

13.4 LAN STANDARDS

The IEEE has published a 'set of rules' standardising on three types of LAN: 802.3 which is CSMA/CD, carrier send multiple access collision detection; 802.4 token ring bus; and 802.5 token ring. The latter two relate to Ethernet, broadband and IBM's cabling system.

802.3 has been adopted by ICL and DEC since it is ideal for transferring large files from one host to another. However, it is difficult to calculate the response as the system changes or grows, as far as display traffic is concerned. It is a non-deterministic network and there are limitations on its physical size.

802.4 broadband is mainly used where there is a larger physical requirement. Broadband has the ability to cater for different forms of traffic, for instance, video and voice, and to date has been sold mostly into the manufacturing environment. It is an expensive technology.

802.5 token ring has been pushed by IBM but it is a long way behind other LANs, in terms of its functionality, because of its comparatively recent release. It has, however, started to overtake 802.3 in the number of kits being shipped worldwide.

Since these three LAN standards conform to rules set down by the 802 Committee of the IEEE, there are bridges, routes and gateways to link them together so a node on one can communicate with a node on another. This enables, for instance, a broadband system in a production facility to cummunicate with a token ring in an office. Communication can also be obtained through public and private networks to remote sites. This is possible because of the adoption of standards pertaining to the bottom two layers of the ISO 7-layer model.

The remaining layers have been defined already in manufacturing environments, enabling a computer running one particular package to communicate with another computer running totally different packages under different protocols. This has been achieved largely through the work of General Motors Corporation in developing the Manufacturing Automation Protocol, MAP.

There are, however, parts of MAP that need to be finalised and these are not due to be released until the end of 1988. However, their eventual adoption will enable computers running under different protocols to communicate with one another even though they are otherwise incompatible.

The remaining layers of the ISO model are also being defined for the office environment in TOP, Technical Office Protocol, which is likely to be available soon.

13.5 PCs IN NETWORKING

In the last three years or so, one name that has become a de facto standard in computing is the personal computer (PC), based on IBM's model. PCs can be used, as stated previously, as a terminal to host a LAN, by direct or indirect means. Although the PC is not an expensive processor, it is more expensive than a simple display device. When Winchester disks, printers and software are added, the total cost can be comparatively high.

PCs that are linked to a network are able to function as terminals in communicating with a host computer. But they can also remove some of the terminal overhead by capturing files on the host and running them locally in conjunction with an application package, for example, word processing, spreadsheet and database management. Once transactions have been completed, these files can be used to update the host.

PCs can also share software and hardware overheads by using a network operating system, capable of supporting a file server. In this way, multi-file servers can be incorporated into a LAN at strategic points. The use of a file server enables application packages and users' data files to be kept on a central disc and maintained by the operating system. This means that there needs to be just one copy of the software. An additional benefit of a file server is that jobs can be spooled for printing, enabling more sophisticated printers to be shared amongst many users.

13.6 TOWARDS THE PAPERLESS OFFICE

The introduction of the LAN has heralded an important move towards the paperless office. Letters, memoranda and reports can now be sent electronically to whoever needs them. The receiver can respond, verifying what has been sent, acting upon the information or passing it on. This is achieved through an electronic mail (EM) system which is ideally suited to a short memo or letter.

EM systems can be tailored to suit the organisation's existing paper-based information systems, thereby limiting the amount of retraining. Information can be marked as urgent so that a prompt to the receiver can be applied, and provided that the PC is switched on, the receiver gets the message at the moment it is sent. Senders should be able to interrogate EM systems to see if a receiver has, in fact, seen his mail and, if so, when. Enclosures can also be sent with EM so that lengthy documents can be entered as an attachment. If there is a requirement to send documents to a number of people, a group can be named and the documents sent to all within that group. Short names can also be used to eliminate the time consuming process of having to key in lengthy names and addresses. This technique can also help when sending documents to the outside world over X.400.

X.400 is a set of rules that will enable two senders using different systems to communicate and is being set up on the public network at this time. The overall objective is to eliminate the requirement for the paper post system. It is costly and will take a long time to progress to the point where the paper post can be eliminated.

A practical application using EM in conjunction with X.400 could take the following form. A letter is created by the word processing package, drawing on information held in, say, a spreadsheet. The document could then be addressed via the database. The letter could be sent to internal parties within the organisation for comment. Once their comments have been received, the finished letter could be sent outside using X.400, with a copy of the letter being sent to the internal database.

Other external services can be attached to a LAN, for example, modems, X.25 and telex, and selected by users. A PC can communicate across the LAN rather than through the file server using protocols such as Netbias or the high layers within the ISO model. Conference calls can also be set up using third party connections.

13.7 CONCLUSIONS

The purchase of a computer for the right job and the ability to communicate from one terminal to all available services can and should be carried out by a LAN. However, all of this does not necessarily come cheaply. Depending on the size of LAN, it is possible that someone will be needed to manage it, with responsibility to change, reconfigure and maintain the service. Whilst this will add to the basic cost of the LAN, it can be justified for the following reasons:

1. Fewer cluttered cabling ducts.
2. Ability of new personnel to attach to the LAN easily without recabling.
3. Provision of statistics about a user, via the network management system.

4. Ability to contend for ports rather than leaving the service idle.

5. Ability to switch from one service to another without needing lots of terminals or leaving the system.

6. Ease with which PCs can be added to the network - their unit cost can be brought down when a file server with suitable operating system is used.

Chapter 14
Telecommunications and Value Added Services

W. NOSEWORTHY

14.1 INTRODUCTION

It is a logical premise that intelligent beings inhabit intelligent buildings and their intelligence is enhanced through the manipulation of intelligent data. A clear pre-requisite is that the intelligent beings must understand the means by which they collect, apply and manipulate the intelligent data.

The first requirement, therefore, is their appreciation of the procedures through which they address the data. In this computer age, a combination of simple keyboard skills and an appreciation of Boolean logic and programmable search techniques is mandatory. Navigation through the computer programs required for such analysis has traditionally been via menu systems where the selection of one then another option will eventually lead to a solution being provided through progressive narrowing of options.

Obviously, such basic processes can become extremely tedious and in consequence skilled users frequently demand the ability to address the programs' logic at a higher (command language) level. This leads to requirements being made of these command languages that they should recognise the syntax and semantics of so called 'natural language'. From this it would follow that the ability to speak to computers and ask appropriate questions, to which the answers would then be instantly provided, must be the ultimate solution.

In this final process we have moved from a strictly defined regime of menued words into areas of dialect, synonyms, homonyms and phononyms which are likely to confuse both the computer and the user more than a little.

14.2 A POSSIBLE SCENARIO

Imagine the user of a computer who asks the system to produce a list of staff in his company who are paid more than £20,000 per annum, where the database in which the data are held recognises staff as employees and pay as salary.

It is certainly possible to employ a thesaurus containing employees as a synonym for staff, and salary, wages, emoluments etc. as synonyms for pay, through which the computer will interpret into an approximation of natural language, the user's request to produce a sensible result.

Moving now to other problems, imagine the difficulty of the machine which is asked to differentiate between full and fool, pool and pull and any other homonym or phononym of which you can think and we are now requiring the machine to second guess the user.

We can now start to enter the world of artificial intelligence. In this case we can include thesauri either in 'workaday' or technical language, which will assist the selection process. We can apply rules or knowledge or expert assistance, which make assumptions based on algorithms derived by knowledge engineers from their analysis of procedures used by experts. We can then ask our programs to make selections with or without these rules, in order to compare the conclusions. But in what area of the intelligent building might they apply? Do we define an intelligent building as one that is equipped with potentially intelligent systems for analysis by intelligent beings?

Surely these systems relate on the one hand to the data and on the other hand to their applications as required by the intelligent users. An intelligent building, for example, might be fitted with smoke or heat detectors which simply sound an alarm when given densities of smoke or excesses of temperature indicate dangerous environments for the occupants and so cause alarms to sound locally and perhaps call the fire brigade. However, human response is required to evacuate the building.

But this relates to just one possible scenario. Suppose the intelligent building is equipped with computers which are connected to the Stock Exchange and that those computers are programmed to buy or sell a particular share when it reaches a 'stop' loss or gain figure, assuming this has been predetermined by an expert investor. Surely the building then contains a different form of intelligence.

Taking another aspect of data input, let us suppose that a marketing manager wishes to analyse the opportunity to sell personal stereo systems in Outer Mongolia. Given suitable data and an appropriate user interface, he can ask of a database, containing appropriate market research, to receive information which represents a geo-demographic analysis of that country's potential users of that product. It might show the existing penetration of competitive products; the potential growth over the next ten years; the likely distributors or retail outlets for the item; the disposable income of the market; and the likely prices of available products based on a given inflation rate on the one hand and a 70% experience curve on the other. But it may fail to tell him that batteries are in short supply in Outer Mongolia.

Yet another application of not dissimilar data may exist with the designer of the last mentioned product wishing to interrogate a central database of available electronic components at the leading edge of technology, which enable his company to produce the item to penetrate the market at the lowest cost. Clearly in this intelligent building, there are many other corporate functions which require the use of information which is either produced internally or available from outside sources, typically on paper. However, the information revolution is set to change all that. Whether the user of the information is the marketing department, the company secretary, the credit control department, the purchasing department or whoever, the traditional paper-based information flow from the organisation's library or outside consultants is proving too slow to provide the response required in today's global marketplaces.

14.3 TELECOMMUNICATIONS

Not unnaturally, the medium of delivery for this sophisticated information is the computer. It is now being linked to more traditional message delivery systems which tomorrow will incorporate FAX with electronic mail, reading the text intelligently so that it can be manipulated in precisely the same way as if it were input through a word processing system. Within the intelligent building therefore, there are now communication networks (local area networks, LANs) which enable a mix of voice and data communications to reach every desk and enable communication from there to the outside world in any form.

It is on this premise that the new digital networks being provided by British Telecom and others, will take us into the 21st Century, and it is happening now.

14.4 VALUE ADDED SERVICES

Soon, British Telecom's Value Added Services will link with these advanced internal and external telecommunications to provide the information and transaction systems for all of our business and leisure applications, and some of these are already in place.

Consider the last time you visited a travel agent who did not have a Prestel terminal, enabling selection of the holiday or business trip and its automatic booking. Similar services exist for agriculture, insurance, retailing, banking and industry and they are being added to at a significant rate as a result of major investments in central computer systems, software and communication networks.

Pilot services are already being launched which will enable manufacturing industry to purchase components and exchange the trade documentation of invoices etc. totally electronically. Such services are already available in the electronics and engineering fields and will be spread rapidly to cover the construction, aerospace, automotive and other industries.

Bringing about the use of this technology requires the determination and adoption of standards to enable totally transparent inter-machine communication. A good example of this exists in the electronic data interchange initiatives developed within specific communities of interest such as the motor industry. These enable the transmission of invoices, statements, credit notes, delivery notes etc., produced by one computerised accounting system to be read through a translator into a totally disparate program on a trading partner's machinery.

In other examples, considerable work is being done to enable the transfer of computer aided design drawings through open standards translators. As the complexity of the task increases, so the timescale becomes elongated. But though these are complex problems they are able to be dealt with through the willing co-operation of the hardware and software suppliers who now recognise that their customers will only buy systems which do communicate with others and which will support an upgrade path seen by the customer to be essential to his developing needs.

British Telecom's Value Added Services are dedicated to an open systems architecture and BT is adding its influence in the marketplace to ensure widespread adoption.

Unless they are easy to use, the value added services - for which there is considerable competition from other major players - will fail. And, like any other business, they must stand on their own commercial success. It is neither sensible nor are we allowed in a regulatory environment to cross-subsidise them from the established telephone networks. Thus, our work on simple and common user interfaces, common machine translation, artificial intelligence and many other ingredients of successful Value Added Services continues apace.

14.5 CONCLUSIONS

The future for these Value Added Services is clearly to provide greater connectivity between applications and to integrate their information and transaction services totally into the pattern of commerce. Stimulating such initiatives will require dedicated collaboration with lead players and communities of interest who have already declared their willingness to participate in these pioneering ventures. As a result, they can enjoy, at the earliest possible stage, the benefits of integration to reduce their costs and provide the competitive advantage that their day to day business requires. Then we will have truly intelligent buildings.

Chapter 15
Planning and co-ordinating cabling requirements

M. STUBBINGS

15.1 INTRODUCTION

Cabling needs to be treated as an important element of a project and construction management should, either themselves or via specialists, ensure that serious consideration is given to this subject. The aims are to achieve, amongst other things:

1. Compatibility between various cabling systems that may be introduced into the project, either during construction or afterwards.
2. Physical co-ordination with the structure and other services.
3. Ease of future growth and reconfiguration works.
4. Accurate recording for maintenance, fault finding and ongoing premises management.

An effective method for achieving the above, particularly on projects with a high concentration of information technology, is to instigate a planned strategy for cabling. The strategy should be provided in conjunction with a specialist in cable management.

15.2 CABLE MANAGEMENT

Over the last few years, it has become increasingly apparent that industries employing significant levels of information technology, for example, banking and financial services, require many more comprehensive skills and services to manage their cabling installations. Business activities in this environment are more and more at risk from their cabling installations. These skills are particularly necessary and have been highlighted in fitting-out (of 'core and shell' projects) and large scale refurbishment works where high volumes of cables supplying many different systems are necessary. The need for a single, highly skilled and experienced professional to provide what is now referred to as 'cable management' has emerged.

Cable management covers a wide range of activities relating to the gathering of relevant information via a multitude of sources, for example, information services providers and equipment manufacturers. The co-ordination of this information is then reproduced on integrated cabling drawings and schedules, and forms the basis of construction and installation works.

The cable management activity covers liaison with clients, users, suppliers, etc. and acts as the focal point for providing information in support of the client's requirements at all stages of the project. The cable management team acts as an interface with the design and construction team, and can provide valuable information to all parties in good time for works to proceed. It is vital, therefore, that the cable manager must have the necessary technical experience, construction experience and diplomacy to combine the above responsibilities, without losing sight of the important time, cost and quality considerations.

Recent experiences of this role have indicated that the cable manager can work successfully alongside the more traditional design and construction team members, that is, the architect, quantity surveyor, consultant engineer, contractor etc. and can contribute to the project without an overlap of skills or effort. The cable manager should also act as the focus for quality assurance and quality control. He should initially establish the quality assurance (QA) procedures with the client and then monitor and control quality through normal supervision line management channels of on-site installations. Finally, the cable manager should (in conjunction with the contractor) monitor on-site progress of cabling to ensure that installations are carried out under the correct conditions and at the agreed programme sequence and rate.

15.3 CO-ORDINATION

The co-ordination of cabling installations, as part of a project, can be thought of at two levels:
1. Co-ordination in time, that is, programming/sequencing of activities.
2. Co-ordination of physical items.

It is necessary and important to review and discuss the sequence of operations with cabling installers (this may involve several organisations covering data, voice, power, alarms, etc. for some highly serviced office environments). It may be that these assorted organisations are responsible to different clients, for example, the fire alarm contractor may be a direct sub-contractor to the electrical sub-contractor, and subsequently he may also be responsible to the main contractor. Furthermore, core and shell works may be separated from the fitting-out of the building, although each arrangement may use the same main contractor.

Client user departments, for instance, telecommunications and administration may also have a relationship with some or all of these organisations and therefore calculating the correct sequence of work may require co-ordination involving a large number of interests; nevertheless, this must be done. Adding these sequences of installation, each with their own particular rates of progress and requirements into a single construction programme, emphasises the importance of planning.

Given the luxury of layout drawings, raised floor grid drawings, under-floor layouts, furniture layouts, equipment positions and services outlets, the establishment of cabling 'highways' and major user and route positions is not difficult. The need, however, is often to produce trunking layout drawings in advance of furniture and equipment layouts. Clearly trunking routes need to be established at an early stage, but with consideration given to the inevitable change which will occur during the development of the project. The more flexible or universal these layouts are made, the more easily modifications during construction and reconfiguration after completion can be achieved. The changes which occur to offices and furniture/workstation layouts, particularly in the high technology (computing and dealing room) environments, seem to increase as organisations need to respond to changing market conditions. To build in future flexibility into layouts can also assist in overcoming the initial co-ordination problems (by offering different and alternative cable routes) and provide clients with an adaptable system which will not restrain future configuration. The inevitable future need to install new or additional cabling on most projects, together with the ability to use alternative routes for those cables, must provide a strong argument for a structured cabling system.

15.4 STRUCTURED CABLING SYSTEMS

A structured cabling system offers a good solution to the complex problem of providing voice and data where it is required, with the minimum of disruption. If planned with expansion taken into account, it can also provide future reconfiguration and office layouts with the necessary services, without recourse to extra risers, hole cutting and other potentially disruptive exercises. Termination density is established on present and future requirements, where these are known. In raised floor areas, density can range considerably, however, distribution outlets at every 40-50 sq. ft. below the floor (and perhaps every 60-75 sq. ft. per floor box outlet), seem to be normal for general office environments. But these can increase dramatically where organisations have a high level of information technology. At the time that cable is laid, for known requirements, the additional cost of extra future cabling should be considered carefully.

A structured cabling system can provide:

1. A functional route for data and voice cabling.

2. Assistance with fault finding of specific routes or cables.

3. A transmission medium that will last in-situ for a good number of years and provide the user with room for future development and expansion.

4. A limit and control to cost of cabling and the consequential damage to the building fabric.

5. A stop to the proliferation of semi-active and redundant cables in risers, ceiling and trunking generally.

6. Consolidation of existing systems, for example, coaxial, twin axial and twisted pair.

15.5 PLANNED STRATEGY

As previously stated, it is essential that major projects include a cable distribution and installation strategy. This strategy should be developed by the design team at an early stage in the planning and should be prepared in conjunction with a specialist cable manager. A checklist of requirements to meet the strategy could include the following questions:

1. Are the riser positions and sizes adequate?

2. Is there sufficient underfloor distribution?

3. Is there sufficient ceiling void distribution?

4. Will the routes be accessible along their entire route?

5. Can the cable be practically installed?

6. Are there potential damage points to cable, for example, acute bends?

7. Can the cables be identified easily; are they tagged   sufficiently?

8. Can additional cables be installed or modifications carried out?

9. Are the cables running in such positions as to cause interference problems?

10. Are the potential crossover points adequate?

11. Is there sufficient space between the horizontal and vertical interfaces, for example, where cables enter distribution risers?

12. What total load will the cables apply to the structure?
13. Should the cables be run in trunking?
14. Are there hazards caused by attaching to the cables, for example, from fire?
15. Can riser closets be worked in practically?
16. Will cables be damaged during installation of other elements of works?
17. Do the cables have adequate fixings?

There are, of course, other questions particular to each project, but each point will prompt an answer which will develop into an overall strategy.

15.5 PLANNING

It is important to consider the nature of data cabling and if possible it will be necessary to discuss with each relevant party the quantity of cable to be installed and its particular requirements. In high rise buildings, it is essential to check whether the cabling system will be 'patched' (a plug and socket distribution board arrangement) at particular points along the route, for example, user cupboards and equipment rooms. It may be that the cabling installation will run on a 'point to point' basis as with fibre optic systems. The problems of running cabling in a main riser position or restricted size equipment room should be considered: a major factor will be the quantity of drums of cable that will inevitably accumulate, causing problems of access, co-ordination and even excess floor loading.

Those responsible for cabling installation should be allowed to review the project programme and introduce realistic time scales. Many projects have suffered from cabling installations because cable installers have not had sufficient input. This is usually the first item to use up any 'slack' or 'float' that any prudent planner will have built into the construction/project programme. Cabling, and in particular data cabling, has often been carried out on a shift basis to meet an already tight schedule.

There are obviously some occasions, for example, working within an occupied area, when out-of-hours work is necessary, but it should not be so for other projects. Often these drastic measures are caused by an initial under-estimate. The cost and other implications of this considerable section of the project probably impacts more on its surroundings than any other element. Cabling may attract up to 5% of a project's capital cost, a figure which is equivalent perhaps to adding suspended ceiling and raised flooring costs together.

15.6 POWER AND LIGHTING

The more traditional building services, that is, power, lighting and controls wiring are well understood and construction planners generally allow sufficient programme time. More often than not the programme reflects this work on a first and second fix basis, and therefore the awareness of the nature of this work is quite high. But when moving to a slightly more sophisticated wiring installation, for example fire alarms, public address systems, security systems and more elaborate building management systems, planning starts to get more difficult.

These systems, although perhaps different in nature to the standard lighting and power wiring systems, generally do not have the same impact on a building as data cabling. The sheer quantity of cabling to be installed for data tends to overshadow the cabling for these other systems. Therefore, whilst fire alarms and security systems do not require the same magnitude of cabling, there are often other problems to overcome. Security systems, for instance, sometimes require walls to be chased to digital lock and keypad positions, and fire alarm wiring needs to be sunk into the walls.

One should also consider the need to run cable to an electric lock on double doors. Drilling through an expensive solid door with a small diameter drill for cabling access requires skill. These illustrations are, by comparison, small when considering the problem of installing several kilometres or so of different cable systems into buildings which are often not designed for such purposes.

The difficulty of getting several hundred cables from a floor void into a vertical riser, which may have three structural walls and be open at the front only, is quite challenging. Add to this the need to install these cables in a correct sequence and maintain access to them for future expansion purposes - plus the potential weight limitations on a structural floor - and the problems begin to increase. Planning a raised flooring installation around these problems without incurring considerable extra expense is not easy.

15.7 INSTALLATION CONDITIONS

It is important to ensure that the cabling installation (particularly data cabling) is integrated within the overall project programme. Often there are only limited opportunities for this work to be carried out. In a raised floor area where the cabling runs at low level, the installation is most likely best carried out towards the end of the flooring panel installation, prior to the partition works. It is often only at this stage (on large projects) that significant areas of clear floor are available for cables to be laid out in an orderly manner before their installation. In most cases, cables cannot be pulled long lengths directly from cable drums, for example, power cables, since they are prone to overloading damage from stretching.

Cables that are run within trunking systems generally offer earlier opportunities for installation and can, for example, be laid before the floor support jacks and tiles, thereby benefiting from the protection of substantial trunking with enclosed sides and covers. Often, however, cables are laid on open trays or indeed are laid directly on to floor slabs to predetermined routes (coloured highways can be painted directly on to slabs).

Installation using either of these methods is vulnerable to significant damage and needs careful planning and possibly even specific protection measures. Cabling can be carried out quickly and efficiently with clear conditions, such as open floor spaces. However, to attempt the same exercise when partitions or ceilings and other high level installations are being carried out is unwise. It is worth remembering that cables may need to be laid through an area where work is being carried out and generally cannot be laid piecemeal, that is, room by room. Few other services or operations suffer this constraint.

15.8 RAISED FLOORS

Raised floors, particularly in open areas, are an asset and are probably one of the single most important developments in building servicing. The fact that increasing numbers of projects do not incorporate raised floors reflects the opinion of most building users who, according to a recent survey, placed raised floors in third place on their list of priorities for new premises. There is no doubt that raised floors, combined with the large quantity of underfloor trunking and floor outlet box systems, offer solutions to cable implementation. However, the raised floor in a cellular office environment may become trapped by partitions, fixtures and even furniture. Raised floors are expensive, therefore, there is little point in having 80% of the tiles trapped.

Finally it is worth noting that the standard of raised flooring manufacture and installation has improved dramatically over the last five years and raised floors generally offer excellent value for money.

15.9 CAD SYSTEM SUPPORT

Cable management can present an information recording and retrieval requirement that is considerably more complex than that for traditional fittings and fixtures. Personal Architect's 3D modelling, drafting and scheduling capability has been used by the author to plan and co-ordinate cable routes in conjunction with other building services, and to produce drawing records and schedules. The Personal Architect system also allows communications and services personnel to carry out relocation, maintenance and routine management after installation, and can be used in conjunction with ECL's Intelligent Building Services (IBS) Division's menu-driven interactive cable and equipment management database system.

The ability to produce clear and easily modified cabling layouts, and at the same time store relevant information, has benefited from the use of CAD. ECL presently use PC-based Personal Architect 3D design and drafting systems to which have been added cost estimating and materials scheduling enhancements. Personal Architect represents a building and its contents through the following associated information:

1. 3D building geometry.
2. A file of structural specifications.
3. Libraries of fittings and fixtures symbols.
4. Schedules of symbol attributes.

It can produce schematic and detailed drawings, colour-shaded internal views, cutaway sections and quantity reports and schedules, because the building database records 3D spatial relationships, technical specifications and symbol information. Symbol libraries may include 2D and 3D structural, M & E, cabling equipment and furniture symbols. Attributes such as catalogue numbers, specifications, descriptions, dimensions and costs, can be associated with each symbol for the automatic generation of schedules and inventories.

Once the structural building model has been generated, the Personal Architect user can design and detail cable routes and equipment rooms. A particular advantage is the ability to engineer and visualise detailed crossovers of multi-cable highways and cable risers in confined spaces.

Cost estimates, environmental calculations, materials and component schedules can be developed directly from lengths, areas, volumes and listings extracted from the model and enhanced using integrated software. Fully detailed and annotated contract and 'as built' structural and wiring drawings are produced by transferring the model to linked drafting software and enhancing the computer generated plans, elevations and sections.

Alternative circulation patterns and layouts may be evaluated and, because the model is a complete 3D structural representation, modifications made in plan will automatically be incorporated in elevations and sections, and vice versa. Cabling implications as well as architectural effects can therefore be considered and layouts can be stored and generated from the database.

15.10 CABLING & EQUIPMENT MANAGEMENT DATABASE SYSTEM

ECL have developed, and use, a menu-driven interactive cabling and equipment database, which can be used during and after installation. This allows communication and service personnel, responsible for information technology related systems, to carry out relocation, maintenance and day-to-day facilities management inside the premises.

The Cable Management Database System consists of three component databases:

1. Outlet User Information Database: concerned primarily with tracing a cable, by its reference number, from its outlet to a device on a workstation via a link cable.

2. Distribution Cable Details Database: outlines the route taken by a particular cable to a patch cabinet (or wiring cabinet).

3. Wiring Cabinet Information Database: traces the route taken by a particular cable within a wiring cabinet. It is concerned with information pertaining to patch panels, communication equipment and any relevant link cables within the cabinet.

The Cable Management Database provides a user-friendly menu-driven interface which is visually displayed on the screen enabling the user to interact with the system. The formation of the menu is such that the screen is divided into distinct areas. The menu bar at the top of the screen displays the main options available such as Report Number, Add Data, Edit, List, Delete and Print. Depending upon the item selected, the database may require additional information: a pull-down menu list appears from which to make further choices. Successive menu options enable the user to form the desired command sequence.

Central to the function of the database is the ability to trace the path taken by a cable, by its unique reference number, through the three component databases. The cable reference numbers are used on the installed cables at relevant points, for example, at each end of the cable run and at strategic positions along the length. By checking the cable reference number from the database, full details of the cable can be quickly obtained including specification, length, route, etc.

The ability to determine a cable route is not only a valuable help to reconfiguration work but can be of great assistance in finding cable faults or damaged cables. Access to the wiring cabinet section of the database allows the user detailed information relating to the patch panel, providing a clear and easily manageable and updated record of 'as installed' and reconfiguration works.

Access to the outlet section provides information on particular workstation equipment, for example, desktop PCs. The ability to store serial numbers, cost folios, maintenance and fault information provides a comprehensive management operation. Naturally spare capacity, in terms of record size, is built into each section to allow the user to store additional information of his choice. Each database can therefore be tailored to specific requirements. By producing and updating the original contract information in database format, clear records of cabling and associated equipment are produced and with regular updating these provide a valuable cost effective service for clients.

The cable database has proved to be an ideal method of recording data during the survey, and amending it as more detailed information becomes available from our survey. The database, when completed, represents the structure of the cabling in the building and links it with the equipment actually installed within the premises. The total database is then used to summarise the information (for example, numbers of PCs by floor, numbers of spare outlets per floor and patch panel utilisation) and from it reports can be prepared for the client.

15.11 CONCLUSIONS

Planning and co-ordinating cable installations into new buildings can be a relatively simple task. There are now sufficient numbers of construction professionals aware enough to give cabling more than a passing thought. Cabling of the much maligned 1950s and 1960s buildings is also comparatively easy, provided that it is planned as part of the refurbishment work. The real challenge is to add 'intelligence' via cabling installation to old and listed buildings. The inability to cut large vertical risers and the inappropriate nature of raised floors and false ceilings demand ingenuity. Flat cable systems and attractive trunking offer some solutions. It is in this area that the greatest need exists for the architect and cable manager to work closely together.

Chapter 16
Building Energy Management Systems: a practical approach to their development

A.S. EASTWELL

16.1 INTRODUCTION

The development history of Building Energy Management Systems (BEMS) is closely linked to advancement in computer technology. This development has also been strongly influenced by the political and economic climate prevailing in the country of origin and this has led to a definite and distinct difference in design approach particularly between the US and some European countries.

16.2 DEVELOPMENT

The US can almost certainly claim to have operated the first BEMS in the early 1970s. As technology had at that time not yet spawned the low cost microprocessor, it was inevitable and natural that the system would be based on a centralised processor with all executive control taking place at the central station, now generally called a 'centralised system'. Systems of this type were most appropriate for installation in single, large buildings where the cable runs between sensors, actuators and the processing device could be most easily achieved. From a political viewpoint, this architecture fitted the scene well as, unlike the UK, large distributed estates were not common, whereas large corporate headquarters were undergoing significant growth.

The UK, however, possessed a different market with many more smaller units operated by estate owners. The slightly later entry of the UK and European manufacturing companies gave them an opportunity to incorporate the (then) emerging microprocessor into their products, and so was born the 'intelligent outstation'. In this configuration the control algorithms, and hence the executive function of the device, could be devolved much closer to the plant under control. This stand-alone ability now freed the central station from the need to maintain continuous communication with the sensors and actuators. It then became feasible to use the British Telecom network to access sites many miles remote from the central station.

To bring the situation completely up-to-date, the cost of processing has dropped to the point where it is reasonable to consider one controller per plant item (as yet largely unrealised), thus devolving the intelligence about as far as it is possible to go.

16.3 ARCHITECTURE

It is worth dwelling for a while on the advantages and disadvantages of the approaches involved in BEMS development. Central intelligence systems have developed a high degree of horizontal integration partly because of their age and partly because of the nature of the companies involved, for instance, Honeywell and Johnson Controls. By integration, we are talking of combining HVAC, fire and security protection, lifts, and access control into a single product. No legislative difficulties arise in the aggregation of these functions as the legislative climate in the US positively favours the linking of HVAC and fire services. In addition, the sensors of both services present similar signals, that is, 'on/off digital' to the processor. Unfortunately, the major drawbacks are concerned with the vulnerability of such a system to catastrophic failure of the main processor. Very few new systems are now installed using a single central processor.

Distributed intelligence systems present a different set of advantages and drawbacks. On the one hand, a greater degree of autonomy and resistance to failure is implicit in the architecture, but this comes at the expense of a loss of 'interconnectability' between systems from different manufacturers. For many years in the UK, it has been customary to separate the various functions and disciplines of the design and construction process, that is, the architect, quantity surveyor, engineer, main contractor, specialists and maintenance contractor. It has also been the custom to consider the various services that we now take for granted as quite separate installations, that is, HVAC, fire and security protection, lifts, and access control.

We have therefore inherited fragmentation on a massive scale. The spectacular lack of enthusiasm for 'intelligent buildings', from potential end users, is reflected in a scepticism based on the inability of the industry to 'get its act together'. This then is the problem.

In the remainder of this paper, several tasks undertaken at the BEMS Centre to remedy just part of the problem will be described. The Centre has no illusions as to the long term nature of the difficulties that we face.

16.4 TECHNOLOGY: A FOUR LAYER STRATEGY

At every conference that discusses intelligent buildings the same old issues are raised, with conversation eventually stumbling over that of compatibility or rather the lack of it. Of course, compatibility means different things to different people. To some it is the ability to connect intelligent outstations from different manufacturers to one central station, whilst for others it is the ability to use a common data wiring loop to connect the totality of the services, thereby reducing wiring costs. The common link is, quite obviously, communication protocols. A four layer strategy is at the heart of the Centre's method for approaching consensus, firstly among manufacturers offering HVAC intelligent controls, but in the long term, to gain common acceptance throughout the other building services functions.

The four elements are:
1. Central station/Outstation.
2. Outstation/Outstation.
3. Intelligent sensor applications.
4. Central station/Central station.

16.4.1 Central station/Outstation

This layer represents the area which has hitherto given rise to the greatest problems for operators of large sites: primarily, central government departments, health authorities and maintenance companies, who wish to avoid being 'locked-in' to a particular manufacturer and who are obliged to invite multiple tenders for additions to their systems. The outcome has been that significant effort has been expended by these organisations to 'do it themselves' in an attempt to design a generic controller which can then be built by any competent electronics company.

It is the author's view that these efforts are doomed to failure. Designs are quickly outdated and without the revenue of profit-making sales, continual development is simply uneconomical. Equipment is also unsupported for maintenance purposes and the in-house expertise required is not only considerable, but unfortunately mobile in a labour market short of exactly those skills.

The logical conclusion which may be drawn is that manufacturers should provide the degree of compatibility that their customers seek. Hitherto, agreement in principle to this objective has not been unanimous amongst the major UK manufacturers although recently an accord has been struck, and the five main UK companies: Trend, Transmitton, JEL, Potterton and Satchwell have agreed to work towards this common aim. The result is that work will shortly be commissioned by the Centre to employ a major software and communications company to draw up a draft standard for BEMS communications. The work programme contains two parts.

The first will deal with the feasibility of the project and will set the scope of the standard. The major BEMS companies, both UK and overseas, will be invited to discuss their own ideas and indicate their own preferences. From this effort the broad specification of the standard will emerge.

The second part will involve detailed drafting of the documents sufficiently to enable a technical implementation of the work to proceed in the foreseeable future. It is envisaged that full use will be made of existing related standards such as the ISO 7-layer model, MAP and TOPS applications, but at this stage no formal attempt will be made to provide full international compliance. It is the author's view that the UK has the undoubted technological lead in this field and it should therefore present firm recommendations to the international community rather than enter into interminable debate.

The project will have a duration of approximately six months and will be funded initially by the Energy Efficiency Office through the Energy Technology Support Unit (ETSU). Further funding will be sought by the Centre, probably in the multi-client research club manner, to ensure that the standard is then fully refined and brought to the appropriate status within BSI, CENELEC or other relevant body.

16.4.2 Outstation/Outstation

Earlier in this paper, it was suggested that intelligence can be devolved completely to a point where individual plant items, such as chillers, AHU's, even individual radiators, have their own processors. There are products now on the market that approach this point. These controls look for all the world like a return to individual stand-alone (SPC) controls that BEMS were intended to replace. The difference is, of course, that the modern control talks to others and its behaviour can be monitored and optimised on a global scale using a data network.

The project mentioned above will look at this issue as part of its remit, but it is the author's view that development along these lines will be influenced more significantly by the emergence in the market of the third layer of the overall strategy.

16.4.3 Intelligent sensors

As far as building services are concerned, intelligent sensors do not yet exist. This may be a 'good thing' if research can be organised as a pre-competitive venture to select the manufacturer who will develop compatible products that will have widespread appeal in the market. Intelligent sensors comprise not only the sensing element, that is, thermistor and photocell humidity element, but also an onboard chip that can perform the translation of sensor information into a digital form. Complex devices can (and most probably will) perform self-calibration, linearisation and mathematical manipulation. An example of this would be a device that measures %RH and dry bulb temperature and provides the information together with specific enthalpy information to a data communication network.

The Centre has set up a project, which is partially funded by the EEO, to examine the feasibility of developing a customised VLSI chip to carry out the functions as described. Naturally, the data transmission protocols must comply with proposals to be examined in the previous project, but with no products currently marketed, the adoption of an existing standard for implementation into intelligent sensors will be attractive to manufacturers. A significant market in these types of products, utilising an agreed transmission protocol, will have a 'knock on effect' on the design of more central intelligent outstations.

16.4.4 Central station/Central station

We come now to the more complex question of integration of separate functional systems into a composite entity. It seems likely that for the foreseeable future we will still buy the equipment separately to fulfil the HVAC, fire and security protection, lifts, and access control functions from separate sources of expertise.

Recently, it has become fashionable for the 'integrated' company to garner expertise by acquisition. However, at present, this can be seen as a convenient marketing tool: truly integrated products are still to be fully developed. What is clear is that it is unlikely that we will ever return to the 'all in one box' approach adopted by the early American centralised intelligent systems of the 1970s.

The problem of integrating functional systems therefore reduces to the electronic exchange of data between 'head end' central stations. As yet, no project is under way to resolve this problem, although its presence has already been felt in the execution of a related project.

16.5 THE FUTURE

The Centre has been developing, with joint sponsorship from the Department of Energy and Shell UK Limited, a real time 'expert system' that utilises the data available from a distributed intelligence BEMS system controlling the boilerhouse of the BSRIA offices. The expert system runs on a IBM PC AT and gathers its data from a JELSTAR II Hewlett Packard 1000 central station. At present the expert system merely diagnoses probable causes of system malperformance, which is little more than can be currently achieved using conventional programming techniques. Future development work will address the task of looking at historical performance to optimise plant operation. The difficulty is essentially one of the exchange of data in a suitable format between the two host processors.

Chapter 17
Using information feedback for energy management

S.L. HODKINSON and D. R. OUGHTON

17.1 INTRODUCTION

Effective and energy efficient control of large buildings is increasingly possible as a result of the development of microprocessor-based building energy management systems (BEMS). The pace of development in the application of advanced control and energy management techniques to building services is extremely high.

This paper describes the application of microprocessor-based technology to the recently completed Administration Centre for a major bank just to the north of the City of London. In particular, three main features will be highlighted:

1. Integration of a large number of room temperature controllers within the energy management system. This provides a highly flexible and energy efficient variable air volume air conditioning system to meet the high demands of a modern office building.

2. Maximising the benefit of the energy management system with the designers having a continuing involvement with 'fine tuning' the performance of the building via a BT Kilostream link from their offices. This allows the engineers direct access to the actual plant operating conditions and to external climatic and internal conditions.

3. A unique arrangement of linking the energy management system with the designers' energy simulation program. The engineering system's performance, over a range of different control philosophies, will be simulated through a typical year's weather and operating conditions. Whereas this operation would take many years by making adjustments to the systems controls on the site (even with the aid of BEMS), by simulation it would be completed in a matter of hours.

17.2 THE ROYAL BANK OF SCOTLAND'S BUILDING

The case study to which this paper refers is the recently completed building for the Royal Bank of Scotland at the Angel, Islington. The building comprises six floors above ground level and has an area floor of approximately 300,000 sq. ft. (30,000 m2). Facilities are provided for office accommodation, data processing areas, a clearing department, catering and recreational facilities. The building houses 1,400 staff and is arranged around two landscaped courtyards.

The design of the engineering systems has aimed to combine flexibility for the needs of a variety of office processes both now and in the future, high standards of user comfort and maximum control over energy use.

The office accommodation is air conditioned by variable air volume systems, supplemented by perimeter natural convectors. Air is introduced through ceiling diffusers integrated with luminaires and arranged together with power and communication systems to provide flexibility on a planning module of 1200 mm. A comprehensive energy management system with distributed intelligence has been installed to control and monitor all mechanical and electrical systems. Extensive use has been made of microprocessor-based Direct Digital Control techniques in the control of the engineering systems.

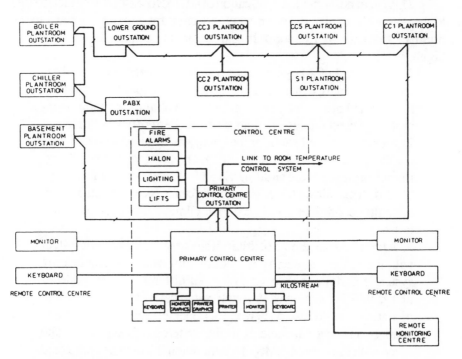

Figure 17.1: Diagram of energy management system

17.2.1 Energy management system configuration

A simplified diagram of how the building and energy management system is configured within the building is illustrated in Figure 17.1.

The system utilises stand-alone outstations to control the central plant and this principle has been extended to incorporate other stand-alone systems which interface with the energy management system. These systems include automatic lighting controls, fire alarms, Halon fire protection systems and an independent room temperature control system associated with the VAV terminal units. The energy management system incorporates dynamic colour graphic displays and comprehensive calculations packages.

17.2.2 Room temperature controls

The usual method of controlling large variable air volume systems has been to set the supply air temperature to meet either the maximum condition or one scheduled from information collected by external sensors. Alternatively, a limited number of strategically placed internal sensors may have been hard-wired back to the central plant. With the increasing use of high heat gain office equipment in buildings, often concentrated in local areas, it is not adequate from control or energy aspect to sense average conditions in a large zone. There is, therefore, a need for monitoring much smaller areas in high technology buildings of today.

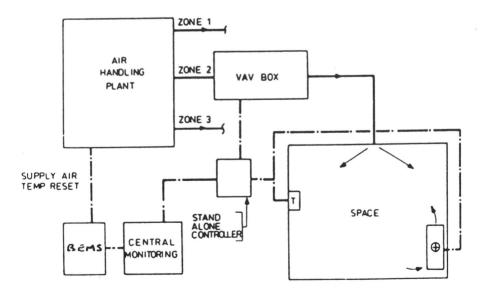

Figure 17.2: Room temperature control system arrangement

The development of stand-alone microprocessor-based controllers with communication facilities for VAV terminal units enabled the designers to provide monitoring of room conditions for the area served by each unit. A central microcomputer is used to handle the data from the 550 perimeter VAV terminals. Figure 17.2 illustrates this arrangement.

The final link in the feedback chain to the central plant was provided by an interface package enabling the room temperature controllers to reset the respective zone supply air temperature. As any terminal unit reaches its present maximum cooling volume, in response to room conditions, a signal is sent via the communication system to adjust the zone supply air temperature downwards. As the cooling demand subsequently drops so the appropriate supply air temperature is then reset upwards. In this way the most efficient supply air temperature/volume ratio can be controlled in the most efficient way.

The perimeter heating control is sequenced with the volume control on the terminal to avoid simultaneous heating and cooling. Figure 17.3 indicates the feedback arrangement to the energy management system.

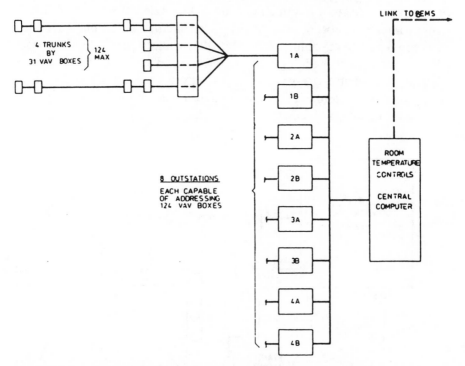

Figure 17.3: Feedback arrangement to the energy management system

Other facilities are, of course, inherent within the system, providing benefits in the operation of the building. These include:

1. Room temperature setpoint adjustments for heating and cooling.

2. VAV terminal maximum and minimum volume adjustments.

3. Room temperature indication.

4. Supply air temperature indication.

5. Velocity of supply air at terminal.

6. High and low temperature alarms.

7. Global command facilities to control groups of terminals either on a system or location basis.

17.3 MAXIMISING THE BENEFITS OF AN ENERGY MANAGEMENT SYSTEM

It is well known that one of the major difficulties experienced on many projects, particularly the larger, more complex ones, is achieving satisfactory completion. This naturally includes correct commissioning and performance testing, preparation of record documents and instruction to the client's staff on operating the systems. Even if all these items are completed to the satisfaction of all parties, in respect of contract requirements, this may not be adequate to ensure the most economical operation of the systems.

At best, it is likely that the systems will be commissioned to satisfy the bases of design. Setpoints, for example, would be based upon theoretical steady-state calculations, modified perhaps by the judgement of the commissioning engineer to reflect the dynamic response of the plant under the particular operating conditions obtained at the time of the commissioning.

Using an energy management system it is possible for the designer to fine tune the systems and controls to the building usage patterns and to the actual thermal response of the building elements and system components.

This activity is currently being undertaken using a direct BT Kilostream link installed between the energy management system and a dynamic colour graphics display and printer modules in the design office (see Figure 17.1). This will allow the engineers direct access to actual plant operating conditions and to the external climatic and internal conditions.

The activities undertaken by the engineers will include:

1. Monitoring energy use and energy cost.

2. Development of energy audit procedures that will be the basis for future monitoring by the client.

3. Involving the client's staff in monitoring procedures over an extended period in order for them to develop a full understanding of the installed systems.

4. Checking the performance of the engineering systems using computer simulation techniques. In this way the client will gain the

maximum benefit from a significant investment in the energy management system.

17.4 LINKING ENERGY MANAGEMENT SYSTEMS AND SIMULATION

For some years now, the use of computer design methods for HVAC system sizing has been fairly common. These design programs are now being extended into the far more complex area of performance simulation. The aim of these new generation models is not only to simulate the performance of the building envelope, but also the way in which the building, with its engineering systems, interacts with climate and occupancy patterns experienced in a real situation.

One can see that with the increasing availability of relatively low cost but very powerful microprocessors, the BEMS will eventually have an onboard simulation facility running in real time. This will have two major benefits: first, it will significantly enhance the monitoring capability of the energy management system in immediately being able to raise alarms if there is a significant departure from the design performance concept; and secondly, it will facilitate self-learning adaptive control.

In order to start this technology moving forward into this exciting new area, energy simulations using the Kilostream link already installed will be carried out using the in-house computer facilities. Figure 17.4 illustrates this arrangement.

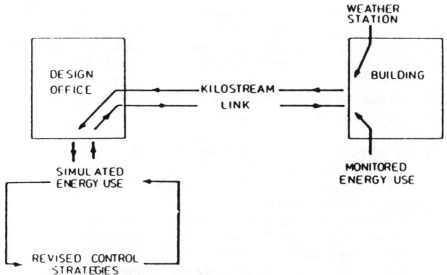

Figure 17.4: Energy simulation system diagram

In order to check that the program is modelling the actual system performance, it will be necessary for the simulation to be based upon the climatic conditions pertaining at the time. To this end, a small meteorological station has been installed on the roof of the building, linked to the energy management system. This will monitor and record temperature, humidity, wind speed and direction, and solar intensity.

The main objective of the simulation study is to investigate possible improvements to the systems controls, with a view to improving the overall energy efficiency. The system performance over a range of different control philosophies will be simulated through a typical year's weather and operating conditions. It will be possible to carry out these studies in a matter of hours. Under normal plant operating and monitoring procedures, this operation would take many years to complete, even with the aid of an energy management system.

In addition, the effect of changing requirements in the occupied spaces, perhaps due to an increase in the cooling load from office equipment, could be simulated and an optimum control strategy established before the change of use is made.

These simulation studies will enable the engineers to monitor the overall affect on energy consumption and advise the client on control setpoints, plant switching times and the like to improve plant operating efficiency. Perhaps more important than these will be the ability to examine in detail a number of key factors relating to the overall control strategy.

For example, it will be possible to examine the relationship between the variable air volume supply temperature and the volume flow rate under various operating conditions, and thus identify the optimum balance between the use of refrigeration energy and fan energy. Also, the spaces that have high levels of internal heat gain and which would determine the supply air temperature for the whole zone, would be identified and, where necessary, action taken to prevent a few extreme conditions adversely affecting overall energy use.

17.5 CONCLUSIONS

To achieve the full benefits of a comprehensive energy management system, it is not sufficient for designers to just be involved with its installation. The complexity of the systems for large, high technology buildings requires a continued effort by skilled engineers to fine tune the system and controls. This period should also include the development of energy audit procedures and involvement of the client's staff in order for them to gain a full understanding of the system's potential.

All too often complex systems are installed at great expense to the client and their full benefits are never realised. The authors believe that a case can be made for the duties of the designer to be extended beyond contract completion to participate in the initial period of plant operation.

Chapter 18
Applying expert systems to environmental management and control

M. R. SHAW

18.1 INTRODUCTION

The introduction of modern building management systems (BMS) has led to significant improvements in the environmental performance, energy efficiency and reliability of building services. While this technology has undoubtedly brought many benefits it has also placed heavy demands on the expertise and experience of those charged with the responsibility of specifying, selecting, commissioning and operating BMS. These demands on premium staff resources are often difficult to satisfy and there are indications that in future this lack of appropriate expertise may represent the biggest single obstacle to the wider application of BMS. The use of expert systems to address similar skill shortages in other analogous engineering sectors suggests that this technology may be capable of providing advice and guidance to BMS users. BRE research into 'expert systems' indicates that this approach may well be viable and the establishment is currently exploring several BMS-related applications.

An expert system is a computer program which contains 'knowledge', in the form of facts, relationships and rules, about some specific area of human expertise. It is capable of making reasoned deductions or inferences for the user and can explain its line of questioning and can justify its conclusions. Expert systems enable computers to be applied to classes of problems which, because of their nature, would be very difficult to tackle using conventional techniques: problems where knowledge is incomplete, the data is uncertain or 'fuzzy', or there is no quantitative theoretical basis.

The concept of an expert system came out of computer science research into artificial intelligence in the mid 1970s. After a rather indifferent start, particularly in the UK (Lighthill, 1973), successful expert systems began to appear in increasing numbers in the late 1970s and early 1980s. These early expert systems, in such diverse areas as medical diagnosis (Shortliffe, 1976), mineral prospecting (Duda, 1979) and mass-spectrogram interpretation (Lindsay et al., 1980), often produced advice of a quality approaching that offered by the foremost experts in the field. From this early success interest has spread and many organisations have recognised the benefits that this technology can bring, and have started to employ it in a wide range of applications.

This paper examines the information management and interpretation problems associated with the implementation and operation of BMS and suggests ways in which expert systems can be employed to address many of these difficulties. Current research by BRE and others into the application of expert systems to BMS-related problems is presented and its likely future commercial exploitation is discussed.

18.2 EXPERT SYSTEMS AND BMS

18.2.1 BMS specification

While the application of BMS technology can undoubtedly lead to significant improvements in environmental performance and energy efficiency there are circumstances when it may not be appropriate. If, for example, the envisaged 'management information' emphasis of the monitoring functions is low, or the plant or building has been badly designed or badly maintained, then a more cost effective solution may lie in the use of conventional controls coupled with improved building management practices. Only a full economic and technical appraisal of a potential BMS application can ensure that the technology represents an appropriate solution (Birtles, 1985).

The increasing use of low cost microprocessor-based stand-alone control and monitoring systems has now filled the middle ground in a complete spectrum of control options which ranges from conventional controls through to full BMS. The point at which BMS technology becomes viable for a particular type of building, and the level of sophistication which is appropriate, is dependent upon a variety of constantly changing factors. These dynamic considerations together with the variability of energy and maintenance costs makes the appraisal of potential BMS applications extremely complex.

The complexity of the appraisal process, and the dynamic nature of the financial and technical framework on which decisions should be based, means that few engineers are likely to have the necessary experience, or be sufficiently aware of current thinking, to make an informed assessment of a potential BMS application. This shortage of engineers with the necessary appraisal experience may well hold back the wider application of BMS in future.

This problem can be addressed by employing expert systems which encapsulate knowledge of the BMS appraisal process to guide an engineer through the task of assessing the suitability of an application and the identification of the most appropriate system. Supported by suitable explanation facilities, such a 'decision support' expert system would also serve an important educational role.

BRE has recognised the potentially important part that expert systems can play in assisting engineers in the BMS appraisal and specification process and is currently investigating means of effectively exploiting the technology to this end.

Expert systems have already been used in a building services selection/specification context. BSRIA have developed a prototype expert system to select heat exchangers for air to air heat recovery (Hamilton, 1986) and the Polytechnic of the South Bank, London have developed a demonstration 'Air Conditioning Expert' (ACE) to select air conditioning systems (Railton, 1985).

18.2.2 BMS commissioning

The most common cause of unsatisfactory BMS performance is incorrect or incomplete commissioning. This is a phase in the implementation of BMS where expertise is essential but is often unavailable or of a low grade. It should be possible to develop expert systems capable of evaluating particular commissioning requirements and of generating advice on the setting up of the plant for efficient and effective operation. In particular, an on-line commissioning expert system could:

1. Iteratively adjust commissioning valves and dampers, and assess system performance against acceptable targets.

2. Identify systems which cannot be commissioned to achieve the designed level of performance.

3. Predict year round performance whatever the season at the time of commissioning.

4. Commission control systems where time delays and variable change rates have been programmed in: delay timers especially could be more accurately set.

As the control systems in BMS become progressively more soft, commissioning expert systems could influence the choice of control response characteristics and generally set the systems to work in a more orderly fashion from actual installed performance.

BRE is currently investigating the potential use of expert systems as commissioning assistants.

18.2.3 BMS information interpretation

If building management systems are to achieve and maintain their environmental performance, energy efficiency and reliability objectives, users must have the necessary building services expertise to interpret and act on the comprehensive, but highly technical, information generated by modern systems. However, many BMS users do not have the time and/or the necessary engineering skills to exploit this valuable information resource fully, and there are indications that in future this lack of appropriate expertise may represent the biggest single obstacle to the wider application of BMS.

At present a BMS user confronted with the interpretation problem has two options:
1. Employ a skilled energy manager to monitor the BMS.
2. Use inexperienced or junior staff to monitor the BMS.

Employing an energy manager is a good solution, but the potential savings offered by BMS can rarely justify the employment of additional specialist staff. Even if the economic considerations are ignored the difficulty of finding and employing good engineers is daunting in itself. If junior or inexperienced staff are charged with the responsibility of supervising sophisticated BMS installations their lack of appropriate skills will prevent them from interpreting and exploiting the highly technical raw information presented by current generation systems. They will not be capable of identifying the more subtle performance deficiencies and cannot be expected to recognise the performance improvement opportunities that form the basis for the justification of BMS.

A longer term, and more attractive, solution is to make the BMS more intelligent, to incorporate some of the interpretive and advisory skills of a senior services engineer. Such a development would give a BMS the ability to recognise malfunctions, poor performance and the need for maintenance action, without delay. Advice would take the form of clear explicit instructions to the operator, and these could be supported by a presentation of the underlying reasoning. The advent of 'intelligent' BMS would significantly reduce the number and quality of skilled staff required for the adoption of this technology and thus would extend the range of cost effective application. Work at BRE (Shaw, 1984), and by others in areas analogous to BMS, indicates that expert systems have the potential to give BMS the intelligence they need.

Expert systems have been employed in the process control industry since the early 1980s to tackle fault location and diagnosis in industrial processes. The cement manufacturer, Blue Circle, has a working kiln control expert system in use at its plant in Abershaw, South Wales; ICI and System Designers are working on a chemical plant alarm monitoring system, as members of a DTI sponsored 'Alvey Club'; Texaco are using an alarm monitoring expert system called PICON at its Port Arthur installation in Texas; Hitachi are developing systems for power system operation and factory automation; and Toshiba and Mitsubishi Electric have built prototype expert systems for nuclear and industrial plant diagnosis. Although few technically detailed papers have been published, sufficient information is available from these analogous application areas to suggest that the application of expert system techniques to BMS is technically feasible.

A building management expert system must simulate an expert engineer, continuously monitoring the information presented by the BMS. It must display the skills and attributes of a good human engineer, that is, it must:

1. Respond to requests from the user.
2. Respond to information generated by the BMS.
3. Form hypotheses based on the information received and test them.
4. Identify trends.
5. Ask for additional information when necessary.
6. Learn from experience.
7. Give advice.
8. Explain conclusions.
9. Produce reports.
10. Recognise its own limitations (a rare human attribute).

In more specific terms the role of the expert system will be dictated by user needs. To assume the role identified for a building management expert system, it should understand or contain knowledge corresponding to the following classifications:

1. Component: knowledge relating to individual items of standard HVAC plant. It is independent of a particular installation and is therefore universally applicable. Typically, it would consist of component attributes, mathematical models of behaviour in par- ameterised form and possibly some general rules relating to status under given conditions. For example, a heating system would have a pump as a component and that would be described by attributes like model number, an appropriate performance equation and rules to decide its on/off status.

2. HVAC configuration: knowledge relating to a particular plant installation that describes how the individual components are connected and how they interact.

3. BMS: knowledge relating to the control functions of the BMS, for example, optimum start, weather compensation and boiler sequencing. It will understand the environmental performance objectives of a control function and the possible reasons for failure to achieve these objectives. It will also understand the effect of a control function on plant operation and the possible modes of interaction with other control functions.

4. Building: knowledge relating to the physical fabric of the building, the use of the building and its thermal performance.

5. Basic physics: an understanding of basic physics of plant and building behaviour will enable the expert system to reason from first principles in the absence of the other more explicit forms of knowledge.

Configuration, BMS and building knowledge all relate to a particular installation and will need to be modified to reflect changes to the plant or usage and therefore must be structured to be flexible and adaptable.

Any viable expert system for building management must be adaptable. It must be capable of being readily modified to reflect different building, plant and BMS configurations. It is envisaged that while this would necessarily involve some manual commissioning for a new installation, the process would be largely self-adaptive with the expert system automatically adjusting a parameterised rule-base in the light of operating experience.

The expert system must be capable of responding to asynchronous alarms in addition to regular time-scheduled status information. The cyclic searching process associated with the reasoning mechanism of an expert system makes the handling of asynchronous information inherently difficult.

An expert system for building management must be capable of requesting information from several sources. It needs to get additional data from the BMS, information from a database of historic performance data to identify trends, and input from the operator on the wider environment. This is an unusual requirement for an expert system, most conventional off-line diagnostic or selection systems consult only the user at the keyboard.

18.2.4 BREXBAS

BRE has recognised the potential that expert system techniques hold for making BMS more intelligent and has developed a prototype: BREXBAS (Building Research EXpert Building Automation System) (Shaw, 1987) to assess and define how best this technology can be exploited.

BREXBAS has been implemented in the PROLOG language on a Digital AI VAXstation II workstation. The overall structure of BREXBAS is shown in Figure 18.1.

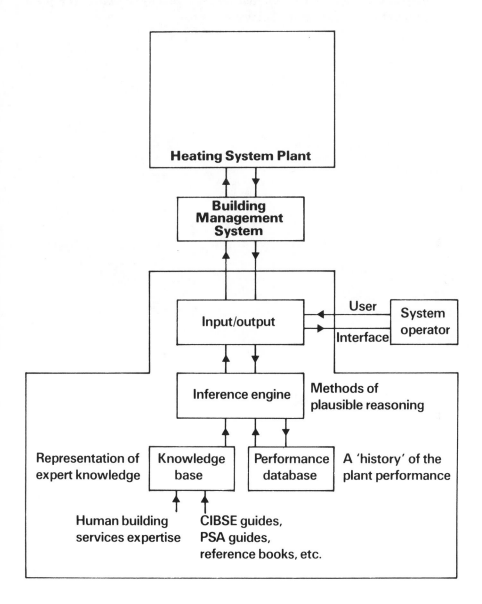

Figure 18.1: Building Research EXpert Building Automation System, BREXBAS

To enable BREXBAS to be incrementally developed and tested, a computer simulation program was written for the workstation to model the time-based behaviour of a simple but realistic heating system. The plant configuration shown in Figure 18.2 was chosen.

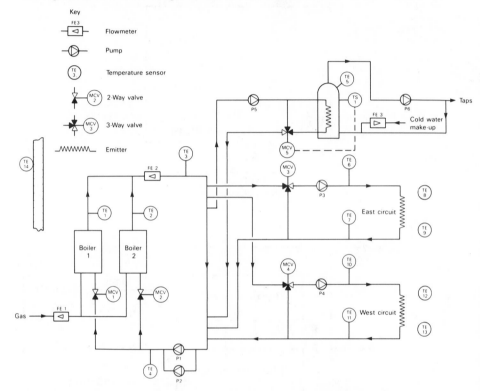

Figure 18.2: Plant configuration used for the computer simulation

The simulation uses the ambient temperature profile as its 'forcing function', that is, the parameter 'driving' the model. All values describing the heating system are dependent upon the magnitude of the ambient temperature and are re-calculated every 15 minutes (simulation) time. Events such as pump failure, valve failure, boiler failure and heat loss variation can also be simulated.

The simulation makes a number of assumptions, the major ones being: an ambient temperature profile for a typical April day, steady flow of working fluid and continuous output from the boiler when on (10% flow increase with two boilers operating).

To generate events for BREXBAS to respond to, the simulation allows the user to specify a series of plant faults or particular environmental conditions at any time during a 24 hour period. The simulation then generates a time-based set of sensor readings corresponding to the conditions selected by the user.

Using the workstation's concurrent processing facilities, the simulation drives BREXBAS with information on flow and return water temperatures, room space temperatures, heat losses, DHWS temperatures and control signals. This input from the simulation causes the reasoning mechanism within BREXBAS to form hypotheses relating to the status of the plant. BREXBAS then gathers further evidence to prove or deny these hypotheses. As an example, if a gradual decline in flow rate is detected in the primary circuit one of the several hypotheses that BREXBAS would form is that the pump strainer is blocked. BREXBAS would then test this hypothesis by investigating valve operation, zone temperature trends, flow and return temperatures, and the results of visual inspection by the operator, if considered necessary.

BREXBAS generates a time-based continuous report on the plant's status, endeavouring to identify malfunctions as and when they occur. Conclusions and recommendations are given as dictated by BREXBAS's reasoning mechanism operating on the knowledge-base. Input is primarily from the simulation, but additional information may be asked of the operator to support a particular line of reasoning. Figure 18.3 shows a typical display from the current version of BREXBAS.

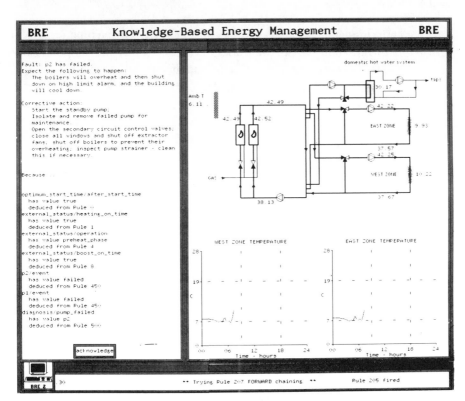

Figure 18.3: Typical display screen from BREXBAS

From the results obtained so far the indications are that BREXBAS, with an extended and refined knowledge-base, will be capable of assisting users with many of the interpretation problems presented by a real BMS. BRE's work will now be directed towards mounting a full practical demonstration. The demonstration will draw heavily on the experience gained with the BREXBAS simulation driven expert system. It will take the form of a large knowledge-base running on BRE's workstation interpreting information from a directly linked commercial BMS central station communicating over the PSTN with one or more outstations in selected buildings.

In addition to BRE's research in this area, relevant research programmes also exist at the BEMS Centre in the UK and at a major supplier of BMS in the US.

18.3 FUTURE COMMERCIAL EXPLOITATION OF BMS EXPERT SYSTEMS

18.3.1 Opportunities

Major improvements have been made in recent years to the functionality, performance and quality of software tools available for the development of expert systems. It is now possible to purchase sophisticated but easy to use PC-based development environments for under £1,000 which will enable non-computer specialists to develop worthwhile expert systems.

Expert systems place considerable demands on the memory capacity and performance of computer hardware. In the past this has presented a barrier to their wider exploitation, but with the advent of powerful low cost 32 bit personal computers and the prospect of add-on symbolic co-processors for such machines, which will execute the code generated for expert systems more efficiently, this is no longer the case.

Research and development into the application of expert systems to BMS is rapidly expanding in the US. A least two major US manufacturers of building services control equipment are currently conducting extensive research programmes, and one US Government organisation is also working in the field. If the UK suppliers of BMS are to maintain their technological supremacy they must start to explore the use of expert systems.

18.3.2 Barriers

Many exaggerated claims have been made for expert systems and most people working in the field would agree that the technology has been oversold. This has resulted in inflated expectations on the part of many potential users which will inevitably lead to a backlash against expert systems if the 'enthusiasm' is not tempered.

One of the most difficult aspects of developing an expert system is the process of knowledge elicitation. Experts often find it difficult to express their expertise and it requires considerable skill and experience on the part of the expert system developer or 'knowledge engineer' to establish the effective dialogue necessary for successful elicitation. Knowledge engineers with the necessary skills are currently difficult to find and are therefore costly to employ.

The ideal environment for the serious development of expert systems is undoubtedly a sophisticated artificial intelligence 'tool kit' mounted on a high performance workstation. Such a configuration, however, is extremely expensive at £30,000 for the workstation and £30,000 for the software.

18.4 CONCLUSIONS

1. There are strong indications that the information management and interpretation problems associated with the implementation and operation of BMS represents a major obstacle to the wider application of BMS in the UK.

2. The use of expert systems to address skill shortages in other analogous engineering sectors, for example, the process control industry, suggests that this technology may be capable of providing advice and guidance to BMS users.

3. Specifying, commissioning and on-line information interpretation represent worthwhile potential BMS applications for expert systems.

4. BRE's development of the BREXBAS expert system has shown that this technology can be used to make BMS more intelligent.

5. The opportunities for the successful development of BMS related expert systems far outweigh the barriers.

18.5 ACKNOWLEDGEMENTS

The work described has been carried out as part of the research programme of the Building Research Establishment of the Department of the Environment, UK and this paper is published by the permission of the Director.

18.6 REFERENCES

Birtles, A.B. (1985), *Selection of building management systems,* BRE information paper, IP6/85, Building Research Establishment, Garston, Watford.

Duda, R.O. et al. (1979), *Model design in the PROSPECTOR consultation system for mineral prospecting,* in Expert Systems in the Microelectronics Age, Edinburgh University Press,153-167.

Hamilton, G. (1986), *Expert systems for building services,* Expert systems for construction and services engineering, CICA/BSRIA Seminar, London, 27-46.

Lighthill, G. (1973), *Artificial Intelligence: a paper symposium (The Lighthill Report),* SRC, Swindon.

Lindsay, R.K. et al. (1980), *Application of artificial intelligence for organic chemistry,* The DENDRAL Project, McGraw-Hill, New York.

Railton, M.R. (1985), *The history of ACE, BSRIA Computer Newsletter,* August, (15), 14-15.

Shaw, M.R. (1984), *Expert systems - an objective view,* Conference on Computers in Building and Services Design, University of Nottingham.

Shaw, M.R. (1987), *Knowledge-based interpretation of BMS information,* CIBSE Technical Conference, Brunel University.

Shortliffe, E.H. (1976), *Computer-based medical consultation: MYCIN,* American Elsevier, New York.

Chapter 19
Life cycle information systems

C. TURK

19.1 INTRODUCTION

In today's excitement for intelligent buildings, it is important not to lose sight of the purpose behind the move towards buildings with increasing intelligence. The overall objectives of creating an intelligent building are:

1. The efficient running of the building through building automation systems.

2. The creation of an environment for effective business through the provision or easy incorporation of information technology.

3. The responsiveness to change to meet the organisation's needs and changes in information technology.

The intelligent building can form the shell which allows these objectives to be achieved. However, to achieve the above requires good facilities management based on sound management information. But why should intelligent buildings be any different from their predecessors in this respect?

In recent years, several changes have occurred which have contributed to the birth of the intelligent building and have reinforced the need for their effective and cost efficient management. The most notable being:

1. *Different life cycles* of the different components of today's building. The structural 'core and shell' of today's building is generally designed for a life cycle of 50 years or more, whereas the building fabric and central services are designed for a life of between 15 and 20 years, with fitting-out components such as raised access floors and ceiling systems often aimed at 10 years or less.

2. *Considerable drop in price of technology* over the past 10 years, when equivalent performance is compared.

3. *Rapid increase in take-up of technology.* In many businesses, information technology has moved from supporting the business to becoming the heart of the business as organisations strive to use information technology to give them competitive advantage in the

marketplace.

4. Emphasis on organisational flexibility, that is, the desire of large organisations to form and disband teams rapidly to meet market needs.

To accommodate these changes and turn them to advantage requires as much managerial skill as the design and construction process itself. In fact, increasingly we see the management of the building through live operation, that is, when it is occupied, as the final phase of the project life cycle. The four phases of the project life cycle being:
1. Concept/initiation.
2. Design/engineering.
3. Construction.
4. Operations.

This paper will concentrate on the information systems which, if installed and used through the first three phases of the project life cycle, will assist in the management of the building through the operations phase.

19.2 REQUIREMENTS FOR MANAGING THE INTELLIGENT BUILDING

High calibre facilities managers and effective information to help them manage are the key, inseparable components required to ensure efficient and effective use of intelligent buildings. In this context, facilities managers refers to the individuals or small teams responsible for providing the appropriate, controlled environment to support their organisation's business, within senior management's policy at an economic cost.

Facilities managers must understand their organisation's business and be able to assess the true effect of failure to provide the required environment. They must also understand the technology employed to control the building and be able to interpret and act on the information it provides. It would be fair to suggest that there are not many facilities managers who fit these demanding criteria and that organisations using intelligent buildings will have to look hard to find the appropriate personnel. However, providing their facilities manager with the right information from computerised systems is something an organisation can plan for and implement.

19.3 INFORMATION NEEDS

Although volumes of data are supplied by today's automated building control systems, there is a danger of being drowned in data but starved of information. There is, therefore, a need to focus the available data into management information and to consider the provision of other key information provided from other sources, such as:

1. *Future organisation and space requirements:* numbers of personnel by seniority and function, space standards, space requirements, and information technology strategy requirements.

2. *Building characteristics:* physical form (drawings), management's design policy, specifications, and test certificates.

3. *Plant and equipment characteristics:* drawings, specifications, operations' manuals, and test certificates.

Information on the future organisation and space requirements gives facilities management the direction for future use of the building. Readily available information on the characteristics of the building, together with its plant and equipment, can be of enormous benefit in facilities planning and maintenance.

In deciding upon the information required and how it should be delivered (for example, building control system, other computerised information system or manual means), it helps to focus on the information requirements for the property/facilities management area as a whole through a framework of major business functions.

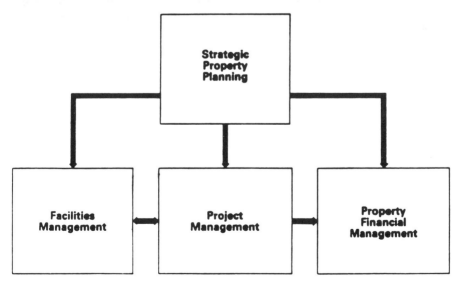

Figure 19.1: Property/facilities management structure

Broadly, these major business functions can be defined as:

1. *Strategic property planning:* long term property planning to satisfy the long term business plan of the organisation.

2. *Facilities Management:* the overall responsibility for making the premises work in accordance with the business needs.

3. *Project Management:* the management of a distinct set of activities to achieve a significant end product. For example, the creation of new facilities by either renovation or new construction.

4. *Property Financial Management:* the procurement and sale of property and the administration of both residential and commercial leases.

Figure 19.2 shows a generic set of information needs for the facilities management business function. This is the most important business function for the management of an intelligent building through the operations phase. The information shown has been built up from several information systems engagements, performed by the author, in the property/facilities management area.

The specific roles and responsibilities of the facilities manager and related functions, such as purchasing and finance accounting, should be mapped against the information needs to help establish the detailed requirements and to assist in shaping the systems solution.

Although much of the information required is generated or collected by the facilities management function, a wealth of information on the physical characteristics of the building and its components is generated in the design/ engineering and construction phases of the project life cycle. The potential benefits to facilities management of using information technology to capture and manage the flow of information through the project life cycle, is only now being realised. Maintenance (of the building, plant and equipment) and facilities planning/utilisation are the key areas of benefit. In addition, the efficiency of the design/engineering and construction phases of the project life cycle is also improved by the use of well designed information systems. The oil industry is probably leading the way in this field, with the need to co-ordinate and retrieve vast numbers of drawings, specifications and certificates rapidly.

19.4 POTENTIAL PROJECT LIFE CYCLE INFORMATION SYSTEMS

The systems required to capture, store and deliver the technical information generated through design and construction phases are relatively simple in

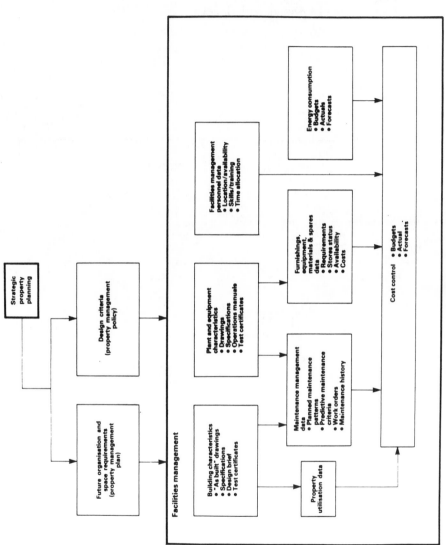

Figure 19.2: Information needs of facilities management

concept, but have to contend with the following generic business problems:

1. Large amounts of documentation.
2. Diversity of data types.
3. Complex inter-relationships.
4. Large number of project participants.

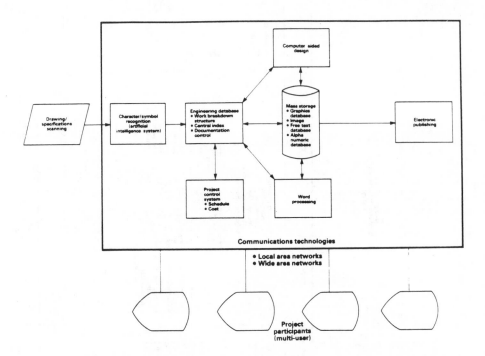

Figure 19.3: Potential systems solution - concept/initiation phase to construction phase

Figure 19.3 shows a potential systems solution which has an emphasis on integration of data types, different systems and project participants. The central hub of the system is an engineering database which can be implemented using one of today's powerful relational database products such as DB2, ORACLE or Ingres. This serves as the custodian of the project's work breakdown structure and an index to where information is stored. The project control system needs to be closely tied in with the relational database through the project work breakdown structure and should be proactive whenever possible. For example, when an activity is to start, the project control system should inform the engineering database of the drawings required. The engineering database should know where the drawings are stored, who should receive them and therefore their distribution in the most appropriate media (on paper or display on a computer screen).

As large quantities of information will exist, mass storage is required. Today, this takes the form of magnetic disk packs, but optical disc storage is of increasing interest as a means of mass storage in the future. The optical discs that are available today work on the Write Once Read Many times (WORM) principle, in a similar way to compact disks. One optical disk can store 2-4 Gigabytes of data, which is equivalent to 1-2 million pages of A4 text, and they can be configured into sets known as juke boxes. However, today's optical discs are expensive, are not yet recognised as legal storage media (which means paper, micro-fiche or micro-film records of key documents must also be kept) and they are currently difficult to integrate with other technology.

However, all the indications are that optical disc storage is set to become the mass storage media of the future as the hardware giants are working on including them in their range of products: research on erasable optical disks is also under way. Therefore, the price should follow the trend of other areas of information technology and drop over time. Whatever the form, mass storage needs to be interfaced with the engineering database so the user can be pointed to the appropriate piece of information.

Computer aided design (CAD) and word processing are the key technology in the preparation of design drawings and specifications. These create different forms of data which should also be interfaced with the engineering database to allow easy user access. Drawings and specifications on paper need to be entered into the appropriate system via a scanning device. For a CAD system to interpret the image generated by a scanner almost inevitably requires manual intervention. For example, the system needs to be told that a series of dots are, in fact, a circle. This manual process can be considerably aided by using a character/symbol recognition system based on artificial intelligence techniques. When information is required in paper form, the document can be pulled together from mass storage via electronic publishing.

Today's communication technology, local area networks (LANs) and wide area networks (WANs), pull together the systems and members of the project regardless of distance. However, communication is an area of rapid change, which now offers a number of alternatives to the traditional dial-up or leased lines for long distance communication (WANs) and a wide variety of cabling systems for short distance communications (LANs).

Value Added and Data Services (VADS) is one of the latest, more interesting developments in WANs. These are communication services offered by organisations who have formed WANs, generally for their own use, and sell the spare capacity as a point to point service based on usage. Unfortunately, communication technology suffers from a number of standards and protocols. These need to be taken into account when designing the network for the project life cycle information systems and when installing cabling into an intelligent building. For example, token ring LANs are best suited to the passage of small packages of information as found in an on-line DP system. Ethernet, on the other hand, is more suitable for large packages of information. In all cases, the type of business usage should drive the design of the network.

For effective management of the intelligent building in the operations phase, the potential systems solution needs to alter (see Figure 19.4) to incorporate a building control system and facilities management application system such as maintenance management and facilities planning/utilisation. The information stored on the graphics, text and alphanumeric databases in mass storage is still required, but in a cut down form. It is not necessary to keep every version of every drawing or every variation order for facilities management. It is, however, necessary to keep all information until after the claims generated during the construction phase have been settled. The timing of a weeding out exercise to form the property/facilities database is a key issue, which needs to be driven by the requirements for the information and mass storage capacity. In general, only a two dimensional (2D) CAD system is required for facilities management in the operations phase. If the intelligent building has been designed using a 21/2D or 3D system, a conversion process to store the building characteristics information as a series of 2D layered drawings must be planned for and carried out.

Figures 19.3 and 19.4 show that the potential systems solutions for the management of technical information through the project life cycle are fairly similar. The information requirements of the facilities management applications shown on Figure 19.4 need to be considered when designing the information systems for the earlier phases of the project life cycle. The expected benefits to justify expenditure on such systems are in essence:

1. Faster design.
2. Improved management control over documentation.
3. Speed of access to the correct version of the required document.

4. Reduction in document storage space.
5. The availability of information for effective management in the operations phase.

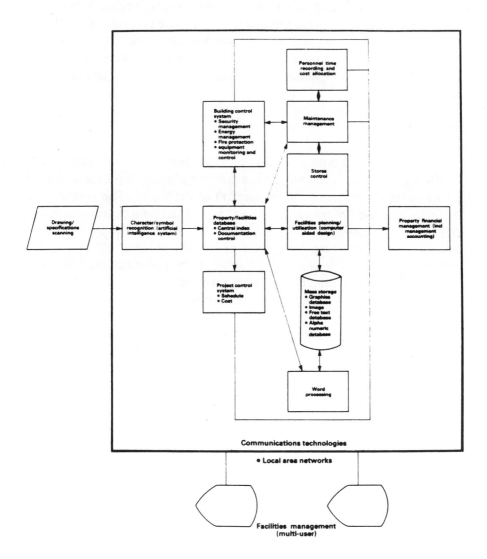

Figure 19.4: Potential systems solution - operations phase

19.5 OBSTACLES TO USING PROJECT LIFE CYCLE INFORMATION SYSTEMS

The benefits listed above are considered sufficient to warrant the use of project life cycle systems in the construction of oil rigs. So why do we not see the same drive and determination to design and install information systems to control technical information through the project life cycle of the intelligent building? People in the building industry will always say it is a different problem and, of course, to a large extent it is. The obstacles to the use of project life cycle information systems can be considered as either organisational or technical.

19.5.1 Organisational issues

The building industry consists of a number of different parties with conflicting interests. Each project is a unique gathering of people who form transient relationships for the completion of the work. The systems and methods they use are governed by their role in the project and established practices. The concept of co-ordinating design information through central systems is foreign to most members of the UK building industry and is perceived with caution as it could take away the individual organisation's 'competitive' approach. The efficient completion of the project and the effective management of the building once occupied, are not always at the top of the priority list.

The use of information systems through the project life cycle for technical information management has a cost and the question of who should 'foot the bill' is a very real issue. Some suggestions of how these issues could be resolved are outlined in section 19.6 below.

19.5.2 Technical issues

Information can be stored in many forms including:
1. *Graphics:* information stored in a vector format, as generated by a computer aided design system.
2. *Image:* information stored in raster format, that is, pictures.
3. *Text.*
4. *Alphanumeric:* the format of most data processing systems.
5. *Process:* machine instructions for automated machinery.
6. *Voice.*

There are clearly problems in transferring information between different forms and, despite considerable effort in establishing standards such as IGES, there are problems in fully transferring information of a similar form between different systems. By fully transferring information, it is meant that information can be used in the new system, rather than just being looked at. This has led to a large array of stand-alone/incompatible systems. The present day solution to this problem is to reduce all communication to the lowest common denominator, that is, print or plot it on paper. This has a number of disadvantages, which are mainly caused by the creation of vast quantities of paper:

1. Storage and retrieval problems.
2. Control of document versions.
3. Re-entry of information into different systems.

The variety of communication standards and protocols mentioned in section 19.4 presents technical issues which must be considered when designing project life cycle systems, as does the distribution of the engineering database and mass storage between the project participants. These issues are not unique to project life cycle systems. They are encountered in any database system used by a number of users in a number of locations. They must of course be tackled and solved during systems design.

19.6 POTENTIAL SOLUTIONS TO ORGANISATIONAL ISSUES

With all the difficulties outlined above it is not surprising that the use of information systems throughout the project life cycle is patchy. However, the benefits listed at the end of section 19.4, although hard to quantify, are recognised in the offshore oil industry and are now attracting considerable attention by leading developers, large owner/occupiers and some multi-discipline design organisations.

To overcome the organisational issues described above requires the owner of the project, whether that is the owner of the resultant building or the developer, taking a firm line on the information requirements for running the intelligent building. The owner must also consider how technical information will be developed, stored and controlled throughout the project life cycle.

There will be additional hardware and software costs involved in the development of project life cycle information systems but they should be offset against:

1. Reduced professional consultant fees through efficient development and communication of information.
2. Reduced contractors' tenders due to reduced effort in handling information.
3. Shorter design and construction durations.

4. Effective business in the completed building (for the owner/ occupier).

5. Increased value of the building (for the owner/occupier) owing to the availability of technical information, which puts him in the position to offer facilities management services, such as facilities planning, to the occupier of the building.

19.7 POTENTIAL SOLUTIONS TO TECHNICAL ISSUES

There are really two approaches to solving the technical issues outlined above. Either the industry must limit the use of information technology, through the project life cycle, to compatible systems using a few of the technical data forms and applying rules as to when each is used; or information technology itself should be used to provide the bridges between systems and forms of data.

The first approach has proved to be ineffective as it does not accommodate the transient relationships established between the parties involved in the project. Different organisations will always want to make use of different systems to meet their own objectives and budgets. It also fails to take into account advances in technology.

Emerging technology offers the potential solution for integrating different systems and data forms. Arthur Andersen Management Consultants has recently made a major commitment to researching integration of the different forms of data listed above and the different systems required for technical information creation, storage and control. A number of prominent suppliers have loaned equipment and software to enable the data integration issue to be determined, and how it could then be interpreted, but above all how the whole process could be controlled. To go into the results of the research in detail would involve a separate paper. However, in summary, the exercise has proved that through careful thought on what logical and physical integration is really required, bridges can be built with varying degrees of manual intervention to transfer data between data forms and systems. The use of artificial intelligence techniques for the recognition of characters and shape characteristics is emerging as a technique with terrific potential to assist in the integration process. Once fully harnessed AI should allow the transfer of data between forms of storage, thus allowing the use of new technology for their most appropriate use, for example, optical disks for high volume storage, in the knowledge that the images can be converted to vector format when required.

19.8 CONCLUSIONS

Much sweat and tears goes into the design and construction of any building. An intelligent building requires even more due to technology considerations, crystal ball gazing to predict future changes and defending the resultant looks of the building for many years to come. But by comparison, little attention is given to the ongoing management of the building, the information required and the systems to capture, store and deliver that information. The benefits are there, if somewhat dissolved amongst the parties involved in the project. For information systems to be effective throughout the project life cycle requires strong, early commitment by the owner of the project. This is particularly important in ensuring that the information requirements are defined and the systems delivering the information are designed, installed and used.

Chapter 20
The role of energy simulation in the design and management of intelligent buildings

J.A. CLARKE and S.V. EMSLIE

20.1 INTRODUCTION

The building industry is Europe's second largest industry, accounting for around 12% of Gross Domestic Product. The capital value of new buildings is exceeded, by an order of magnitude, by their recurring costs, with heat energy representing in excess of 35% of Europe's delivered energy (50% or eight billion pounds stirling annually in the UK). Energy conservation in buildings therefore has significant potential, equivalent in kind to a substantial, untapped energy resource. Also, as a consequence of the extended life cycle of buildings, the ration of our existing building stock to new is increasing so that energy retro-fits, in the form of innovatory re-designs and advanced control systems, will surpass, in conservation potential, the new design market.

With the emergence of low cost, advanced information technology, buildings of the future will be expected to incorporate a greater level of automation. In particular, there is the possibility of pursuing an approach in which the various sub-systems - for safety, movement, access control, communications, energy systems and lighting - are truly integrated: this is the intelligent building scenario.

But, in view of the complex interactions which underlie building systems, deciding on the best control strategy or the optimum arrangement of design features is an extremely complex business. It is a task which does not lend itself to simple paradigms or rules of thumb.

This paper describes these complexities in relation to the energy sub-system. The form and content of two advanced simulation models is then described. The implication is that simulation, by allowing designers and operators to preview future reality in terms of performance, will allow the prototyping and efficient running of future intelligent buildings.

20.2 THE BUILDING AS A COMPLEX SYSTEM

Figure 20.1 shows the interacting energy flowpaths encountered within buildings and their environmental control systems. Such a system can be thought of as a network of time varying resistances and capacitances, subjected to varying temperature differences. Rooms and constructional elements are volumes of fluid and solid matter characterised by thermophysical properties such as conductance and capacitance and variables of state such as temperature and pressure. Since these properties and state variables vary with time, the problem is a temporal one: regions of differing time constants competing to capture, store and release energy at different rates. Such a system is termed 'stiff' because of the large range of time constants. For example, the time constants of multi-layered constructions can be measured in days, plant components in minutes and control actions in seconds.

Superimposed on this network is a complex set of interacting energy impulses. This set will include several spatially- and temporally-dependent processes:

1. Surface convection as caused by buoyancy and mechanical forces and influenced by surface finishes, geometry and temperature distribution.

2. Inter-surface longwave radiation exchanges as caused by temperature differences and influenced by geometry and surface finishes.

3. Surface shortwave gains caused by the date dependent sun path and influenced by site location and conditions, building geometry and the transmittance, absorbance and reflectance characteristics of constructional materials.

4. Shading and insolation as caused by surrounding and facade obstructions and influenced by site topology and cloud conditions.

5. External surface longwave exchanges as influenced by sky conditions and the degree of exposure to the site.

6. Air movement in the form of infiltration, zone-to-zone air exchange and intra-zone circulation as caused by temperature and pressure differences and influenced by leakage distribution, occupant behaviour and mechanical phenomena.

7. Casual gains - those stochastic processes associated with internal heat sources created by people and equipment, and influenced by social and comfort factors.

8. Plant interaction in the form of convective, radiant or mixed heat exchange and influenced by control action and occupant response.

9. Control action involving distributed sensing and actuation, various response characteristics and the processing of a potentially vast

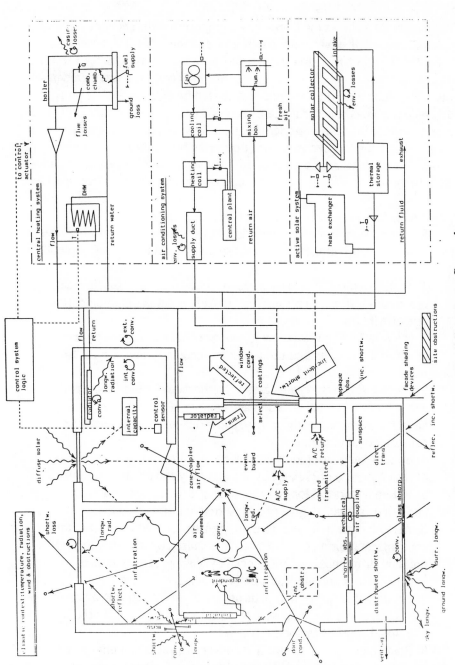

Figure 20.1: The complexity of building energy flowpaths

array of signals.

10. Moisture effects as caused by internal generation processes and a migration from outside.

11. Movable features such as window insulation and solar screens.

12. Other complexities as caused by thin film technology and a variety of solar capture and processing features: the so called passive solar elements.

20.3 BUILDING ENERGY MODELLING

From a mathematical standpoint, several equation types are required to represent accurately the dynamics of such a network. Parabolic and hyperbolic partial differential equations can be used to define transient conduction and air convection paths respectively; and shortwave and longwave exchanges, infiltration and control require non-linear, perhaps complex, equation structures. And because these equations are inter-related, it is necessary to apply simultaneous solution techniques if the performance prediction is to be both accurate and preserving of the spatial and temporal integrity of the building system.

In a simulation approach, accuracy and flexibility is determined by the way in which the governing equations are treated. Often, some portion of the network is neglected in whole or in part, for example, the use of environmental temperature to represent longwave radiative exchanges. Time invariant values may be assigned to one or more of the state variables or network resistances; for example, the use of constant, user supplied air change rates or boiler part load efficiency curves. Simplifying boundary conditions may be imposed, for example, the steady cyclic assumptions of the frequency response function method; or all derivatives may be eliminated to produce a steady-state system.

Traditionally, building designers have accepted these simplifying assumptions as the basis of manual calculation methods in support of system design. With real energy systems the foregoing complexities are present and act to expose the deficiencies of these traditional methods. In response, a number of advanced, computer-based energy simulation models are now appearing in the marketplace. These are the systems which will increasingly underpin decision making in the field of energy conscious building design.

20.4 WHAT IS SIMULATION?

This question is addressed by describing two simulation models. The first, the ESP system, is concerned with the energy behaviour of a building and its associated plant when constrained to conform to some control action. The second is a system known as DIM which is capable of simulating the behaviour of light in an architectural space. Both systems are designed to operate in tandem so that a designer can determine the energy, cost and comfort parameters of a proposed design when subjected to realistic occupancy behaviour and climatic influences.

20.4.1 The ESP system

Figure 20.2 shows the program modules of ESP; a tool for the simulation of the energy behaviour of buildings. Within ESP, all heat and mass flowpaths (as identified in Figure 20.1) and flowpath interactions are assigned a counterpart mathematical equivalent in an attempt to emulate reality. The entire system, however specified, is then contained within a single numerical framework. The theoretical basis of ESP is fully reported elsewhere (see, for example, Clarke (1985)). The following is a summary overview only.

At program run time, a building and its plant, as described by a user, is made discrete by sub-division into a number of interconnecting, finite volumes. These volumes then possess uniform properties which can vary in the time dimension. Volumes represent homogeneous and mixed material regions associated with room air, room surface and constructional elements on the building side, and component interface heat transfer on the plant side.

It is not uncommon to have as many as two hundred and fifty such volumes per building zone, with around five volumes per plant component. Then, for each of these finite volumes in turn, and in terms of all surrounding volumes deemed to be in thermal or flow contact, a conservation equation is developed in relation to the transport properties of interest - heat energy or mass exchange, for example.

This gives rise to a whole system equation set where each equation represents the state of one finite volume (or space) as it evolves over some small interval of time. These are termed state-space equations. Control equations are then added to this equation set to prescribe, limit or impose conditions on system behaviour. Once established for a particular increment in time, the equation set is simultaneously solved - by a numerical method - before being re-established for the next time-step. In this way, ESP time-steps through some user-specified simulation period to produce a time series of state variables which characterise building performance.

Many algorithms are required to compute such information as solar and casual gains, sky and ground temperatures, heat transfer coefficients, control states and so on.

If the whole system (building + plant + controls) equation set was set down in matrix equation form, these matrices would be topologically sparse

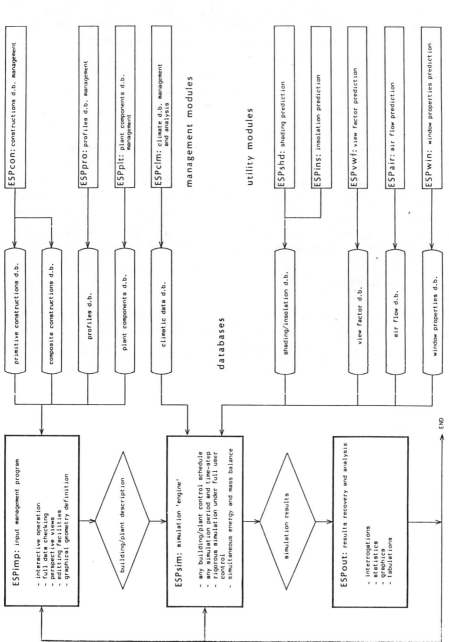

Figure 20.2: The ESP system - a suite of inter-relating, interactive program modules

and very diagonally dominated. In ESP, the problem of processing a matrix of this type is overcome by sub-dividing the matrix into a series of smaller partitioned matrices, each one representing a small portion of the overall system including inter-matrix links. The solution of the entire system - now held in partitioned form - need only address fully populated matrices as opposed to sparse ones. Throughout a simulation, all finite volume time constants are evaluated at each time-step and the nature of the related equation, or the processing frequency of the corresponding matrix partition, adjusted to ensure a stable solution of high accuracy.

To minimise computing time, partitioned matrix re-processing can even be disabled after the first time-step if matrix contents do not change significantly over time. With contemporary hardware, such computational efficiency is the key to providing a simulation-based design tool. As an added advantage, the method is able to accommodate any time-varying excitation and can accurately represent control systems in terms of the spatial position of control loop sensors and actuators, as well as the temporal factors inherent within controllers. Figure 20.3 overleaf shows a typical output from ESP.

20.4.2 The DIM system

This simulation model (Stearn, 1987) is comprised of four program and four database modules as shown in Figure 20.4. As with the energy simulation model, the objective is to represent in a rigorous manner, the underlying physics. With DIM this entails the tracking of light vectors as they inter-reflect between the surfaces comprising a space.

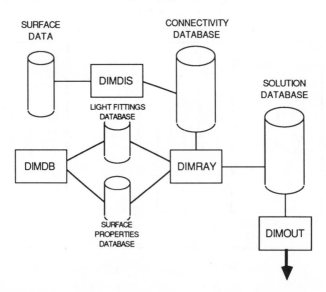

Figure 20.4: The DIM system - a suite of inter-relating, interactive program and database modules

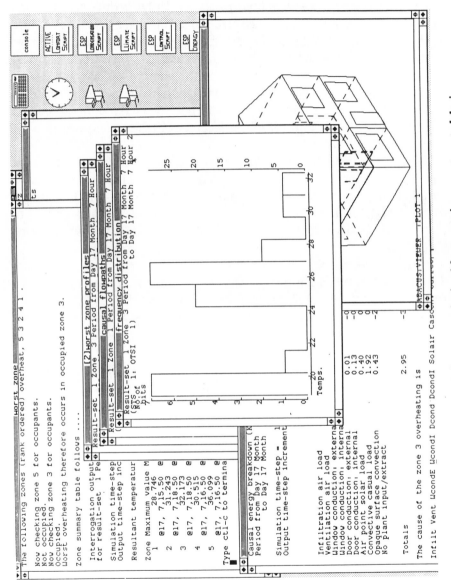

Figure 20.3: Example ESP output obtained from running an automated design appraisal methodology for comfort assessment

A zone's topography and topology is transformed into a discrete numerical equivalent in a manner which maximises numerical accuracy. This is done by applying a finite element grid to each polygon. A unit hemisphere is generated and, by slicing this equally in the horizontal and vertical planes, its surface is represented as a set of finite patches, each subtending an equal solid angle at the base centre point. When placed over a polygon cell, these surface patches then represent the cell's discrete radiosity field to a controlled level of accuracy. The patched unit hemisphere is then placed over each bounding and obstruction polygon grid cell in turn and a number of rays formed by connecting the cell's centre point with the centroids of each hemispherical patch. Each ray is then projected to locate the point of intersection with another polygon grid cell. In this way, each projection gives rise to a ray and each ray has a source and sink cell.

At the end of this 'discretisation' process a number of rays exist, each one with a distinct source and sink cell. These comprise the discrete equivalent of the initial continuous zone. Now the user extracts luminaires from the fittings' database and positions these within the space. The spatial distribution of luminance intensity is represented as a number of intensity vectors, and each vector exists at a number of mono-chromatic wavebands to represent a luminaire's spectral characteristics. Each vector (representing a particular direction and waveband) is then locked into the discrete ray equivalent of the specified zone and the multiple inter-reflections tracked.

At each surface reflection a mathematical model is invoked which depends upon the reflection properties of the surface - diffusing, off-specular or specular. This gives one or more exit or reflected rays, termed secondary vectors, which are added to the list of vectors to be processed. The ray tracking process continues until, eventually, new exit rays can be discarded because their intensity has diminished below some insignificant threshold value. In this way, the ray stack is processed until exhausted. The next mono-chromatic waveband or light source vector is then processed.

At the end of this stage, a database exists containing, separately for each initial light source vector and waveband, the reflected flux distribution for each polygon cell. DIMout is the analysis module which allows the recovery and presentation of these performance data. It has two capabilities. The first allows the performance data to be integrated by fitting and by surface. This yields, for any mix of fittings, surface illuminance or luminance.

The second capability concerns the transformation to terminal RGB to enable, via a scan-cell algorithm, the production of an enhanced screen image. This requires a display driver possessing a subjective and terminal colour mapping operation. For any given eye and focus point, a perspective transformation is applied to each polygon cell before terminal display. When combined, as in DIM, with a visibility priority algorithm (such as z-depth sorting), this gives rise to a perspective image. Note that if the initial polygon cells are set small enough, the technique becomes equivalent to scan-line pixel addressing. Figure 20.5 shows a typical image as generated by DIM.

20.5 AVAILABILITY OF SIMULATION MODELS

Simulation models are usually large systems which, until recently, were confined to mainframe environments. Now, with the advent of low cost workstations, this situation is changing and systems are available at low cost, for as little as £15,000, including a modestly powered (1MIP) workstation comprising:

1. Multi-tasking computer unit with 4 Mbytes of RAM.
2. 125 Mbytes Winchester disk.
3. Ethernet and RS232 serial input/output ports.
4. Floppy disk or tape unit.
5. Floating point unit.
6. High resolution, bit-mapped screen.

7. Window manager.
8. Programmable keyboard.
9. Mouse.
10. UNIX operating system licence.
11. Numerous software development and word processing tools.

This juxtaposition of low cost workstation technology and advanced simulation software not only improves model accessibility, it also permits considerable improvements to the user interface. For example, multi-window, multi-tasking capabilities allow several tasks to be undertaken at the same time - perhaps several simulations are in progress while some previous results are being analysed. Pop-up menu command selection, and process initiation by icon (picture) selection, makes program control much easier. In practice the *modus operandi* is as follows.

A design hypothesis is arrived at and specified to the model. With ESP, for example, this would include information on building geometry, construction, usage, plant and control. This process can take from less than half an hour to many days depending on the objectives of the performance assessment and the availability of relevant data. Much work is underway to install more intelligence within models so that they can operate on incomplete descriptions (MacRandal, 1986).

A rigorous, first principles simulation is now performed. This produces a string of performance variables which represent the building and plant energy behaviour in the case of ESP, or the illumination levels in the case of DIM. Simulations may take from a few minutes to many hours depending on the extent of the simulation, the complexity of the problem and the number of design variables to be studied.

System performance is assessed by interrogating the simulation output to obtain an insight into the underlying causal relationships and so identify cost effective changes to the design hypothesis. This process may take from a few minutes to many days depending on the skills and experience of the analyst. The initial design hypothesis can now be modified and further simulations requested.

20.6 SIMULATION AND INTELLIGENT BUILDINGS

Given the emergence of simulation as a viable prospect, how might it be applied in practice, especially in the context of intelligent buildings? The following two generalised examples will help answer this question.

20.6.1 The basics: form and fabric

It is entirely possible to determine, by simulation, the optimum combination of zone automation. Several simulations are conducted to determine a zoning strategy which not only satisfies the functional criteria, but will also accommodate sophisticated multi-zone control and the re-distribution of excess energy. Some simulations might focus on the choice of construction materials, and their relative positioning within the multi-layered constructions, so that load and temperature levelling is maximised. Alternative facade fenestration and shading control features may be investigated in terms of comfort and cost criteria.

20.6.2 The intelligence: control and response

Once a fundamentally sound design has emerged, well tested in terms of its performance under a range of anticipated operating conditions, a number of alternative control scenarios can be simulated. For example, basic control studies will lead to decisions on the potential of optimum start/stop control, appropriate set-back temperatures, the efficacy of weather anticipation, the location of sensors and the inter-relation of thermal and visual comfort variables. Further analysis might focus on smart control, where the system is designed to respond to occupancy levels or prevailing levels of luminance intensity. As the underlying relationships emerge, the designer is able to assess the benefits and the problems of any given course of action before it is implemented.

The appraisal permutations are without limit. For example, a model such as ESP could be used to answer the following questions.
1. What are the maximum demands for heating, cooling and illumination and where and when do they occur?
2. What will be the effect of a particular design strategy, such as adopting super-insulation, specialist glazing systems or sophisticated control regimes?
3. What is the optimum plant start time or the most effective algorithm for weather anticipation?
4. How will thermal and visual comfort levels vary throughout the building under alternative lighting management schemes?
5. How will infiltration or temperature stratification be affected by a particular management strategy and will condensation become a problem?
6. What is the contribution to energy saving and comfort level of a particular passive solar feature?

The approach allows a designer to improve his understanding of the inter-relation between design and performance parameters, to then identify potential problem areas, and so implement and test appropriate building, plant and control modifications. The design to result from this procedure is more energy conscious with better comfort levels attained throughout.

20.7 THE FUTURE

The appraisal of building performance by simulation is now a real possibility. Proven systems are emerging and these are, increasingly, being offered on low cost, powerful workstation technology. The opportunity now exists for the design and construction team to test the consequences of various design and operational proposals before they are implemented in practice.

At the present time, a second possibility is being pursued at the research level, that of incorporating the elements of simulation within the building's control systems. At one level, it would be feasible to incorporate process models within HVAC controllers. This would allow these controllers to compare any deviation of the control condition from some predicted state on a continuous basis. In the case of energy management systems, for example, this would provide a look-ahead capability so that control actions could first be appraised in a software environment before being applied to the real system.

To facilitate this possibility, it is necessary to re-cast the methods of simulation in a modular manner so that building specific models can be readily configured (and reconfigured). One current research project is addressing the notion of an advanced machine environment - termed the Energy Kernel System ('eks') - designed for this purpose. The 'eks' (Clarke, 1987) is a software/hardware product which is capable of constructing a program from internal, accredited methods. Figure 20.6 shows the elements of the 'eks'.

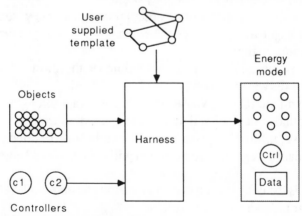

Figure 20.6: Elements of the 'eks'

It is imagined that a template can first be constructed to define a model in terms of its methods. This template is passed to the harness which automatically constructs the program, outputing it in the form of a multi-object model, expressed in source or executable form. This is done by transferring the selected objects from the object's library, and automatically generating the control object which will co-ordinate the methods at program run time. The output is a program aimed at a specific machine.

20.8 CONCLUSIONS

Simulation models are now emerging which are well equipped to handle the microcosm of complexity which is the energy sub-system within buildings. The demands currently being placed on designers, in terms of the technology now demanded by clients, will require such an approach as the basis of future design decision making. The possibility exists to harness computer simulation as a device to allow design prototyping at the design stage and, in the longer term, as an integral element of advanced real time control.

20.9 REFERENCES

Clarke, J.A. (1985), *Energy Simulation in Building Design,* Adam Hilger, Bristol.
Clarke, J.A. (1987), *The Future of Building Energy Modelling in the UK: The Energy Kernel System,* Report to the UK SERC, ABACUS, University of Strathclyde, Glasgow.
MacRandal, D. (1986), *The Application of Intelligent Front Ends in Building Design,* Informatics Group Report, Rutherford Appleton Laboratory, Didcot.
Stearn, D.D. (1987), *DIM System Manual,* ABACUS Publication, University of Strathclyde, Glasgow.

Chapter 21
The application of stochastic modelling to environmental control in buildings

D. L. LOVEDAY

21.1 INTRODUCTION

The 'oil crisis' of 1973 signalled the end of the era of cheap fossil fuels. This, together with the realisation that reserves of such fuels were finite, caused attention to be focussed on methods of conserving energy and hence reserves of fossil fuels. Efforts to this end have been made in many areas, the built environment being no exception. Since 1976, the UK Building Regulations have progressively reduced the U-values deemed appropriate for walls and roofs in both dwellings and other buildings.

The trend has been, and is likely to continue, in the form of reducing ventilation heat losses. This has led to a situation where other factors begin to take on an increasingly important role as regards progress towards further reductions in building energy consumption. One such factor is solar gain, which has resulted in greater awareness of passive solar design. Another factor is occupancy, especially the need for more detailed knowledge of occupants' presence and activities. This is necessary if further improvements in energy and comfort conditions are to be achieved. A major factor to which more attention is now being paid is that of control. The environment within buildings is being greatly improved by accounting for the factors described above within a control strategy. Control systems have thus become more complex - the 'intelligent building' has arrived.

21.2 INTELLIGENT BUILDINGS

At present there appears to be no single definition of the term 'intelligent building', though several descriptions have been suggested (Building Services and Environmental Engineer, 1987). For the purpose of this paper, the following definition is proposed:

'An intelligent building is one in which the services can make their own decisions for the control of the environment'.

The objective of the control would usually be to maintain internal comfort conditions for the occupants with the minimum of energy consumption. In intelligent buildings, the ability to take such decisions is provided by taking account of an increasing number of factors which can influence the thermal performance of the buildings. Hence, knowledge of external climatic variations, thermal response of the structure, plant performance characteristics and patterns of occupancy is required for effective environmental control. This often involves the monitoring of temperatures in strategic locations and the processing of data at a central control point followed by the implementation of appropriate control action. This is the basis of many building energy management systems (BEMS) (Building Services and Environmental Engineer, 1987b).

To a large extent, BEMS rely on the instantaneous sensing of temperatures and the setting of time controls. Optimum start controllers, though, do take account of rates of rise or fall of temperature when starting up heating systems in commercial premises so that comfort conditions are achieved in time for the arrival of occupants. However, climate and occupancy patterns not only show daily and seasonal variations, but also exhibit random changes. Improved control and greater energy savings may result if forecasting of temperatures, heating loads, occupancy profiles, and climatic conditions inclusive of random and sequential effects were possible, with the system operating in response to the forecasted values.

Forecasting of future values of a variable is possible from a mathematical model of the system. If values can be forecasted exactly, the system is said to be purely 'deterministic'. However, randomness as mentioned above can occur. Such random variations are termed 'stochastic'. When these influences are present stochastic modelling can be employed.

The objectives of this paper are:
1. To outline stochastic modelling in general terms and to relate its application to the currently held concept of intelligent building.
2. To illustrate the use of stochastic models in forecasting of external and internal air temperatures for an occupied dwelling, and to validate the models derived.
3. To compare the results with those from two deterministic models, BREAM and ESP, in order to highlight the differences of the two approaches.
4. To discuss possible applications and future developments in

relation to intelligent environmental control in buildings.

This paper is a further development of work presented earlier (Loveday and Craggs, 1986) and places that work within the context of BEMS and intelligent buildings.

21.3 WHAT IS STOCHASTIC MODELLING?

Stochastic models can be derived by analysing the history of values of a variable. A dataset consisting of values of the variable taken at regular intervals over a period of time is called a time series. The use of time series analysis techniques such as those of Box and Jenkins (1978) allows the dependence of the variable on its previous values to be investigated. The model fitted to the dataset is said to be univariate if the present value of the variable is related only to past values of the same variable.

As an example, the present external air temperature could be related to the previous values of external air temperatures. A model is said to be multivariate if it related the present value of one variable to previous values of other variables. For example, such a model could show the relationship between the present heating load of a building and past values of external temperature, internal temperature and solar radiation. For both univariate and multivariate cases, the relationships would be inclusive of time-dependent and sequential effects. The models could then be used to forecast future values of the variables. (For a fuller discussion refer to Loveday and Craggs, 1986; Box and Jenkins, 1978; Chatfield, 1984).

21.4 EXPERIMENTATION AND MODELLING

This paper describes an application of the above modelling technique to data from a monitored building. Univariate stochastic models, as presented by Loveday and Craggs (1986), were fitted to a time series of hourly measured values of external ambient and internal lounge dry-bulb air temperatures for an occupied dwelling. The validity of the models was tested by using them to forecast ahead, in steps of one hour, future values of ambient, TA, and lounge, TL, dry-bulb air temperatures for a period of 36 hours. Forecasted and measured values were then estimated using the deterministic thermal models BREAM and ESP, and the differences between them and the stochastic approach highlighted.

The building under investigation was a detached domestic residence near

Basingstoke, UK. Heating was provided by a solar assisted heat pump situated in the roofspace (Neal *et al.* 1979) - refer to Figure 21.1.

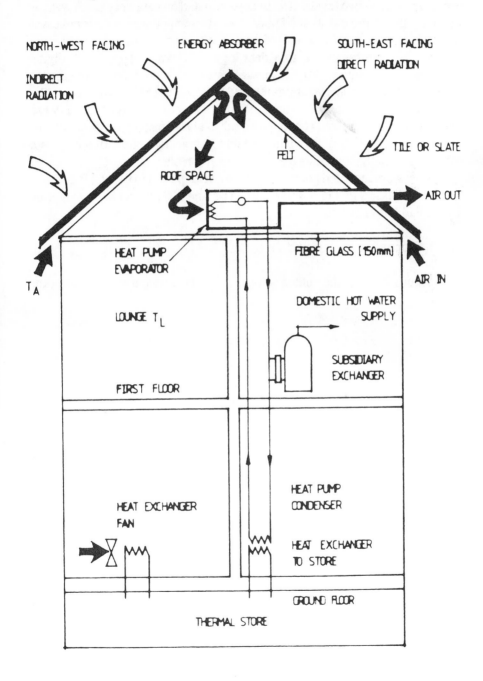

Figure 21.1: The system being monitored

The unit supplied heat to a 22,000 litre water store which in turn provided space heating via a ducted warm air circuit. Accommodation was for three occupants and on two levels. The lounge, situated on the upper level, was the subject of this particular study. The dry-bulb air temperature in the lounge was recorded hourly over a period of two weeks using a thin film platinum resistance sensor connected to a data logger (Newport Type 267A digital pyrometer, and printer). The sensor was located near the room thermostat on an internal wall at about two-thirds the wall height. The lounge was rectangular and comprised two external walls, one facing south-east, the other south-west. The south-east facing wall contained a double-glazed patio door. Both sensors were encapsulated within radiation-shielded housings, the external sensor being additionally housed inside a Stevenson screen.

Data were recorded hourly over a two week period in the heating season providing datasets of 336 observations. The first 300 observations were used for the validation exercise.

21.4.1 Stochastic models and forecasts

Figure 21.2a is the autocorrelogram for the ambient temperature time series.

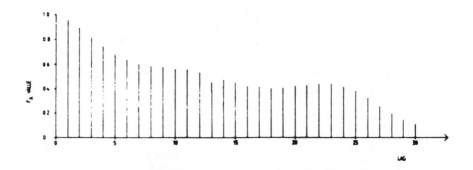

Figure 21.2a: The autocorrelation coefficients for the ambient air temperature series

This consists of a plot of autocorrelation coefficient, the rA values, against the lag k. The autocorrelation coefficient at lag k may be regarded as the correlation coefficient between the value of a variable at time t and its value at time (t - k), where k is the time lag in question (for example, one, two, three or more hours ago). It can be seen that the correlation between the present value of ambient temperature TA and earlier values steadily decreases as the lag k increases, with the temperatures of the previous few hours having the major influence. In other words, and as one might expect, the present value of TA is more strongly related to its value one or two hours ago than to its value, say, five or six hours ago. The peak at lag 24 indicates that the value of TA at the same time on the previous day is related to the present value.

Using techniques described by Box and Jenkins (1978), a univariate model was fitted to the time series of 300 observations. This model (Tables 21.1a and 21.1b) shows that the main influences on the present ambient temperature were the values for the previous four hours, and its value 24 hours ago.

SERIES AND TYPE OF MODEL	FITTED MODEL
AMBIENT ($T_{A\ t}$) ARIMA $(4,1,0) \cdot (1,0,0)_{24}$	$\nabla T_{A\ t} = 0.3168 \nabla T_{A\ t-1} + 0.0268 \nabla T_{A\ t-2} - 0.0443 \nabla T_{A\ t-3}$ $- 0.1773 \nabla T_{A\ t-4} + 0.1644 \nabla T_{A\ t-24} - 0.0521 \nabla T_{A\ t-25}$ $- 0.0044 \nabla T_{A\ t-26} + 0.0073 \nabla T_{A\ t-27} + 0.0291 \nabla T_{A\ t-28}$ $+ ET_{A\ t}$
LOUNGE ($T_{L\ t}$) ARIMA $(1,1,1) \cdot (1,1,0)_{24}$	$\nabla \nabla_{24} T_{L\ t} = 0.7594 \ \nabla \nabla_{24} T_{L\ t-1} - 0.3522 \ \nabla \nabla_{24} T_{L\ t-24}$ $+ 0.2675 \ \nabla \nabla_{24} T_{L\ t-25} - 0.9718 ET_{L\ t-1}$ $+ ET_{L\ t}$

Table 21.1a: Box and Jenkins univariate models

SERIES AND TYPE OF MODEL	ERROR TERM	ESTIMATED VARIANCE OF RESIDUALS	% VARIATION ACCOUNTED FOR BY FITTED MODEL
AMBIENT ($T_{A\ t}$) ARIMA $(4,1,0) \cdot (1,0,0)_{24}$	$ET_{A\ t}$	0.2450	94%
LOUNGE ($T_{L\ t}$) ARIMA $(1,1,1) \cdot (1,1,0)_{24}$	$ET_{L\ t}$	0.7290	83%

Table 21.1b: Error term, estimate of variance of residuals and % variation, for each of the Box and Jenkins univariate models

The model was then used to forecast future values of TA for the
succeeding period of 36 hours, in hourly steps.

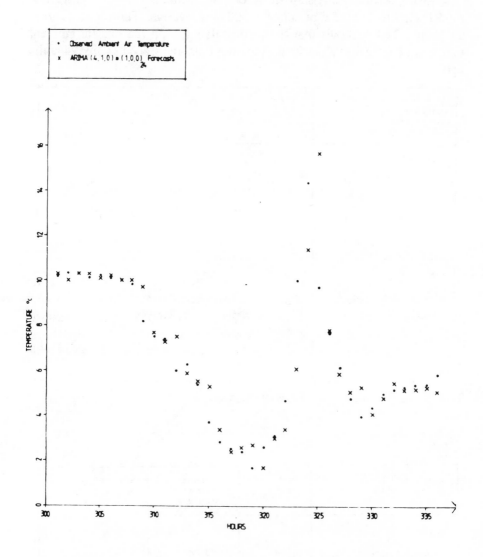

Figure 21.3a: Comparison of observed and forecasted value for ambient air
temperature

In Figure 21.3a is shown the comparison of forecasted and actual values, while the summary of residuals (the difference between the actual and forecast values) is shown in Table 21.2.

TEMPERATURE SERIES AND TYPE OF MODEL	NUMBER OF FORECASTS	RESIDUALS FROM FORECASTS		% VARIANCE OF OBSERVED VALUES ACCOUNTED FOR BY FORECASTS
		MEAN	VARIANCE	
AMBIENT ARIMA (4,1,0)*(1,0,0)$_{24}$	36	-0.0965	2.2062	76%
LOUNGE ARIMA (1,1,1)*(1,1,0)$_{24}$	36	+0.0075	0.3603	93%

Table 21.2: Summary of residuals from one-step-ahead forecasts

All terminology is as defined by Box and Jenkins, unless otherwise stated. Figure 21.2b presents the autocorrelation coefficients, the rL values as a function of lag k for the time series of lounge temperatures. This shows the presence of a 24 hour cycle.

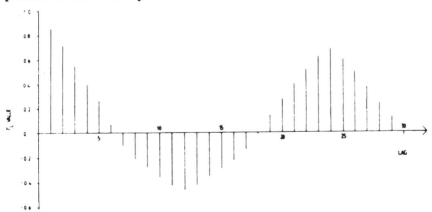

Figure 21.2b: The autocorrelation coefficients for the lounge air temperature series

The negative rL values show that there is a negative correlation between values of lounge temperature TL for some lags, the maximum occurring at a lag of 12 hours. In simple terms, while the value of TL may be increasing at 17.00

hours, for example, its value is decreasing at 05.00 hours. There is evidence of a strong positive relationship between the present lounge temperature and its values 2 to 3 hours ago, and 24 hours ago.

The univariate model fitted to the lounge temperature series is given in Tables 21.1a and 21.1b. It shows that the temperatures 1 and 24 hours ago, and also one hour ago error term were the main influences on the present TL value. Using the model, values for TL for the next 36 hours were forecast, in steps of one hour. Figure 21.3b shows the comparison with the actual values, and Table 21.2 the summary of residuals.

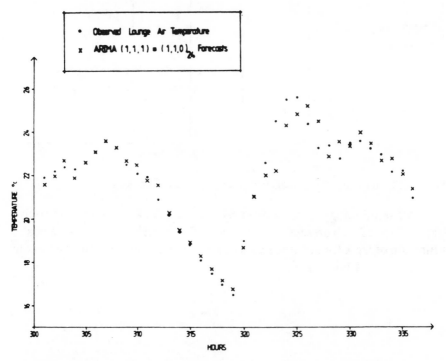

Figure 21.3b: Comparison of observed and forecasted values for lounge air temperature

21.5 WHAT IS DETERMINISTIC MODELLING?

A deterministic model is one in which it is assumed that no random influences affect a system, thereby allowing the values of a variable to be calculated exactly. Most building design engineers in the field of thermal modelling are familiar with this type of model. Such models range in complexity from the simple steady-state techniques (manual U-value calculations), to the intermediate models (simplified treatments of dynamic thermal performance using admittance and time-lag), and finally to the fully dynamic thermal models requiring computer usage. However, in most models, simplified treatment of some of the input is required, such as occupancy profiles and gains; these are often known only approximately and are inserted in 'blocks'. Using two such models, values for lounge temperatures were estimated and compared with the stochastic approach.

21.5.1 Deterministic models and results

To compare deterministic and stochastic approaches, the lounge temperatures were estimated over the same 36 hour validation period as in the previous section. Two models were utilised:
1. The admittance procedure (Milbank and Harrington-Lynn, 1974) in the form of the package BREAM, an intermediate level model.
2. The program ESP (Clarke and McLean, 1986), a fully dynamic model.

In each model, appropriate thermophysical data relating to the lounge construction were inserted, as were details (as far as they were known) of occupancy and plant operation. Climate information was, in the main, drawn from standard average data as available within the programs; it was made to fit, as closely as possible, the actual weather over the period in question. The problem was modelled as a single zone configuration in BREAM, and as a two zone configuration (lounge and loft) in ESP (the latter model being able to handle more detailed information).

Figure 21.4 compares the values of lounge temperature TL estimated using BREAM with the actual values over the 36 hours. The maximum lounge temperature of 25 debrees Centigrade results from the thermostat setting required in the program. The relatively low temperatures estimated between 314 and 318 hours (not shown) result from the assumed periodic variation in external ambient temperature TA necessary for program operation, and thermal capacity effects.

Figure 21.5 compares the values of TL estimated using ESP with the actual values over the same 36 hours. Once again, the maximum estimated temperature of 25 degrees results from the program thermostat setting requirements.

21.5.2 Comparison of techniques

The temperature estimates using the deterministic approach (BREAM and ESP) are reasonably close to the actual values, showing that the models capture the general thermal behaviour of the lounge. However, both suffer

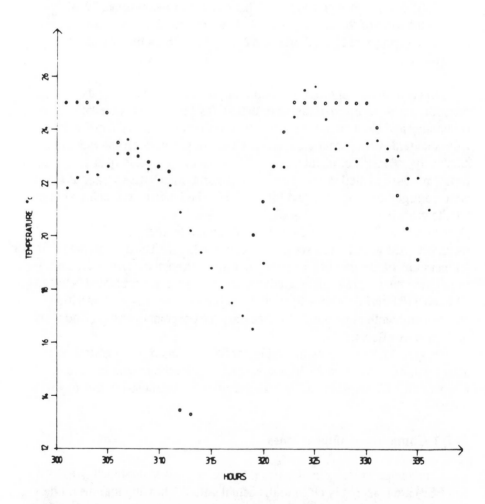

Figure 21.4: Comparison of observed lounge air temperatures with those calculated by the admittance procedure

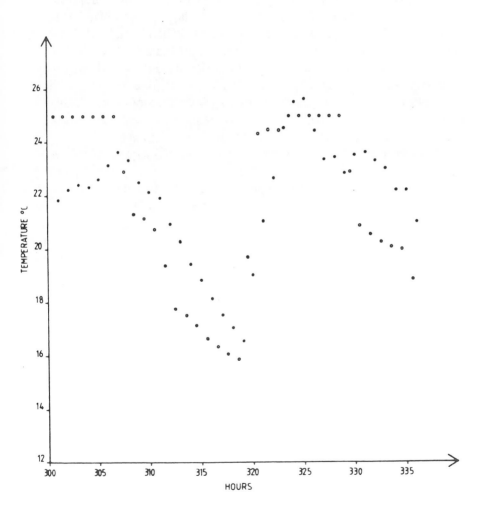

Figure 21.5: Comparison of observed lounge air temperatures with those calculated using ESP

from a lack of fit between 301 and 306 hours. This is thought to be due to variations in occupancy and plant operation which cannot be modelled in detail. This illustrates a difficulty with deterministic models. Without highly detailed data on occupancy, plant usage or climate, for example, they cannot estimate detailed temperature variations in buildings, since these data are subject to random (stochastic) disturbances. On the other hand, ESP is able to produce an overall better estimate of lounge temperature compared with BREAM, such as over the period 312-318 hours. This is because ESP can handle more detail in the input data, and offers a more rigorous treatment of time-varying heat transfer.

Using BREAM, it has been shown (Loveday and Craggs, 1986) that variations in the number of air changes per hour between 0.5 AC/h and 1.0 AC/h can cause fluctuations of up to 2 degrees in the estimates of lounge air temperature. Similar variations in air change rate, when input to ESP, cause fluctuations of up to 1.3 degrees. Variations in air change rate of the above magnitude can occur frequently and intermittently in buildings and hence may be regarded as a stochastic effect. The air change rate for a room or building is difficult to quantify accurately, especially when that room or building is occupied. Note, that the data necessary for deterministic estimates must be known or assumed beforehand before modelling can commence.

Stochastic models can take account of random and sequential variations in the influences mentioned above, provided such variations occurred during the period from which the model was produced. If another disturbing influence suddenly acts on the building, the forecasts produced by the model will be adversely affected (though the model can 'self-adjust' as more data become available). This is illustrated in Figure 21.3a. The external ambient and lounge temperatures rose suddenly between 322 hours and 326 hours as a result of a period of sunshine.

Throughout the 36 hours, forecast and actual values of TA and TL were in excellent agreement, but were worse for the above period. This is because relatively little solar radiation had occurred during the preceding 300 hours, the period from which the models were derived. This highlights a shortcoming of the stochastic approach. Forecasting accuracy could be improved by basing models on longer, more representative datasets, or by using a self-learning model which modifies itself as more data are recorded. A 'forgetting factor' may be included to place more emphasis on recent data rather than older data. In contrast to this 'batch' type of modelling, a recursive method may be used.

21.5.3 Summary

Autocorrelation coefficients have been determined for time series of the ambient and lounge air temperatures. Univariate stochastic models fitted to each series were validated by using them to forecast ahead, in steps of one hour, for a period of 36 hours: no data from this period were used in formulating the models. Agreement between forecasted and actual values was excellent, showing that adequate models of this type can be developed for applications in building thermal analysis. Two deterministic models, in the format of the computer programs BREAM and ESP were used to estimate lounge temperatures for the same 36 hours. It was shown that the fit to the actual temperature variation is improved if greater detail can be added to the data input to the model.

It is concluded that deterministic analyses are sensitive to lack of detailed data (for example, occupancy gains, plant usage and air change rates as functions of time), whereas stochastic analyses are sensitive to non-representative data (for example, solar irradiance) over the period from which the model is derived. Usually, such analyses consider stochastic processes to be 'white noise' (Box and Jenkins, 1978) in nature. Should this not be the case, then models based on white noise can give erroneous forecasts. It becomes necessary to model the stochastic processes more accurately (using generalised least squares, see (Astrom and Eykhoff, 1971)).

21.6 APPLICATIONS AND FUTURE DEVELOPMENTS

The deterministic approach is normally adopted at the design stage in the life of a building to assess its thermal behaviour and likely energy consumption. Only when built does the stochastic approach become available with regard to monitoring, modelling and then forecasting temperatures, loads, etc.. It may be possible to develop a combined deterministic/stochastic approach for use at the design stage. In the case of occupancy, for example, this could be achieved by developing stochastic models of occupancy patterns for a series of building types and typical numbers of occupants. These models could be incorporated within existing deterministic thermal models. Benefits in the form of improved estimates of energy consumption in buildings may result, since more realistic occupancy profiles, inclusive of sequential effects, are being utilised. At present, errors in estimates of energy usage of up to 40% can occur due to the simplified treatment of occupancy in current thermal models. Similar approaches to that described could be devised for climate, appliance usage, and lighting.

The possibility of basing control of a system on stochastic models is attractive. Energy consumption may fall if the control system operates on a forecasted value rather than an instantaneously-sensed value. One step ahead forecasts as shown in this paper have been very accurate, but forecasts up to five steps ahead have also given good agreement (Braun *et al.* 1987) where a methodology has been devised using a deterministic/stochastic approach for the optimal control of a large cooling plant. It is necessary not only to develop suitable stochastic models for climate, temperature or load prediction and to validate them carefully, but also to assess any energy savings that may result if they are used in specific control devices. This is particularly important if on-line control using multivariate models is proposed (the models arising from identification of the parameters with the strongest influence).

It may be possible to develop several specific control devices to operate as described above and save energy, but application to building energy management systems could result in enhanced energy savings. The development and implementation of stochastic-based software for on-line operation in such systems may lead to the development of the 'super-intelligent' building. Such a building would not only be able to make its own decisions to maintain occupant comfort and save energy, but could do so with an element of 'foresight'. It has been pointed out (Building Services and Environmental Engineer, 1987b) that it would be prohibitively expensive to develop BEMS for individual buildings. However, if control is based to some extent on stochastic models, it may be possible to develop software which is tailor-made for a particular building. Such software could be produced after a period of monitoring of a particular building; the software could then be retro-fitted into the energy management system. Provision for this would be necessary in the hardware.

The installation of a BEMS may be regarded as converting a 'primitive' building to an 'intelligent' building. The application of stochastic techniques could represent the next step in the development of computer-aided environmental control. Further work is needed in the preparation and careful validation of suitable models for system control purposes, not least the assessment of the magnitude of any energy savings brought about by their use. If such developmental work is successful and is exploited, the era of the 'super-intelligent' building will have arrived.

21.7 ACKNOWLEDGEMENTS

The assistance of Dr C. Craggs, School of Mathematics and Statistics, Newcastle-upon-Tyne Polytechnic, Mr S.V. Emslie, ABACUS CAD Unit, University of Strathclyde, Glasgow and Dr G. Virk, Department of Control Engineering, University of Sheffield, is gratefully acknowledged.

21.8 REFERENCES

Astrom, K.J., and Eykhoff, P. (1971), *System Identification - A Survey*, Automatica, 7, 123-162.

Box, G.E.P. and Jenkins, G.M. (1978), *Time Series Analysis Forecasting and Control*, Holden-Day. London

Braun, J.E., Mitchell, J.W. and Klein, S.A. (1987), *Performance and Control Characteristics of a Large Cooling System*, ASHRAE Transactions, 93, (1).

Building Services and Environmental Engineer (1987), 9, (10), 17-18.

Building Services and Environmental Engineer (1987b), 9, (7), 24-32.

Chatfield, C. (1984), *The Analysis of Time Series - an Introduction*, 3rd edition, Chapman and Hall, London.

Clarke, J. and McLean, D. (1986), *ESP - A Building and Plant Energy Simulation System*, Version 5, Release 3, ABACUS CAD Unit, University of Strathclyde, Glasgow.

Loveday, D.L. and Craggs, C. (1986), *Short-term Stochastic Modelling of Internal and External Air Temperatures for an Occupied Residence*, in Proceedings of the International Conference on System Simulation in Buildings, Leige, Belgium, 391-413.

Milbank, N.O. and Harrington-Lynn, F. (1974), *Thermal Response and the Admittance Procedure*, Building Services Engineer, 42, 38-54.

Neal, W.E.J, Loveday, D.L. and Pabon-Diaz, M. (1979), *A Solar-Assisted Heat Pump and Storage System for Domestic Space and Water Heating Using a Conventional Roof as a Radiation Absorber*, Proceedings of the ISES Congress, Atlanta, GA., 1, 822-826.

Chapter 22
Implementing smart strategies for climate control systems

R.M.C. DE KEYSER

22.1 INTRODUCTION

Energy conservation in building heating can be realised by taking several well known measures: better heat insulation techniques, an appropriate heating plant and a performing control system. Each of these methods can also contribute to a more comfortable environment or at least a preservation of the comfort conditions, but with a lower energy account.

The objective of this paper is to present some conventional and new control algorithms in increasing order of complexity. In order to have a basis for comparing the several strategies, it is necessary to state clearly the main effects by which a control policy can contribute to energy saving. These effects are: decreasing the operating time of the heating plant, utilising the free energy sources and increasing the plant efficiency.

A decrease of the plant operating hours is essentially realised by floating start/stop instead of programmed start/stop. This can be implemented by means of optimal start/stop procedures based on prediction techniques, taking into account the building dynamics and heating plant dynamics. Making the most of freely available energy sources (such as solar radiation and other heat sources within the building) means that the control algorithms compensate for their effect. This can be done explicitly by measuring them or implicitly by measuring their effect on the inside room temperature. Finally, the overall heating plant efficiency should be increased by a performing control strategy for the boiler and a minimisation of the heat transportation losses. The next section will consider some control strategies according to the above criteria.

From a control engineering point of view, a heating plant can be represented by the block scheme of Figure 22.1. A number of feedback loops are omitted from this model for simplification and to aid clarity of detailing.

A basic principle that must be fulfilled by the control system is a continuous accommodation of the heat supply to meet needs. This is realised by two measures: first, by arranging a building in occupation zones and secondly, by specifying a schedule for the occupation time of each zone which may then be controlled independently according to needs.

The subsequent heating plant control methods will be evaluated according to the above concepts, that is, optimality in space (the zone concept) and optimality in time (the occupation schedule or start/stop concept). It will be shown that none of the existing methods fulfils all requirements. A novel system based on smart advanced control strategies will then be introduced and evaluated.

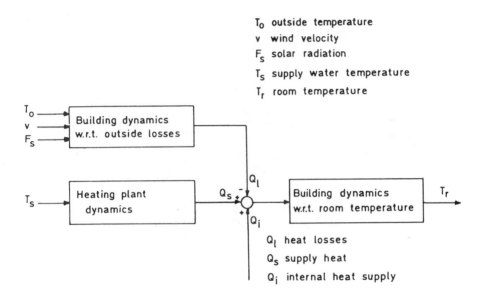

T_o outside temperature
v wind velocity
F_s solar radiation
T_s supply water temperature
T_r room temperature

Q_l heat losses
Q_s supply heat
Q_i internal heat supply

Figure 22.1: Block scheme of heating plant

22.2 CURRENT CONTROL SYSTEMS

22.2.1 The central room thermostat

This is the most simple method. According to the sign of the control error (desired room temperature - real room temperature) the supply water pump (or boiler) is started or stopped. It is a pure feedback control system (see Figure 22.1). Moreover, it is an on-off controller with the well known disadvantage of steady-state oscillations around the setpoint. This is well illustrated in the experiments of Figure 22.2.

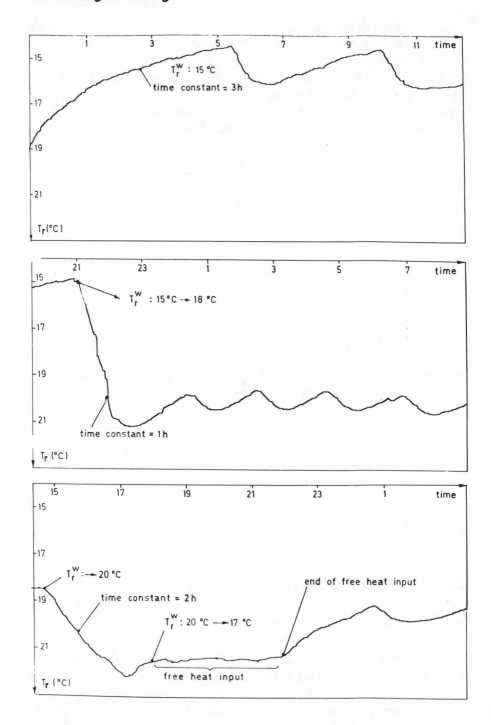

Figure 22.2: Experiments with heating plant controlled by thermostat

In order to decrease the amplitude of the oscillations, heat anticipation elements are used in the thermostat, but it remains a primitive (although low cost) control system. The concepts of optimality in space or in time are totally non-existent because the heat supplied to the several zones depends entirely on the requirements of the central room where the thermostat is placed. As a result, it is frequently necessary to apply corrections manually in the other rooms, that is, by changing radiator valve positions.

22.2.2 Thermostatic valves plus boiler aquastat

Each heat emitting element (for example, radiator) has its own thermostatic valve that changes the supply water flow according to the needs of the particular room. The water supply temperature is fixed and controlled by a boiler aquastat. This is the first step in the right direction as far as optimality in space is concerned. Apart from the doubtful performance of the individual slave controllers (a thermostatic valve may not always lead to a performing closed loop system), the system has essentially two notable disadvantages: first, the valves are almost totally open when it gets colder outside or closed when it gets warmer, because of the fixed supply water temperature.

The valves do not regulate well in these extreme positions. The second shortcoming, which is important from the point of view of energy saving, is that optimality in time is totally neglected. The only way to decrease output during non-occupied periods is to change the setpoint manually for each individual thermostatic valve. Finally, it is interesting to note that this method is again a pure feedback solution from a control engineering point of view.

22.2.3 Thermostatic valve plus weather dependent boiler control

The distinction that may be drawn with the control system described in the previous section is the dependence of the supply water temperature on the outside temperature. This relationship is given by the well known heat curves illustrated in Figure 22.3. It is a further step towards the optimality concept introduced already. By this step, the first disadvantage stated in the previous section is solved. However, the second important shortcoming remains. Moreover, a new problem is introduced, that is, the user has to select a proper heating curve on which the heating plant is to operate. It is worth noting that in Figure 22.1, the heating curve concept is a (static) feedforward control of the outside temperature, a strategy that is well known in process control. The selection of an appropriate heating curve then corresponds to the tuning of the feedforward control gain.

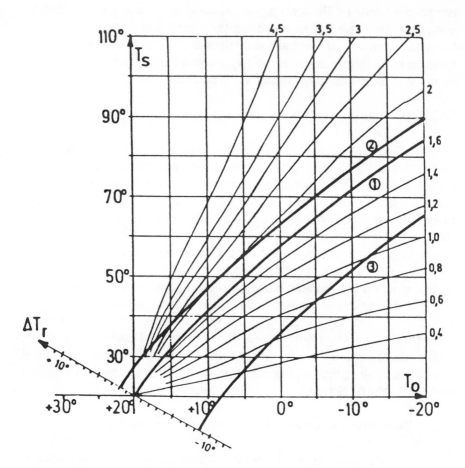

Figure 22.3: Heat curves

22.2.4 Digital self-learning control

The availability of cheap microprocessor chips and peripheral interface chips creates new openings for building a low cost intelligent controller. It is now possible, therefore, to implement smart advanced control strategies, that is, self-adaptive control.

This section describes the results of a demonstration project. The objective of this project was to illustrate by means of real life experiments, the feasibility of certain concepts of modern control theory and digital instrumentation to low cost applications.

The capabilities of advanced control strategies, that is, self-tuning and adaptive methods, and computer-based control instrumentation to industrial process control systems have become well established over the last decade. However, this paper focusses on another potential field of automation and control applications, that is, in the non-industrial sector such as building automation. In order to end up with a product which is economically viable, the designer has to keep in mind the objective of minimising cost from the very beginning. Although this may seem like a severe strait jacket, it has the effect of stimulating the designer into thinking about smart hardware configurations as well as writing efficient software, but without the assistance of a powerful operating system.

This demonstration project illustrates two important points: first, micro-processor-based digital hardware is today a valuable alternative to classical analogue electronics for low cost automation equipment; and secondly, as a result of this, the availability of advanced digital control algorithms is no longer a privilege of the larger process control projects.

22.2.5 System hardware

The general structure of the Adaptive Microcomputer Controller, AMC, is shown in Figure 22.4.

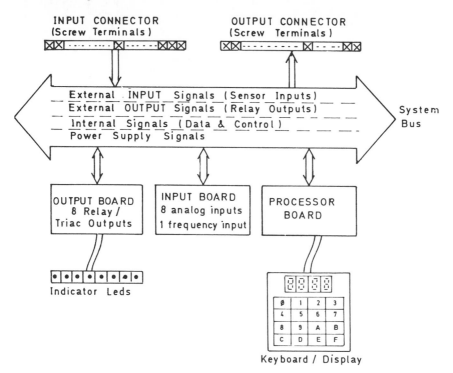

Figure 22.4: Hardware structure of the AMC

Apart from the main board with system bus and power supply, there are four smaller boards which implement specific functions: three are identically sized (12 cm x 7 cm) boards which can be plugged into any of the four bus slots (the processor, input and output board) and a keyboard/display board which is mounted on the front panel for interaction with the operator. The whole system is very compact and is contained in a (11 cm x 13 cm x 26 cm) wall-mounted case.

A block scheme of the processor board is given in Figure 22.5. The well known MC6809 8/16 bit microprocessor chip is surrounded by four other popular VLSI chips.

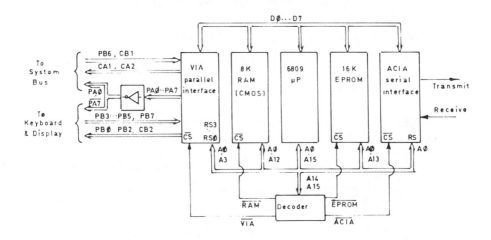

Figure 22.5: Block scheme of processor board

The program code is stored in a 16 Kbyte EPROM chip; the program data in an 8 Kbyte RAM chip. The CMOS static RAM chip is plugged into a 28 pin DIP socket with a built-in CMOS watch function, a non-volatile RAM controller circuit and an embedded lithium energy source. This provides a complete solution to problems associated with memory volatility and uses a common energy source to maintain time and date.

There is no battery backup on the system level, therefore when there is a power shut-down the processor stops running. This is not considered to be a serious drawback for the kind of applications that were envisaged (there is indeed a good chance that the power for the actuators will be off as well). However, it is important that after power start-up the control system should restart automatically, having the exact time of day available (because the operator setpoint, for example, a heating schedule, may be a function of time) and with the same data as just before shut-down. This is especially important when using self-adaptive control algorithms, because the controller actions are based on the estimated numerical process model, which should not be lost.

The ACIA chip (Asynchronous Communications Interface Adapter, MC6850) allows for serial communication with any computer (usually a PC) which has a standard RS232 interface. In this way, it is possible (albeit not essential) to send all measured and internal data from the AMC system to a PC for supervision or further processing, or to receive data and instructions from the PC: for example, for remote operation instead of local operation via the keyboard. This option has turned out to be a valuable feature, especially when co-ordinating several AMC systems in a larger application environment.

Perhaps the most important chip on the processor board is the VIA (Versatile Interface Adapter, SY6522) because it is the interface between the processor and all other system functions such as sensor inputs, relay outputs, keyboard input and display output. The control and data transfers for all these functions have been realised through a relatively low number of binary input-output lines. This was possible only when using the same signals for different functions and multiplexing them in time, resulting in a less straightforward, but low cost hardware design and essentially more complex software.

The input board contains three main parts:

1. The electronic circuits to translate the input signals coming from the external sensors into a suitable 0-5 V DC signal; as the system was initially built for climate control applications, the currently available input sensors are for temperature and relative humidity.

2. An electronic multiplexer to convert the selected 0-5 V DC signal into a 0-5 KHz block wave; the frequency is measured directly by means of a counter in the VIA chip - in this way the analogue sensor signals are converted into a digital value.

The output board contains eight output switches (relay or triac) which are controlled from the VIA binary output signals PA0...PA7 by means of the CA2 signal which acts as enable input to an octal D-type latch. When the enable is high, the latch outputs will follow the data inputs PA0...PA7. When the enable is taken low, the outputs will be latched at the levels that were set up at the inputs. Each of the eight output switches has a corresponding LED indicating its state on the system front panel.

22.2.6 System software

All software is developed on a MC6809 microcomputer development system. The executable code is then stored in the 16 Kbyte EPROM chip of the target system. As the target system itself does not run under the supervision of an operating system, the software for the self-adaptive microprocessor controller has to include the low level procedures for the real-time control of all system hardware.

Normally, this is done in a low level computer language such as assembler. However, in this project all software (including the low level procedures such as timer control, interrupt processing and input/output port manipulation) is programmed in PASCAL. The PASCAL compiler has some extensions to the standard language which permits this low level programming.

The heart of the AMC system is a timer in the VIA chip which is interrupting the processor every 20 milliseconds. The time critical tasks that are initiated by the timer tick are, for example, keyboard input, display refreshing, time of the day updating, sensor measurement and control. The remaining part of the processor time - between the finishing of the interrupt service routine and the arrival of the next timer interrupt - is for eventual dialogue with the user. This can be referred to as the background program, while the interrupt handling part of the software is called the foreground program.

The background program consists of two parts: first, the initialisation procedures and a loop executing the user interface (dialogue) software which is running as a low priority task and which is interrupted every 20 ms by the foreground (high priority) tasks. At power-on, the necessary RAM locations are initialised with default values, the VIA and ACIA chips are properly initialised and the time of day is read from the battery protected CMOS watch. From now on, the VIA timer is allowed to interrupt the background program every 20 ms, while it is waiting for keyboard input from the user.

The main part of the foreground program contains the control algorithms, including the sensor measurements, the relay setting and the communication procedure. This part is repeated every five seconds. It can take one or more seconds to execute depending on the number of measurements, the complexity of the control algorithms, and whether or not PC communication is requested etc.. Obviously, the other parts of the interrupt service procedure (for instance, keyboard scanning and display refreshing) must be executed strictly every 20 ms (and take only a few milliseconds to execute). The control part should start by allowing new interrupts, thus resulting in a program structure with nested interrupts and several priority levels.

22.3 APPLICATIONS

The system described thus far is essentially a small general purpose microcomputer controller. It offers some nice application possibilities for low cost automatic control and regulation in the field of climate control. This section contains a brief summary of some recent applications. The control of a building heating system will be described in detail using a specific example.

22.3.1 Greenhouse climate control

Temperature and relative humidity (%RH) are important parameters that should be kept close to a desired value in order to stimulate growth and quality of the crops. The main disturbing effect is outside weather (solar radiation, temperature, rain and wind). The actuators that can be used for control are essentially heat supply and ventilation windows. The popularity of minicomputers and microcomputers for the control of greenhouses is steadily growing. In practice, control procedures are improved by adding decisions. The combination of one or more AMC systems for basic temperature and humidity control with an optional PC for monitoring and rule-based control has an obviously promising future.

22.3.2 Incubator control

Here, temperature is an extremely important parameter which should be kept within a range of +/- 0.1 degrees Centigrade around a reference value that slowly varies with time during the incubation period. Also humidity has to be controlled to within a few %RH. The air is ventilated around the eggs and is heated by means of electrical resistors. The temperature is kept within a specified range by switching the heating power on and off frequently by means of the AMC triac outputs: there is no mechanical wear.

The air is moistened by means of blades turning in and out of a water reservoir. The driving motor is controlled by the AMC system on the basis of the measured and desired humidity. The setpoint for temperature and relative humidity can be pre-programmed by the user for the whole incubation period and for several different types of egg.

22.3.3 Building heating control

A typical configuration that can be controlled by a single AMC system is illustrated in Figure 22.6.

The residence is divided into four heating zones (each consisting of one or more rooms) which are controlled independently. Three of them (1, 2 and 3) are underfloor heated, the fourth being heated by a large surface (low temperature) radiator. The following instrumentation is available for the control of the heating system: temperature sensors for the outside air; the boiler water and supply water; a valve motor for the four-way mixture; a temperature sensor in each zone for the room air; and an electro-thermic valve which can shut-off the circuit. The seven temperature sensors are connected to the input board of the AMC system. The eight relays (triacs) of the output board are used to switch the circulation pump, the boiler, the mixture valve (open/close) and the four shut-off valves on or off, as appropriate.

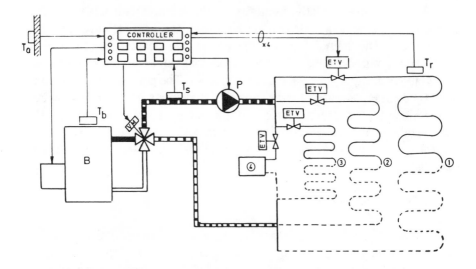

Figure 22.6: Configuration of building heating control system

The desired room temperature is pre-programmed independently as a function of time for each zone, which ensures that a zone is heated only when occupied. This is the only information which the user has to enter in order for the system to operate. Specific characteristics about the building (such as heating curves that have to be tuned by the user in current weather dependent control systems or gain constants for a modulating mixture valve regulator) are totally absent. All parameters are identified and optimised by the control software itself from information in the measured data, resulting in a self-learning or self-adaptive control system. This software can be described as being a simple rule-based expert control system (Astrom et al., 1986; Sutton, 1984) in which an essential part of the knowledge is obtained by means of self-learning algorithms.

22.4 REAL-LIFE EXPERIMENTS

The operation of the hardware and software of the AMC system has been thoroughly investigated by means of simulation studies and by real-life demonstration projects. Some results are described by De Keyser (1985).

Typical real-life results of the building heating control application are sum-
marised below.

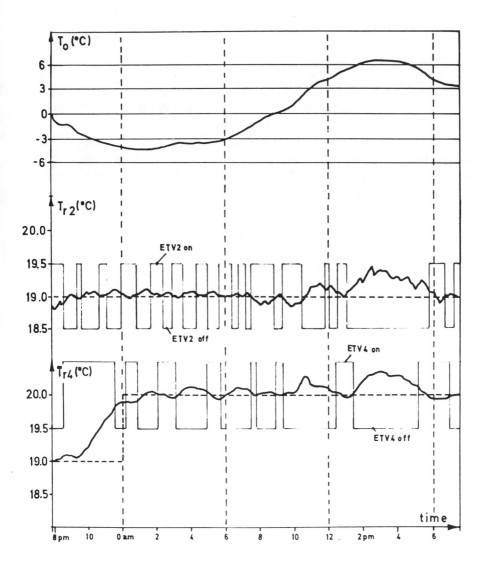

Figure 22.7: Experimental results

The upper part of Figure 22.7 shows the variation of the outside air temperature To during a 24 hour period. The day/night difference is over 10 degrees. The middle part shows the measured temperature in zone 2 during that day as well as the position (open/closed) of the zone shut-off valve. The desired temperature was 19 degrees all day long. Obviously, the control performance can hardly be improved, the natural variations during the night (no disturbances of sun or occupants) being +/- 0.1 degrees. The lower part of Figure 22.7 shows how a setpoint increment (19 degrees to 20 degrees) is realised in zone 4.

22.5 CONCLUSIONS

A low cost self-adaptive microprocessor controller has been presented through a description of its system hardware and real-time software. The controller is somewhat general purpose in nature and could be applied to several real-life control problems in the field of heating and ventilation: two applications were briefly described. A further application, the control of a multi-zone building heating system was presented with the controller proposed as a viable solution.

22.6 REFERENCES

Astrom, K.J., Anton, J.A. and Arzen, K.E. (1986), *Expert Control*, Automatica, 22, (3), 277-286.
De Keyser, R.M.C. (1985), *Adaptive microcomputer control of residence heating*, CIB-W79 Recent Advances in the Control and Operation of Building HVAC Systems, SINTEF Trondheim, 154-164.
Sutton, R.W. (1984), *Expert Systems for Process Control*, in Bennett, S and Linkens, A. (eds), Real-time Computer Control, Peter Peregrinus Ltd., London, 247-251.

Chapter 23
Towards the integrated environment for intelligent buildings

J.A. POWELL

23.1 INTRODUCTION

People want to be in control of their own lives, their own environments and their own futures. They have begun to realise they no longer have to rent or own buildings that fall apart, are unhealthy or are just plain 'sick'. Neither do they have to work or live in uncomfortable conditions, ones which are difficult to make secure, or conversely provide inadequate means of escape in case of fire. As earlier papers in this volume detail, they no longer have to. For we now undoubtedly have the technology to design intelligent buildings which, for a small extra initial capital outlay, can be mindful of building occupants' needs by effectively controlling conditions to maintain equilibrium under most commonly occuring situations.

Recent media coverage of the above, together with trade and white collar union pressures, especially in Canada and the US, have resulted in increased occupant demands for buildings which truly respond to users' present and future needs. This has led those acquiring buildings to become more discriminating in the buildings they choose to occupy. Even developers have caught on to the concept of intelligent buildings as a benefit in the marketing of new and sometimes old premises. For as one New York developer recently commented "a building only becomes an intelligent building to me when it is fully rented". For him, and others, there is no doubt that if buildings have to become more intelligent in order to be sold they will become more intelligent, and quickly.

But what form should that intelligence actually take and who should be given the task of designing intelligent buildings? The primary purpose of this paper is to examine these two questions in some detail, on the assumption that the technical means do exist to build workable designs. Later in this paper, the argument will be put forward for user-intelligent buildings, where individual users can selectively control their own environments and indicate why only certain multi-discipline design teams could even begin to produce such buildings and 'stage manage' them properly into the real world.

23.2 WHAT ARE INTELLIGENT BUILDINGS AND WHAT SHOULD THEY BECOME?

23.2.1 Conventional intelligence

Currently, the most generally accepted definition of an intelligent building, according to the general manager of Intelligent Building Services (Stubbings, 1986) is "one which totally controls its own environment". In such a definition the emphasis is seen to be on the building, or rather its management computer system, taking control by technical means over: heating and air conditioning, lighting, security, fire protection, telecommunication and data services, lifts and other similar building operations. For those who accept this conventional definition, 'intelligence' tends to be remote from the users and presently focusses on to two functionally independent facets of providing a suitable technical fix: integration of environmental building controls; and distribution of voice, data and video communications by means of new information technology (Sennewald, 1986). These facets and their associated problems are now discussed in a little more detail.

(A)   AUTOMATED BUILDING ENVIRONMENTAL CONTROL
The environmental conditions in a conventional intelligent building (or zones within a large one) are typically served by a dedicated microcomputer (outstation) supervised by a central controller. Here, electronic management systems based upon the concept of distributed intelligence are starting to be introduced in the UK to control particular, known and easily controllable performance characteristics of many buildings, such as temperature and lighting (to effect energy saving), security and smoke detection.

Under such building control regimes, while temperature and lighting could be selectively controlled by occupants or smoke detector systems could become part of an early warning information system for all users, the favoured strategy is conventionally to direct all information through a central control. Access to information about a building's performance, whether it is through smoke detectors or thermal sensors, resides within the self-correcting computer programme controller, which is open to the influence of its guardians only (for example, engineers, building security officials and safety officers).

While there are important reasons for this being an efficient way of providing information to those who have certain responsibilities in a building, it is important to stress that this building management solution is part of a social, as well as technical, system. Such systems cannot work independently of the social organisation of a building. The technical solution can create or reinforce a network of communication and information in which certain individuals only are in control.

In terms of life safety, and smoke detection, research of human behaviour in public building fires suggests that people should be given far more accurate and timely information than is often supposed (Sime, 1986). While computer-managed information warning systems could work much more efficiently than fire alarm sirens in alerting the public, their effectiveness in increasing life safety will diminish if information is restricted to building managers. In the same respect, computer-based energy management may extend the scope of managerial control at the expense of the freedom of action of an individual (Cooper, 1983; Powell, Sime and Perkins, 1986).

The problem is that most microelectronics are being applied with the aim of not only maintaining a level of building performance within buildings to make environments more comfortable (for example, consistent with recommendations such as an acceptable temperature margin in schools of within 2 degrees Centigrade of 18 degrees: (DES, 1987)), but of controlling energy consumption or other important resources. Indeed, the introduction of control technology into non-domestic buildings is being actively promoted for that purpose with strong government backing (Cooper, 1982, 1983).

Managerial staff are being exhorted to install in their premises equipment, described as being Energy Management Systems (EMS), which a government spokesman hopes will lead to maximum cost effective energy efficiency (Jonas, 1979). According to such criteria, EMS systems have anecdotally been shown to produce considerable short term savings in some homes, schools and offices.

To date, the amount of systematic research on user response to EMS is fairly limited. To give one a flavour of what has so far been found let us turn to the most rigorous analysis that has been undertaken, for schools. Between 1981 and 1983 an Electronic Energy Management System for monitoring heating systems was introduced by Hereford and Worcester County Council into some 50 of its schools. The energy efficiency performance (including costs of installation and energy consumed) of a sample of the schools was monitored on behalf of the Energy Technology Support Unit (ETSU) by the Building Services Research and Information Association (BSRIA).

A complementary assessment of teachers satisfactions with environmental conditions was carried out by Interlogos Ltd as part of the same appraisal on behalf of ETSU. Here, user knowledge of the EMS and desired degree of control over the temperature and heating were assessed before and after the introduction of the EMS in a comparative survey of teachers opinions using a questionnaire issued in 20 of the county schools. These 20 schools cover a range of age groups: infants, juniors, middle and high. The schools were constructed between the interwar period and the late 1970s and include single and multi-storey structures of conventional and lightweight construction. Heating was fuelled by oil or gas, or a combination of the two. In general, the research on behalf of ETSU revealed a fuel cost saving for 1982/83 in 26 schools of 13.3%. Furthermore, the survey of teachers revealed ''no overall and significant change in the quality of the working environments in the schools''.

The ETSU energy saving demonstration programme has produced similar, though not as systematically rigorous, findings for both homes and offices. We can therefore conclude from these that, at least in the short term, electronic environmental management systems can work to produce savings without lowering environmental quality. However, unless thoughtfully designed, well and humanly managed, and fully accepted by a building's occupants, the sort of automated environment provided by an EMS can make users feel they are being watched and controlled.

As a result there may be a longer term social and psychological 'price to pay' as users begin to submissively fight against their controlling influence. Such criticisms are increasingly being voiced by those who have studied such systems in use (Cooper, 1983; Haigh, 1982; Powell, Sime and Perkins, 1986; and Mill, 1986). As a result of their observations, these social scientists now strongly argue that it is almost a psychological necessity for building occupants to have the ability to control their own surroundings.

Nevertheless, the tendency is for building designers and managers to try to socially engineer people's behaviour - treating people not as active participants in the running of a building, but rather like the physical environment itself as a 'non-thinking object'. Architects, engineers and, indeed, policy makers may feel they can easily control people through such means (Sime, 1985). If people do not like to be controlled in this way, it is hardly surprising that they may feel disinclined to conserve energy.

As Cooper (1982) has poignantly argued: ''for those whose ultimate aim is to persuade people to accept the necessity of conserving energy and other costly resources in non-domestic buildings, the introduction of controlled environments, and of centralised electronic management systems may prove counter-productive, in the medium to long run. Deprived of, and denied, the means and experience of altering their environmental conditions, occupants may respond by feeling that they have been relieved of responsibility to ensure that resource consumption is reduced''.

Furthermore, when such systems 'go down' users do not go out of their way to inform management of problems unless it is in their interest. Rather, as shown by Powell et al. (1986) for teachers using school buildings and Hartkopf et al. (1983) for office occupants, users tinker with parts of the system open to them for their own benefit. This often has disasterous effects counter to the ones desired by the control system. Furthermore, Powell et al. and Hartkopf, et al. have also found problems with the hardware itself. They repeatedly observed uncalibrated sensors; improperly functioning linkage networks between sensor and controller; systems improperly installed; systems not being operated as intended (lack of training and user 'cussedness'); and local sensors not corresponding to local needs due to frequent spatial layout changes.

Many architects/owners are unaware of just how long it takes to get a building system to work effectively: you don't just buy it and turn it on. Furthermore, if users do not fully accept the system or feel themselves not to be fully integrated into its use, their negative feelings will act to overthrow the system or at the very least be made aggressively known to their managers: not a good organisational environment to get greater co-operation and enhanced productivity.

(B)   AUTOMATED BUILDING INFORMATION TECHNOLOGY

The aspirations for advanced information technology systems are profound: full televisual and data communication, information handling and computation constructively linking all users within the system. The systems available today are far from being so profound and in their somewhat restricted form are usually only found in the most high technology office situations.

Automation of information systems expressed in their correct form has the paradoxical effect of vastly enhancing the power and capacity of data storage, retrieval, transmissions and calculation while at the same time incorporating a new set of constraints imposed by the need to formalise, that is, to create explicit, precise, regular and inflexible meanings and relationships that can be programmed (Weizenbaum, 1976).

Providing office users with the capacity, through information technology, to call up more analyses and more data inevitably puts pressure on them to do so. However, this may only increase their sense of incoherence and insecurity because their difficulty is to know what the real problem is - only then can they have the proper premises for information definition and selection. More information may only confuse and obscure this, especially since in most systems information is anonymous and impersonal, rendering impossible the use of personal reference as a credibility check. The end result may well be delay, increased stress and reduced management effectiveness.

Furthermore, when automated information systems are based upon falsely rationalistic models of information and decision making, they begin to demand a more precise definition for their information. This itself leads to an increased differentiation, in terms of autonomy and flexibility of task, between top and middle management in almost any office organisation. The path to define the agenda, to set organisational goals effectively, which, in turn, implicitly defines what counts as information, will move even further up the organisation with the increased formalisation that the information system will demand. This could easily deprive middle management of whatever formal and informal flexibility, autonomy and responsibility it is usually able to cultivate.

The result could be a de-skilling of much of management with a lessening of personal identification with the job, increased alienation and consequent destruction of loyalty, counter to the desired effect of the information system. This in itself will create a further requirement for external supervision and control, leading to a greater pressure on higher level managers who must administer it, but also to an increased sense of alienation at lower levels in a vicious cycle of escalation and polarisation.

Consciously or not managers are likely to adapt their role, style and outlook to correspond with the system in which they work. If they do so adapt, conflict and extra pressure is likely to manifest itself as a result of authoritarian and remote styles of management; if they do not, they are in conflict with the automated information system that is supposed to be their aid.

Systems designed on empirically unsound models of the real social world of managers and other building users simply succeed in placing them in what has been called 'psychological failure and double bind' in which organisational success means personal failure, and the reverse. As Wynne and Otway (1983) have noted, such automated information systems may even offer those at lower levels the explicit opportunity to engage in 'creative insurgence', the creative interpretation of directives in ways which contribute to the time effectiveness and goals of the organisation and, at the same time, give meaning to their own working lives.

The advent of microelectronic technology in advanced building control and information provision was meant to liberate the human condition and make it more effective. Unfortunately, as discussion of the above facets highlight, there have been worrying observations in the first generation of buildings which try to make use of such technology to control people - the automated or conventionally intelligent buildings.

So far, such buildings only seem able to provide automated, rather than user responsive, control over a fairly restricted range of environmental factors; to provide access to a rather formal and managerially centred information system which heavily constrains user autonomy and flexibility. On both counts such conventionally intelligent systems are often seen by workers or users to be an overt manifestation of traditional managerial authority, where environmental or information edicts emanating from on high are simply reflected in the systems monitoring and control functions. Lower level users of buildings in which such systems operated are only involved in responding to the systems environmental wishes, in translating policy edicts into specific form and enactments, in monitoring and maintenance of the system or in producing raw information for the system to analyse. Such conventionally intelligent buildings in no sense appear to be neutral to their users. Rather they become a serious invasion of privacy, providing possibilities for continuous, but discrete surveillance and control at a distance. A frightening potential for abuse which it is hoped the next generation of user-intelligent buildings should move towards overcoming.

23.2.2 Appropriate intelligence

An alternative view of building intelligence suggests itself from the Latin roots of the word intelligence itself: inter, meaning between and legere, meaning to see, to gather and to choose. From this base an intelligent building would be one that enabled users to see, gather and choose information relevant to their own handling of their own environmental and organisational problems - problems and considerations often novel to themselves occuring between those recognised at a building's inception.

In cybernetic terms, the building should provide requisite variety to match the spectrum of variety in those using it, namely the building's occupants. In my mind this can only occur when the occupants are fully integrated into the system, where system and user blend to form a whole. Of necessity and because of the human dimensions, such systems must be dynamically responsive and provide a co-ordinated strategy in which users can actively control their own environments and their access to the information in the system that they want (not simply that predefined by the systems managers). This would be a tall order if the system were to take on full responsibility for its control. It is perfectly possible if users become more actively involved in the process. For both system and occupant need to be equally involved in control to create a workable dynamic equilibrium that affects aware resource management while maintaining environmental comfort.

The key factor in whether the intelligence system of a building will prove constructive or otherwise to users and their organisations is probably that of autonomy: how flexible will the 'official' system be (how flexible can it afford to be) to autonomous local definitions of relevance to a user? Those who have substantial discretion in the decision about whether, when and how to use a building's intelligence system will feel enhanced by it because they can utilise it as a relatively flexible resource to fit their many social agendas (Kling, 1980).

This returns us to the question of power and control in any humanly related systems, whether they be an electronic building controller or otherwise. We have seen the problems that occur when such a controller is based upon the somewhat authoritarian classical and rather hierarchical model of an organisa-

tion. An alternative model for such systems is that of 'pluralistic power
coalition' proposed by Wynne and Otway (1983). The essence of their model
is openness and negotiation towards shared goals which all accept. In any
organisation this model suggests there will be several information cultures
each probably competing to achieve its own desired ends. Their model
recognises that authority and coherence can only exist through negotiation
which requires repeated human interaction for reaffirmation. Therefore,
building intelligence systems, as value systems, must be open in principle to redesign and re-orientation (not just technical data input) from junior levels
(including middle management).

In other words, such systems must recognise and relate meaningfully to
local environmental and informal informational needs. If they are not in this
way open, then those local value and information systems will simply create
their own autonomous means of survival, alienated from the organisation's
overall values and purposes. They will need continued suppression, surveillance and formal control, engendering more devious strategies of evasion,
which in turn engender more elaborate regulations and so on in a gradually self-
destructive spiral.

Recognising that all organisations (taken here simply to mean more than
one individual working with others) using buildings are coalitions of diverse
interest, more or less legitimate, is to accept that to have positive effects, any
building intelligence system will have to allow for human negotiation and
interpersonal differences. It will also have to recognise, make explicit and
attempt to understand, no matter how crudely to begin with, extact human
relationships within the system and the emotional roots of many rational
actions, processes and responses. It should be able to embrace the different
interpretations of those who have decided to exist within the system as part of
their everyday lives.

In short, to be successful, it would have to reflect real man/environment
contexts and be open to evolution in the face of changing but proper and
valuable uses. As such these changes should slowly be revealed by the users
rather than be imposed on the basis of a questionable or negative framework
about these users. Such an approach would have to be more cautious, modest,
sensitive and selective to the implementation of intelligence systems than
hitherto seen or promised.

A suitable user-intelligent approach to building intelligence design has
been developed and tested by Hartkopf et al. (1983) in the Canadian context.
The involvement of users in the plan of work for design, construction and
facilities management of a user-intelligent building is the key to its success.
The particulars of extra user involvement are:

1. The building design and its user controlled intelligence is conceived and developed with the help of the eventual users during the

planning and design stage. Even at these early stages users are allowed to explore alternatives through full scale mock-ups and to take part in the design process using specially developed techniques (O'Brien, 1981).

2. Users are allowed to continue this intervention at all stages during the design process, through its construction and in its commissioning. This is truly a decision making involvement, backed up by building 'walkthrough' surveys and adequate briefing; all given in a language appropriate to the user's understanding.

3. The design team attempt to provide users with as much autonomy and flexibility as possible in their design of localised user controlled task and living environments.

4. During both commissioning and routine maintenance, a series of building diagnostic techniques are employed to determine if the building is actually working to specification.

5. The final 'honing' of the individually or user contolled building intelligence takes place during and after the commissioning process. Each individually based environmental control system is made to integrate fully with local use patterns and needs. This requires the design team, not only to produce user sensitive designs, but also to 'stage manage' those designs into the real world - adapting, extending and focussing them where necessary in response to user's demands.

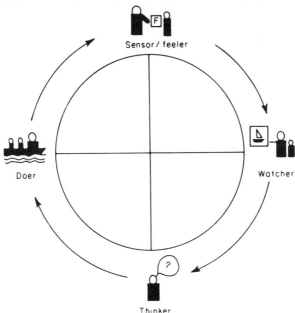

Figure 23.1: The learning cycle (after Kolb)

The design, construction and proper commissioning of user-intelligent buildings, so that they reflect the fullest integration of current building intelligent technology, with individual and organisational needs, can add up to 25% to the capital cost of a building. Nevertheless, organisations increasingly think this to be worthwhile because of the large 'cost in use' savings that can eventually result.

For instance, Brill *et al* (1984) have suggested that appropriate environmental contexts in offices (enclosure and layout) can have a yearly organisational worth amounting to almost one seventh of a manager's/professional's productivity. Furthermore, Powell *et al* (1986) have observed that where school building designs allow appropriate selective teacher control of the environments, the savings on energy are as great, if not greater, than for automated centrally controlled schools. What is more, the teachers are content with their environment and as a result these savings seem to continue with time.

It appears that when users feel themselves to be in control and where they know how to intervene constructively, they are able to generate comfortable, and supportive environments without wasting resources. Ensured of support and comfort, even with changing occupancy, task function or living conditions, users become truly part of the organisational team and not a 'mechanical cog' in its relentless roll onward. They may even become more productive - an extremely constructive behavioural modifier indirectly, rather than directly, influenced by the building design.

The above discussion indicates that fully maximised user intelligent buildings meet this requirement, but who should clients get to design them? The next section portrays the characteristics clients should look for in a good design team, to ensure that a dynamically responsive user-intelligent building is achieved.

23.3 THE ROUTE TO WELL DESIGNED USER-INTELLIGENT BUILDINGS

Studies by Powell *et al* (1982) indicate that the single most vital role the client has is his choice of designer. For no matter how professional the client, once designers are engaged they use all their subtle and subversive skills to move the client, slowly but surely, towards an overall solution consistent with their own attitudes and ways of thinking.

23.3.1 Designers' constrained strategies

Studies by Thompson (1982) and Newland *et al* (1987) of designers' approaches to thinking and designing suggest they employ a particular set of strategies. There appear to be four 'strategy sets' which are viable and the particular 'strategy set' taken onboard by each designer is closely related to the way each learns about his/her world. The ideal for learning has been portrayed by Kolb (1976) as a cycle (see Figure 23.1).

A learner senses the world, stands back to reflect on this feeling, thinks to create an abstract model and tests this in doing: it is the re-sensing that takes place in this action that initiates a new learning cycle.

In the context of architectural design, however, this ideal cycle is very much curtailed. As Newland *et al* (1987) have shown, good decision makers tend to operate on shorter cycles. They align themselves with a strategy set which allows them to make faster decisions. Some operate mainly within one arc or quadrant of the circle.

For instance, entrepreneurial types move on an arc between sensing and doing; whereas design engineers and technologists, such as lighting experts and acousticians, tend to watch the world and then think about it. 'Watching' here implies systematic observation. 'Sensing' is more intuitive and feeling based. It is important to stress that these observations are of architectural designers' preferred action styles. Someone who is mainly a thinker-doer is perfectly capable of sensing or watching.

However, in practice, within the pressures of conventional design time, designers will normally operate with a design style and manner conforming to their preferred way of learning about the world. They are rarely prepared to change the way they learn about new ideas, it takes too much effort. As a result, architectural designers tend to think about and design using one of four rather different and independent strategies. Powell (1987) has styled these designers as Dynamics, Focussed, Rigorous and Contemplatives. Each of these architectural designers is now briefly discussed.

(A)   DYNAMIC DESIGNERS

These are entrepreneurs and innovators whose learning is rooted in 'sensing and doing'. Their real world is the concrete, physical world. For them the incidents of life, the dynamic, dramatic, active events and the continuous awareness of the changing present and the future possibilities they create, are taken as the basis for understanding. They are in a continual process of being shaped by their surroundings and are gregarious for variety in an attempt to widen their perspectives trying anything new as long as they are actively and personally involved.

Independent and assertive, their world perception allows an opportunistic nature; an adventurous attitude which gives them the ability to switch swiftly from a capacity to be entrepreneurial, initiating profit centres, to an ability for rapidly producing innovative designs. Those dynamics who become entrepreneurs move their basic learning towards abstract patterning; those who become innovators towards reflective observation. They make the brief fit their ideas for the building; in other words they influence the world as much as is necessary to accommodate their ideas. These designers are the ones encapsulated, or at least desire to be encapsulated, either in the architectural glossies or within the professional, financial and management pages of national newspapers. If you want an unusual design you would seek out the excitement of a dynamic designer who would 'shape' you something novel.

(B)　　FOCUSSED DESIGNERS

The real world for the focussed designer is the concrete, physical, objective world. Focussed designers are those who started by watching and sensing the world, and have often ended up wanting to do something about it. Down-to-earth types, rather than abstract thinkers, they often become campaigners for alternative energy technologies or the 'small is beautiful' philosophy. They worry about the depletion of natural resources and ask questions like "can or should we do this...or this...or this, and what will happen if we don't get it right?" For them objects, and especially nature, must be seen for what they are.

They will take people into account so long as it does not conflict with nature's interests (which, according to them, should be in all people's interests in the long term). They are good at practical evaluation and resource investigation. They are also guardians of society's rights. If you want something built that will actually work and work well these are the designers for you. They turn concepts into practical solutions (as long as they agree with these concepts in the first place).

(C)　　RIGOROUS DESIGNERS

The real world for the rigorous designer is understood through abstract thoughts and mental constructions. These designers have learned to exist as effective designers by combining this abstracting propensity with either sensing needs (becoming managers who can turn strategies into manageable tasks) or with controlling action (becoming good bosses, making the best use of their colleagues' full potential). These designers are self-disciplined. They attempt to construct a reasonable understanding of the world by seeking out underlying patterns.

They can handle complex theories, their analysis is good and they like things to be objective. Within these constraints they need to be stretched. They are efficient planner designers who are the establishment's guardians of professional standards. They strongly believe they can create a suitable technical fix for every situation including creating environments that will control human behaviour. They have learned to be good organisers, make sure a job is completed on time and can be valuable chair persons. They would produce the ordinary but competent solution as long as the right guidance and tolerances were there on which it could be based.

(D)   CONTEMPLATIVE DESIGNERS

Contemplative designers are watchers and thinkers who may feel no powerful urge to get involved in the world. They are continually analysing data thoroughly, looking for abstract patterns to explain the world. Often the grand holistic insight eludes them. They therefore have difficulty in reaching decisions, usually working best if there is someone else there to help make the decisions or to define their role and job precisely. Most contemplative designers make good job architects, for instance. They make their building fit the brief as exactly as is possible, modifying their own ideas to be acceptable to the bosses whether they be a fellow designer or client.

22.3.2 All-round designers

There are some designers who exhibit combinations of the above strategies but those who tend towards the 'all-round' turn out to be unable to make decisions fast enough to survive as designers. Paradoxically, to ensure the successful design of a fully integrated building and its stage management into the real world, we need an all-round but fast acting decision maker: someone who is good with people and can listen; can be innovative and shape ideas; can organise and evaluate; can understand resource implications and how to optimise; prepared to work selflessly to get the work finished on time; and finally can co-ordinate all this into a new, unique and humanly responsive whole.

The aforementioned studies by Thompson, and Newland and his colleagues, clearly indicate that such abilities, skills and understanding cannot reside, with any quality, in the mind of one design individual. The pressures of time dependent decision making almost exclude this as a possibility. However, there is no reason why a good design team should not possess all the above functional skills necessary for the design of user-intelligent building design and be a workable synergistic team: such teams already exist.

23.3.3 Successful design teams

Almost twenty years ago the author undertook a year's postguaduate course leading to a Masters Degree in Design. This course trained a small group, from different disciplines, in the art of combining as a team to produce better designs. Those responsible for the course had a vision of the future where designing would no longer be a typically individualistic pursuit, rather it would be undertaken by teams of caring individuals having differing but complementary skills. In the author's continued working relationships with colleagues from that course it has become apparent that we had been taught a very rare skill in design - the ability to work as complementary team members rather than as individualistic designers or team leaders. Experiences of working in several multi-discipline teams, together with observations of other successful design teams, confirms the author's view that it is only they, and not individuals, who can effectively orchestrate the sort of rich and humanly responsive architectural ensemble appropriate for user-intelligent building design.

There are several multi-discipline design practices operating in the UK who could field a multi-discipline group capable of such designing. Potential clients, and those designers who want to form good teams, need to be aware of the right characteristics for team membership. Belbin (1983) has shown that all professional team members exhibit a dual role. The first, the functional, is obvious, individuals belong to the team for the specialist experience they can bring to bear on any problem. The second role, the team role, is less obvious but equally important if a team is to be successful in meeting its objectives well.

(A) FUNCTIONAL ROLES

Any team required to design a user-intelligent building clearly needs much of the same experience and technical expertise as is available in traditional architectural design. There needs to be an architect, a quantity surveyor and both structural and service engineers. There also needs to be at least someone who has: social science skills, who can elicit user needs and have sufficient design knowledge to help the design team produce user responsive designs; social skills, to help the stage management of the design into the real world; building diagnostic skills, to access, and improve a building's physical and control characteristics; design knowledge of current building intelligence systems and the ability to commission them.

Particular building design problems will also suggest designers having other functional expertise. Clients should seek the appropriate combination for their problem. When looking for a good team they should ask several design practices to indicate the functional skills of the team members the practice intends to involve in the scheme design. They should compare such a skills' profile with the performance profile required for their building. These can be arrived at quite simply using the criteria given in the paper by Mill, elsewhere in this volume.

(B) TEAM ROLE

It is clearly necessary to have team members with the appropriate functional skills to ensure successful intelligent building design. However, functional expertise is not in itself sufficient to ensure success. Belbin has shown that effective teams are invariably comprised of individuals showing a balanced mix of personalities or team skills. Characteristics which would be incompatible in one individual, (see previous section), can combine well in a group: drive, prudence, enthusiasm, understanding, opportunism and reliability are all needed. It is a fact of life that each of us has strengths and weaknesses and that we can only play certain roles effectively. Seen in this context of a team, this is not a negative idea. None of us is perfect, but a group of people, whose team and functional strengths and talents complement each other, can be. Belbin has isolated just eight roles as the only ones available to team members:

1. *Chairman:* ensures that the best use is made of each member's potential. The chairman is self-disciplined, dominant but not domineering.

2. *Shapers:* look for patterns and try to shape the team's efforts in this direction. They are out going, impulsive and impatient. They make the team feel uncomfortable but they make things happen.

3. *Innovators:* are the source of original ideas. They are imaginative and uninhibited. They are bad at accepting criticism and may need careful handling to provide that vital spark.

4. *Evaluators:* more measured and dispassionate. They like time to analyse and mull things over.

5. *Organisers:* turn strategies into manageable tasks which people can get on with. They are disciplined, methodical and sometimes inflexible.

6. *Entrepreneurs:* go outside the group and bring back information and ideas. They make friends easily and have a mass of contacts. They prevent the team from stagnating.

7. *Team Workers:* promote unity and harmony within a group. They are more aware of people's needs than other members. They are the most active internal communicators and cement of the team.

8. *Finishers:* are compulsive 'meeters' of deadlines. They worry about what can go wrong and maintain a permanent sense of urgency which they communicate to others.

Belbin has shown that for a group to be successful it needs to be comprised of people having the right balance of the above role characteristics. Certain roles - that of the chair, shaper, and innovator - involve a higher profile in design than others and apparently involve greater kudos and prestige, but all eight roles are equally significant. Hart (1986) have developed a 'group skills development game', known as 'Teams', that can be used to clarify team roles for individuals and groups in any organisation.

This could be used by clients to assess the 'skills ability' of their chosen team or by design groups themselves in order to determine which team role characteristics their team is lacking. The advantage of 'Teams', as a game, is that although simple and enjoyable to play, it provides a context in which complex and emotive issues can be discussed and analysed in a positive and non-threatening way.

The work of Powell *et al* (1982) for housing associations, and Belbin (1983) show how teams balanced with respect to both functional and team roles will be most effective. This will require a balance of dynamic, focussed, rigorous and contemplative designers who have functional specialisms appropriate to the building design in hand.

23.4 CONCLUSIONS

This paper argues for user-intelligent buldings - those which enable good user control and encourage positive feedback. Such buildings will lead occupants to generate their own comfort and support without undue resource wastage. This may even lead to increased productivity as users feel themselves to be a greater part of the team - a team in which pluralistic negotiation is forged. Teamwork is also important in those who are chosen to design such user-intelligent buildings for it is only through such teamwork that major problems are perceived as challenges for which teams have the inherent ability to solve. Design teams having the right balance of functional and team role skills will galvanise to become the most effective when it comes to the design and stage management of fully integrated buildings into the real world. Fair warning to clients: it is in their choice that the balances rests.

23.5 REFERENCES

Belbin, R.M. (1983), *Management Teams: Why they succeed or fail,* Heinemann, London.
Brill, M., Margulis, S. and Konar, E. (1984), *Using Office Design to Increase Productivity,* BOSTI, Buffalo, N.Y..
Cooper, I. (1982), *Occupant control over energy consumption in non-domestic premises: a question of perspective,* in Consumers, Buildings and Energy, Stafford (ed), CURS, University of Birmingham, Birmingham.
Cooper, I. (1983), *Energy Conservation in Non-Domestic Buildings,* Design Policy, Design Council, London.
Haigh, D. (1982), *User response in Environmental Control,* in The Architecture of Energy, Hawkes, D. and Owers J. (eds), Construction Press, Lancaster.
Hart (1986), *Teams,* Hart Ltd, (The game is available direct from Hart, 56 Covent Garden, Cambridge, for _12.90 plus P & P).
Jonas, P. (1979), *Energy and Microprocessors,* British Institute of Management, London.
Kling, R. (1980), *Social Analysis of computing: theoretical perspectives in recent empirical research,* Computing Surveys, 12, (1).
Kolb, D.A. (1976), *The Learning Style Inventory Technical Manual,* MacBer and Company, Boston, MA..
Hartkopf, V., Loftness, V. and Mill, P.A.D. (1983), *The Concept of Total Building Performance and Building Diagnostics,* ASTM E6.24 Conference Proceedings, Bal Harbor, Florida.
Newland, P.M., Powell, J.A. and Creed, C. (1987), *Understanding architectural designers' selective information handling,* Design Studies, 8, (1).

O'Brien, D. (1981), *Design and evaluation methods: variations on a theme*, in Design: Science: Methods, Jacques and Powell (eds), Butterworths Scientific, London.
Powell, J.A., Platt, S., Piepe, R., Paterson, B. and Smyth, J. (1982), *Control or Charade*, SERC Final Report, SERC, Swindon.
Powell, J.A., Sime, J. and Perkins, M. (1986), *A Systemic Interdisciplinary Study of Energy Utilisation in British Primary Schools*, SERC Final Report, SERC, Swindon.
Powell, J.A. (1987), *Is Design a Trivial Pursuit*, Design Studies, 8, (4).
Sennewald, B. (1986), *Smart Buildings*, Architectural Technology, March-April.
Sime, J. (1985), *Designing for people or ball-bearings?* Design Studies, 6, (3).
Stubbings, M. (1986), *Intelligent Buildings*, Contracts Journal, August.
Thompson, M. (1982), *A Three Dimensional Model*, in Essays in the Sociology of Perception, Douglas, M. (ed), Routledge and Kegan Paul, London.
Weizenbaum, N. (1976), *Computer Power and Human Reason*, Freeman, London.
Wynne, B. and Otway, H. (1983), *Information Technology Power and Managers*, in Office Technology and People, Elsevier.

Chapter 24
The shape of the future

F. DUFFY

24.1 INTRODUCTION

Lack of depth is the usual price paid for breadth of ambition. However, in order to make sense of the current enthusiasm for the intelligent office building it is necessary not only to investigate what is happening in countries as widely dispersed as Japan, Sweden and the US but also to indulge in a rather liberal interpretation of what office buildings actually are. The first benefit of this point of view is that a great deal can be learned by architects and clients from contrasts between offices built in different countries (and for different organisations) particularly about values held by the individuals and about the social structures which make up the modern office organisation. The second benefit is that a better understanding of how offices are built and serviced, over time, is of great practical advantage to those who must manage rapidly changing organisations.

The phase 'intelligent building' means many things to many different people. A futuristic view would lead one to imagine buildings which had learned to walk towards the sun, or away from its burning rays, depending upon the latitude for which they were built; buildings which could anticipate not only the extremes of climate but also the likely pattern of diurnal use so that scarce energy could be expended with the utmost parsimony; buildings which know where everything and everyone was at any time of day or night; buildings which recognise you and are sufficiently clever to hand you your raincoat and umbrella when you leave the door not because they don't know it is sunny in London but because they have learned from your diary that you are off on a trip to Manchester where rain, it so happens, is falling today.

Although these speculations are far from unrealisable, it is best to push them aside for the moment because they are so entertaining that they obscure several other themes in building intelligence which are much discussed but often confused.

24.2 FOUR DIMENSIONS OF BUILDING INTELLIGENCE

The clearest, if not absolutely the most complete, exposition of these themes is contained in an excellent document produced, naturally enough, in Japan, by the newly deregulated and privatised Nippon Telegraph & Telephone Company (NTT, the Japanese BT). NTT distinguishes three major aspects of building intelligence:

1. Office automation: a high level of office automation as provided by the building owner, either for his own organisation's use, or for tenants. Such features include built in Local Area Networks (LANs, or data highways to use a more colourful expression) together with a wide selection of high technology office equipment such as word processing, large volume printing, electronic filing, electronic diaries, credit card access for timekeeping or for access to cafeteria and common office services, software support, and even 'war rooms' where data is assembled and manipulated in electronic form for big decision makers.

2. Advanced telecommunications: the potential offered to tenants or user organisations to have ready access to a far more up-to-date and wider range of telecommunication services than they would normally expect. This wider range is achieved through digital switching and fibre optic cabling and leads not only to considerable advantages in volume and cost, but also to particular services such as FAX, voice mail, computer graphics, as well as voice, video and computer conferencing.

3. Building automation: the oldest and most reliable form of building intelligence which is based upon the integration, through electronics, of various sub-systems useful for running buildings such as building management, security protection, power and data, as well as energy.

NTT are quick to point out, not only in their documentation but also in their prototype intelligent building projects, such as their new Shinagawa complex, that these three aspects of intelligent building have important implications for the way in which buildings are planned and managed (for example, emerging methodologies in facilities management and space planning) as well as in the development of new kinds of building components (for example, better ducting systems for cables and air conditioning, more responsive lighting and furniture, building skins which react to light) and building techniques (life cycle costing, fast tracking of construction, greater responsiveness to changing demands).

But there is an irony here. Despite this wonderful shopping list, the reality is that the kinds of office building currently occupied by organisations such as Honda, Mitsubishi, Mitsui, Daiwa, Toshiba and Shimuzu are not only crushingly similar but, by advanced Western standards, elementary not just in quality but also in the application of information technology to office tasks. For a variety of complicated reasons (not least of which is the refractory nature of the Japanese language, especially its characters) the bulk of office technology used in Japan tends to be centralised and top-down rather than distributed and dynamic. Hence the environmental stress generated in many Western organisations by PCs and LANs seems still rare in Japan.

Perhaps this is why NTT fail to mention what seems to DEGW to be a colossally important aspect of building intelligence, that is the ability to adapt or change a building during its lifetime.

4. Responsiveness to change: the ability of buildings to accommodate, over time, changes in individual requirements and organisational demands.

24.3 RESPONDING TO CHANGE

Responsiveness to change is a more subtle, more qualitative, aspect of building intelligence, the need for which is well illustrated by the Dutch management consultants, Twijnstra's, projection of the changing mission of the office building. In the 1960s the design of office buildings was influenced primarily by organisational efficiency (remember O & M studies, the endless arrays of elementary steel furniture, and the appearance of the office before carpet came into general use). In the 1970s a new factor emerged which overtook but did not displace operational efficiency in office design: the need engendered by the energy crisis to cope with 'costs in use'.

Costs in use in their turn have been overtaken in the 1980s, but not supplanted, by a new wave of concern for office quality. Why this should happen just now is explained by the substantial changes in the structure of the office population brought by information technology: obedient, poorly paid clerks have been more or less replaced by better educated, more demanding, less easily satisfied professionals and managers who expect a better quality working environment. Twijnstra argue that the office environment of the 1990s will be influenced by another factor, the need to stimulate creativity, that is, to galvanise inert office organisations into greater teamwork and more demanding intellectual effort.

Architectural devices such as the atrium, which are often thought of simply as spatial gimmickry, can alternatively be interpreted as a powerful means of making people in large organisations more aware of the totality of the organisation and the relationships between its pacts, that is, a means, if used correctly, of stimulating organisational change.

There is little evidence of such environmental ambitions in Japan. In fact the reality is that most Japanese offices are stuck firmly in the era of operational efficiency, the only interesting feature of which is the use of the office environment to emphasise collectivity and teamwork. However, it is also clear that the Japanese are less than happy with their existing offices. In this sense, the Japanese are thus prepared to acknowledge what NTT omitted from its otherwise extremely comprehensive list of the features of the intelligent building - the fourth dimension of intelligence, the capacity to respond to new kinds of demand. Intelligent buildings mean 'better' buildings.

24.4 DEFINING 'BETTER' BUILDINGS

'Better' is defined by the four kinds of intelligence described above. However, a word about buildings is necessary; they are not quite what they seem. Indeed, in a time of rapid organisational and technological change, buildings cannot continue to be regarded as large, heavy permanent entities - slow to build and expensive to run. Office buildings, in particular, are contrived by the weaving together of four major factors:

1. Information technology: the storage, processing, and transmittal of information, primarily by electronic media.
2. Organisation: the social structure which holds people together to carry out office tasks.
3. Building technology: the means available for constructing and servicing the building fabric.
4. Facilities management: the software by which the use of buildings is programmed and managed over time.

No one building is ideal for all organisations. Depending on each user's particular mix of information technology and organisational structure, entirely different kinds of building technology and facilities management will be required. For example, the contemporary Japanese and Swedish office buildings are totally different in appearance precisely because the office cultures of Japan and Sweden are so far apart. Such mixes change over time, never more so than at present, and in order to facilitate such change it is enormously helpful to look at office buildings not as complete entities but as a series of superimposed life cycles:

1. The shell, skin and structure designed customarily (although this is increasingly in question) to last for at least 50 years.

2. The services, the primary mechanical and electrical systems which are increasingly important, and which have a life span usually no more than 15 years.

3. The scenery, the ceilings, partitions, furniture and finishes which constitute the fitting-out which is necessary to accommodate a particular division or tenant. Such elements are often cleared away within 5 to 7 years of being installed, that being the customary length of a lease.

The more independent of each other these major time cycles are, the easier it is to change scenery, for example, without reconstructing the basic servicing structure or rebuilding the long term shell, the easier it is for a building to accommodate change.

Interest in different kinds of organisation and different patterns in the use of building resources is not simply fascinating from a comparative anthropological point of view. It is now of the utmost pragmatic importance in determining which building has the capacity (or the intelligence) to cope with different degrees of acceleration in organisational and technological change.

24.5 THE DEVELOPMENT OF INTELLIGENT BUILDINGS IN THE US

The most intensive discussion of building intelligence in the US has not been on building automation, although great advances have been made in energy management and in the development of automated building systems by firms such as Honeywell and Johnson Controls. What has caught the headlines is the contribution of office automation and advanced telecommunications in the aggressive marketing of real estate. The most common name for this is 'shared tenant services', that is, value added by information technology services to multi-tenanted property.

There are three reasons for this characteristically North American emphasis on tenancy and service:

1. The large scale and volatility of the US real estate market and particularly the very important role of the speculative office developer. While such developers exist in most European countries nowhere, except perhaps in the UK, is their importance so great.

2. The excellent US tradition of building management, the result of a buyer's market and a much more responsive approach by landlords to tenants than exists, for example, in the UK. The importance of building management is also obviously more important in a

situation where office buildings tend to be much bigger than in Europe and multi-tenancy is far more common. It is also true that US tenants are more mobile, more sophisticated and more demanding.

3. The deregulation of the great US telephone monopoly, the Bell System, which had introduced competition and a bewildering variety of choice for users of telecommunication services. The legal reality is that not only is there competition between prime services but that each large building can, in effect, become a private utility company as far as telecommunications are concerned, run for the benefit of tenants and the profit of the landlord.

There were in the US in mid-1985, at the height of the shared tenant services craze, approximately 100 office projects to which shared tenant services were offered and several hundred more under construction. Most were large (over 500,000 sq. ft.), high rise office buildings in major urban centres such as Houston, Dallas and Atlanta, the cities which had been overbuilt since the 1982 recession and which exhibit high vacancy rates. No one has yet become wealthy through providing shared tenant services and there is considerable doubt about the profitability of some already installed. There have been some notable failures and a gradual realisation not only that some tenants resist the concept of sharing (they have their own preferred systems), but also that the management of shared tenant services is a considerable and labour intensive necessity.

The movement tends to be vendor driven - a combination of anxious developers and eager telecoms salesmen - and there is little evidence of increasing demand from critical end users. However, recently the most active of the associations which have grown in this field, the International Intelligent Building Association, seems to be moving in a consumerist direction.

To Europeans, used to monopolistic and slow moving PTTs and very often used to custom built office buildings, the amount of 'hype' has been astonishing. Nevertheless it is quite clear that shared tenant services are likely to survive as a long term concept. In cities such as Dallas, shared tenant services have become a feature which no premier office development can be without. The chief achievement is a product of the integrating culture of the communication's age: the linking of two entities which previously had been conceptually quite distinct, that is, real estate and telecommunications.

24.6 JAPANESE DEVELOPMENTS IN BUILDING INTELLIGENCE

Attention has already been drawn to the comprehensive presentation by NTT of building intelligence. There is considerable interest in Japan in what intelligence means for building design. At least one of the three factors which explain the rise of the intelligent building in the US exists in Japan: the deregulation of the telephone monopoly, NTT in late 1986.

The paradoxical context is a society which is dependent on trading in high technology products which is not yet using them as extensively as many organisations in the US and Europe; a stock of office space in Tokyo, for example, which includes some advanced buildings but many others of poor quality which are at least as vulnerable to obsolescence caused by information technology as those in the UK; as well as generally conservative and labour intensive forms of office organisation which are nevertheless extremely effective.

What strikes the outsider as different to Europe or the US is:

1. The vision (expressed frequently in the brochures and publicity of organisations such as Toshiba) not simply as a collection of semi-autonomous units, nor as organisation charts which stress control and power, but as interactive networks of communications that can overcome geographical dispersal and divisional specialisation.

2. The concreteness of the idea of the intelligent building as a product or a series of products, quite different from the American emphasis on marketing, and much more precise than European equivocation. Behind the obvious commercial motives, there seems to be for the Japanese a drive towards an aestheticism of complete electronic capability.

3. A willingness to extend the idea of the intelligent building beyond the isolated site, beyond the particular organisation, to a much larger scale. A new kind of city planning is seen to be a logical extension of the intelligent building: hence plans for Tokyo Bay, for the Osaka Teleport, and for the competition for the City of Kawasaki in which electronics turns the city into a gigantic, continuous, university level seminar.

Given the close knit structure of Japanese industry, and the ability of the great trading houses to take ideas and turn them into products, it is not too fanciful to anticipate that the Japanese will succeed in exploiting building intelligence: first, to regenerate their decaying city fabrics, which are suffering from the relative decline of the old capital industries; and secondly, to capture a vast potential market for a new generation of products based on building intelligence, such as superior lifts, air conditioning units and office furniture.

24.7 THE EUROPEAN CONTRIBUTION

European offices, particularly those in Scandinavia, Germany and Holland have developed in a quite different way to those in the US and Japan. The difference is not so much technological as organisational, and is due in particular to the enormous influence of widespread industrial democracy on the quality of working life.

Northern European offices tend to be custom built. Consultation between employers and employees about the office environment is so common that the Northern European office has taken a dramatic step away from the big open plan towards highly individualised, cellular offices in which the need to give direct aspect to nature is the strongest determinant of form.

Consequently, the new generation low rise, cellular, finger like offices in Northern Europe are quite unlike those found anywhere else in the world. In this the developer has played an insignificant role. The PTTs themselves are making slow progress towards deregulation so that the duopoly in the UK between BT and Mercury is liberal by European standards. What influence therefore has the intelligent building had? In fact, there is not one influence, but three:

1. Building intelligence has been linked, as in Japan, very firmly to large scale economic planning and redevelopment. Examples include the use of advanced telecommunications (Wide Area Networks and the like) to provide a locational edge for developments like the Amsterdam and K_ln teleports, for whole cities like Milton Keynes and for areas of urban regeneration like the London Docklands. The teleport movement is itself a covert step towards deregulation of the PTTs, by providing, for the first time on a large scale, competitive pricing for telecommunications services.

2. The use of building automation, not just at whole building level, such as the design of energy efficient perimeter skin walls or all comprehending security systems, but at the micro level of the workstations, allowing each individual office worker to adjust lighting, air conditioning and access to data.

3. A significant contribution, at least as important as that in the US and far more advanced than that of Japan, in thinking about how buildings can be made more responsive to change. This contribution has largely been in inventing ways of measuring building performance on a rigorous, comparative basis.

24.8 BUILDING EVALUATION

Measuring building performance is one aspect of the increasingly important software of facilities management. It depends upon powerful, well organised users who are anxious to achieve buildings which meet their changing demands over time.

Facilities management, which developed first in the US, has been given an enormous boost by the take-up of information technology in the office. As a result, the importance of the building as a means of achieving organisational success has been enormously enhanced.

The ORBIT 1 study, carried out by DEGW, Building Use Studies and EOSYS in the UK in 1982 and 1983, established design criteria for offices in the era of information technology. ORBIT 2 (DEGW, Harbinger, and Professors Sims and Becker from Cornell University, 1985) developed these criteria in the quite different context of the US into a technique for aiding building users and developers to assess how demand for office space, by different kinds of office organisations with different kinds of technology, was changing.

The ORBIT 2 technique also allows the same users and developers to measure supply in terms of the capacity to accommodate changing organisational and technological demands of any given building. The method can be applied at the level of an individual building, the stock of space held by an organisation or existing in a city, and related to the needs of divisions, organisations, or whole sections of the office market.

In terms of building intelligence, this is the most important task - linking supply with demand. No building, however automated with whatever enhancement of office automation or advanced telecommunications, is intelligent unless it can cope with change. Such measurements as those in ORBIT 2 are the first real tests of that intelligence. ORBIT 2 completes the loop between building hardware and software, and brings the four factors mentioned at the beginning, that is, information technology, organisation, building technology, and facilities management, into one complete system.

24.9 THE CITY OF THE TWENTY FIRST CENTURY

A prediction was made in the course of the completion of ORBIT 1, rather rashly it seemed at the time. This was that the introduction of information technology into office buildings built in the office boom of the 1960s and early 1970s, in the UK, would be so demanding and stressful that for many users their existing office stock would become prematurely obsolete. What premature obsolescence means is quite precise: the moment when the cost of bringing an office building up to date to make the new demands of emerging information technology exceeds the cost of tearing the building down and beginning again.

The prediction has come true in London with a force that was not anticipated. The City of London is today a remarkable proof of how closely architectural form is linked to social and technological change.

The ostensible cause is 'Big Bang', the deregulation on October 27, 1986 of the London Stock Exchange. Underneath lie the internationalisation of the financial services sector and the concentration in a limited number of world cities, of which London is one, of unprecedented levels of telecommunications and computing power. The result is huge pressure on the existing office stock rendered, as predicted, prematurely obsolete. The inevitable consequence is a rapid programme of construction of a new generation of office buildings, of a far superior order to those they replace. Office buildings of the 1960s are being torn down to make way for the new. The prototype of the new kind of office is the new building for the Corporation of Lloyd's, a building which contradicts most of the traditional rules of office development. Needless to say, it exhibits all four dimensions of building intelligence:

1. Office automation.
2. Advanced telecommunications.
3. Building automation.
4. Responsiveness to change.

The peculiar needs of the Corporation of Lloyd's (a marketplace in which shared information for member firms is critical) and excellent briefing, resulted in London's first intelligent office building. It is, no doubt, the precursor of many more.

Tom Cross, of the Intelligent Buildings Corporation in Denver, says (from an obviously US marketing perspective) that the intelligent building is the one that is fully let. To his basic definition, the Japanese would add a dimension of technological completeness and the Europeans one of responsiveness to individual needs and organisational change.

We have a long way to go before the perfect building, whether in Japan, the US or in Europe meets the completely satisfied user. Nevertheless, it should be clear that the challenge ahead is at least the equivalent to the invention of the office building in Chicago one hundred years ago, when a new office technology of typewriter and telephones was necessary to open up the Midwest. What faces us today is not only the invention of a new kind of office but also the City of the Twenty First Century.

Index